October 9, 1939, Berlin

[*The Polish war was over in less than six weeks. At its conclusion Hitler made a "peace offer" to England and France. He offered to guarantee the British empire and French possessions in perpetuity in exchange for cessation of hostilities and allied recognition of Germany's new position in Europe, including, of course, its Polish gains. Since the allies were now convinced—finally—that Hitler's ultimate aims were of Napoleonic dimensions, no serious consideration was given to the offer, and the war continued. Today American revisionist historians are calling Roosevelt war-monger; they are charging that America was tricked into entering World War II—that Hitler could have been "stopped" at a peace conference in 1939 Says one of the leading exponents of this thesis—Charles C. [ ]sill—in his back Door to War (p. 607): "During the meetings [ ] peace conference in Washington (Goering had agreed to holding [ ] conference there—ed.) there would have been an opportunity to foc[ ] the eyes of the world upon the ills of Europe and attempt to remedy them. If the president had possessed real courage and vision he would have welcomed these German overtures and staged a peace conference that would have saved both Poland and Czechoslovakia. . . . In the long chapter of historical might-have-beens, Roosevelt plays a prominent and dismal part." Elsewhere Tansill refers to Hitler as entering the war with "many misgivings," and as offering to the world on October 6, 1939—the date of the peace bid referred to above—a "sane and moderate program."*

# The Hitler Conspiracy

## JOHN L. STIPP

MANOR
BOOKS
INC.

**A MANOR BOOK**

Manor Books, Inc.
432 Park Avenue South
New York, New York 10016

*Library of Congress Catalog Card Number:* 55-7749

Originally Published as The Devil's Diary. Copyright, ©,
1955, by John L. Stripp.

Revised, with additional material. Copyright, ©, 1977, by
Manor Books, Inc. Published by arrangement with the
author. Printed in the United States of America.

ISBN CODE 0-532-19153-6

*to Cleo*

# Editor's Foreword

"No nation is allowed to live in ignorance with impunity." Over one hundred fifty years ago Thomas Jefferson so warned the young American republic.

By now the once sharp lines of the Hitler age have faded before the current world picture shaped by the continuing capitalist-communist cold war. A group of revisionist historians, moreover, led by the late Charles A. Beard, Charles C. Tansill, and Harry Elmer Barnes, have busily and rather effectively engaged themselves in the business of revealing that Franklin D. Roosevelt tricked the American people into the unnecessary participation in World War II. In addition, a world renowned historian, for reasons difficult to assess, has published a much read work "proving" that Hitler was no more responsible for bringing on the Second Great War than any other national leader. If we forget, or if we come to place full faith in partial truths or, worst of all, if we both forget and falsely believe, our tomorrows hold little hope for that measure of security and serenity that even the cynic's heart yearns for.

A nightmare, however real it may seem to the suffering victim, is the very essence of unreality—a phantom divorced from reality. The Hitler Age is slipping into the nightmare framework and one day may be remembered as a phantom thing, a grotesque thing. But it was not a nightmare; it happened. It can happen again if we forget or if we are fooled by the distortions of the history fraternity.

This book is presented in the belief that contemporary Americans need a refresher course in recent history. During 1945-1946 the United States government captured and collected tons of documentary material within Germany dealing with Nazi affairs, plans, programs, directives, etc. This material when combed through, translated and compiled, constituted the basic evidence used in the trials of the leading Nazis at Nurenberg. It was published in nine volumes (with supplements) under the title *Nazi Conspiracy and Aggression.*

A no less important purpose in collecting this material was to give to the world an opportunity to come to an understanding of the Nazi state and spirit, a state and spirit which have shaped events for one of the most important periods in man's entire history. He who reads and absorbs these documents will, in Lincoln's words, politically know where he has been and how he got there and thus better be able to know where to go from here, for the Nazi spirit—and the state which sprang out of it—is an integral segment of the modern temper.

But while the documents fulfilled successfully the first purpose they have failed to achieve the second and surely more important one. Two reasons account for this failure. First, the very scope and comprehensiveness of the material have prevented their general use. These volumes, averaging over a thousand pages per volume, do not constitute reading material easily handled. Secondly, the organization of the documents is such as to discourage use by any but the professional and even he must have a hardihood and patience exceeding the normal. For the "refresher course," the editor of this book has selected from this indigestible mass documents which tell, mostly in their own words, the true story of the Nazis' acts of conspiracy and aggression. Here is not labored interpretation but historic fact. Here is not a thesis developed by this ambitious historian or that for one purpose or another, but the naked Nazi record, against which all interpretation may and should be checked.

This record shows when and how European World War II was planned and, with considerable precision, how the plans were executed. It begins with a Hitler conference in late 1937 when general war as an instrument of national policy was officially (and of course, secretly) announced by the German Fuehrer to a group of his intimates. It then takes up the first step of aggression—against Austria—and reveals in the minutest detail the pattern of deceit and violence carefully and intricately woven by the makers of the "new order." In the Nazis' own words there follows then the Nietzschean conniving that led to Munich and the incorporation of the Sudetenland. Next come the behind-the-scenes details concerning the complete conquest of Czechoslovakia in the Spring of 1939, a conquest publicly and repeatedly repudiated by Hitler when he was nursing along the fatal appeasement policies of the Western powers. Some of these details, apart from inclusion in the government's unwieldly collection, have never been presented to the general public before. At this point the Nazi record shows the vacillation that went on in Hitler's mind as he sought to determine where—in the East or in the West—his next blow should fall. Always, as this record plainly demonstrates, his large aim was clear, but the steps by which it was to be achieved frequently had to be improvised out of the sometimes surprising developments of the hour and of the week. The record also shows the resolution of this vacillation, with the reasons for it. Thus comes the decision to invade Poland, a decision which officially opened World War II and led to German mastery over most of Europe. The secret planning to spread the war to Norway and Denmark, the break through the lowlands into France, the never-executed plans to invade England (and Gilbraltar), the fatal planning that led to the "end of the beginning"—the invasion of Russia—are set forth in the final portions of this work. Again it must be repeated, this material is "evidence" of historical development in its truest sense; its historical value cannot be overestimated. If the purpose of the historian's craft is to "let the people know," the editor frankly states his satisfaction that here, in the Nazis' own record, that purpose is achieved.

## ACKNOWLEDGMENTS

Grateful acknowledgment is made to the United States Department of State for permission to rework, in an entirely free and unhampered fashion, the mass of material collected by the United States and allied governments to prosecute the major war criminals at Nurenberg, and subsequently brought out by the former under the title *Nazi Conspiracy and Aggression*.

Appreciation is expressed for the words of encouragement given me by various colleagues across the country. I wish particularly to mention Dr. Samuel J. Hurwitz of Brooklyn College, the late Dr. Quincy Wright of the University of Chicago, and Dr. Jeanette P. Nichols of the University of Pennsylvania.

Mr. Freeman Champney, then manager of The Antioch Press, counselled me with friendly advice, and my association with him was of the greatest importance throughout.

For errors of judgment in selecting and condensing, and for any inadequacies in editorial treatment I must, of course, bear sole responsibility.

JOHN L. STIPP
Professor Emeritus
Knox College
1977

# Preface

[Over thirty years] have passed since the days of the Nurenberg trials. [By now] the meaning and purpose of those trials have faded and, even worse, the brutal deeds which gave rise to them are [largely] forgotten. The trials themselves were not—and never should have been interpreted as being—an indictment against a particular nation given by nature to nefarious aberrations. Rather their purpose was to uncover the personal responsibilities of individuals who, by deliberate violation of law and abuse of power, consciously brought about national and international catastrophe. Needless confusion has arisen out of the controversies over procedural matters, indictments, sentences, etc., matters of primary concern to the legal profession only. The flurry of charges and counter-charges has tended to obscure what for the historian, the political scientist—indeed for everyone interested in human history—is the chief value of the trials, namely, the original documentary evidence—of an unbelievable abundance and wealth—brought forth during the trials.

These documents exposed what happened and how it was conceived. They warned of what could happen again if the doctrine that might makes right is not nullified by international accord.

Thus far the chief stumbling block in all man's efforts to declare aggression a crime, and to eliminate war as an instrument of national policy, has been man's obvious failure to define aggression. The definitive definition has been spelled out for him in the 22 truckloads of documents hidden in secret places by the German Foreign Office and found at war's end by American and British troops. Here indeed is a perfect blueprint for diplomatic, economic, and military preparation for conquest in flagrant violation of treaties and international law.[1] The proposed plan, its execution and its consequences, provided ample material for indictments against those who had willfully based national policy upon aggression.

Irrespective of procedural questions and differences of opinion as to the application of substantive law, the Nurenberg trials have rightly been interpreted as the thus far "most concerted effort to make aggressive war a crime in international law."[2] They have set a precedent for international criminal jurisprudence. Though they have by no means eliminated, by themselves, the danger of another world war, they have given clear emphasis to the personal risks involved in political gambling.[3] It is not necessary to subscribe wholeheartedly to Livy's "Vae Victis" to believe that the Nurenberg sentences will deter future aggression.

But if the Nurenberg—and for that matter Tokyo—trials mark indeed a new departure in International Law, if they reverse our former thought which found nothing wrong with serving national interests by conquest and aggression, then this is true because *crimes against the peace* were indicted. Strictly speaking, war crimes, atrocities, and organized crimes against humanity, despite their unprecedented monstrosity, are in this context of secondary importance. In the last analysis they constituted but ugly end-products of total war (and they could have been dealt with just as well, perhaps even better, before a national forum.) Of permanent interest

---

[1]Palmer, N.D., Perkins, H.C.: *International Relations,* Houghton Mifflin Co., 1954, pp. 296, 850.

---

[2]Eagleton, Clyde: *International Government, Ronald Press,* 1948, pp. 118, 119.

[3]Palmer and Perkins: *International Relations, loc. cit.*

are those parts of the record which allow the objective reader, irrespective of his nationality, to form his own individual opinion regarding the motivation and shaping of policies of conspiracy and aggression.

These questions are just as acute today as they were in 1946, although the general political atmosphere has greatly changed and [long since] broken down. This should not have been surprising, since alliances between heterogenous elements never survive victory. The conspiracy of the Thirties to plan and wage aggressive war has been brought to the bar of international justice. But the [subsequent years] have seen the shaping of another conspiracy against world peace hardly more respectable than the Nazi pattern which it follows. The Nurenberg trials are "in fact an inestimable lesson to all those who are willing to perceive the true nature of any totalitarian regime; German National Socialism belongs to the past, but its history affords us the key to almost everything going on in Russia."

This presentation of selected documents begins with the famous "Hossbach Protokolls." Here are set forth the approximate dates for the planned invasion of Austria and Czechoslovakia, the opening moves in Hitler's pattern of aggression; moves without which the following steps detailed in the documents and which today we know and yesterday we *should* have known, could never have been taken. This first document the reader may find a difficult and tedious hurdle; he may become disgusted at its arrogant and repetitious language. But he should not be discouraged.

Our future depends upon whether or not we learn lessons from history. Nothing can serve us better and more impressively as a text today than this condensed and readable edition of the Nurenberg documents.*

KURT VON SCHUSCHNIGG
[Former Chancellor of Austria]

---

*Bracketed material is editorial emendation.

# The Hossbach Notes

## *How to Plan a World War*

November 5, 1937, Berlin      1. Document 386-PS

[*This document is unique in the annals of modern statecraft. Never before—so far as historians have discovered—has the head of a state called together his chief advisors and set forth plans for a world conflict. At one time Kaiser William II was charged with this kind of plotting but subsequent research has shown the complete emptiness of the charge. Indeed, the very idea has quite commonly come to be regarded as fantastic. In our own times, however, in the Hitler age, the fantastic has materialized. This document, commonly referred to as the "Hossbach Notes," after the Fuehrer's adjutant who took minutes on the conference in which plans for conflict were detailed, exhibits the schemes of the German leader for all to read who will.*

*On this day Hitler grouped around him the five individuals who would be most concerned with the disclosures he intended to make—Field Marshal von Blomberg, Reichsminister for War; Freiherr von Fritsch, Commander-in-Chief of the Army; Grand Admiral Raeder, Commander-in-Chief of the Navy; Colonel-General Goering, Commander-in-Chief of the Air Force; and Freiherr von Neurath, Reichsminister for Foreign Affairs. The meeting lasted over four hours. In it Hitler announced that Lebensraum—living space—was Germany's paramount need, that without it Germany not only could not increase her prosperity and power but actually would be unable to preserve such gains as had been made since he had become chancellor; that space was never found empty, hence it would have to be taken from others (as Roman and British rulers had in their times discovered), that the immediate, basic question was when to apply force, i.e., aggression, with the least risk; that Austria and Czechoslovakia were the first "spaces" to be occupied; that ultimately England, France and Russia would become involved, but proper leadership would determine a pattern of action which would reduce risk to a minimum; that he had worked out such a pattern which was of three parts, or "cases."*

*At that time these far-reaching decisions were being announced to Hitler's rather astonished advisors, affairs throughout the world generally were in rather bad shape. The depression had finally caught up with France; this, coupled with her chronic feeling of insecurity and her tragic condition of internal political dissension made her a frail reed for the champions of peace and democracy to lean upon. Britain was fidgeting under the amateur leadership of the awkward Chamberlain; Russia was frantically changing her course under the new third Five Year Plan to meet the Nazi aggression she incessantly harped upon. The United States was busy creating isolationist safeguards in the form of neutrality acts (which were virtually scrapped before the war, when it came, was six months old), and fearfully watching an industrial civil war as the new C.I.O. fought it out with company police. In Spain a shooting civil war was raging, and in China, Japanese aggression flared anew.*

*It is quite possible that the world, had it known of Hitler's plans, which of course it didn't, would have considered them too fantastic to be worth seriously bothering over or, had it wanted to bother over them, would have found itself too occupied at the moment to make more than paper protests. But such is only conjecturing, for new news of the conference's destiny-touched decisions leaked out; eight years and another world war later Allied troops, combing Berlin's ruins, came upon them, filed with typical Teutonic care. For yesterday, the discovery of the Hossbach notes was good only for helping to convict certain Nazi leaders at Nurenberg; for tomorrow, they may, if pondered, have a greater significance.*]

The Fuehrer stated initially that the subject matter of today's conference was of such high importance, that its further detailed discussion would probably take place in Cabinet sessions. However, he, the Fuehrer, had decided NOT to discuss this matter in the larger circle of the Reich Cabinet, because of its importance. His subsequent statements were the result of detailed deliberations and of the experiences of his 4½ years in Government; he desired to explain to those present his fundamental ideas on the possibilities and necessities of expanding our foreign policy and in the interests of a far-sighted policy he requested his statement be looked upon in the case of his death as his last will and testament.

The Fuehrer then stated:

The aim of the German policy is the security and preservation of the nation, and its propagation. This is, consequently, a problem of space.

The German nation is composed of 85 million people, which, because of the number of individuals and the compactness of habitation, form a homogeneous European racial body which cannot be found in any other country. On the other hand it justifies the demand for larger living space more than for any other nation. If no political body exists in space, corresponding to the German racial body, [*this void*] will represent the greatest danger to the preservation of the German nation at its present high level. An arrest of the deterioration of the German element in Austria and Czechoslovakia is just as little possible as the preservation of the present state in Germany itself. Instead of growth, sterility will be introduced, and as a consequence, tensions of a social nature will appear after a number of years, because political and philosophical ideas are of a permanent nature only as long as they are able to produce the basis

3

for the realization of the actual claim of existence of a nation. The German future is therefore dependent exclusively on the solution of the need for living space. Such a solution can be sought naturally only for a limited period, about 1-3 generations.

The only way out, and one which may appear imaginary, is the securing of greater living space, an endeavor which at all times has been the cause of the formation of states and of movements of nations. It is explicable that this tendency finds no interest in Geneva and in satisfied States. Should the security of our food position be our formost thought, then the space required for this can only be sought in Europe, but we will not copy liberal capitalist policies which rely on exploiting colonies. It is NOT a case of conquering people, but of conquering agriculturally useful space. It would be more to the purpose to seek raw material producing territory in Europe directly adjoining the Reich and not overseas, and this solution would have to be brought into effect in one or two generations. What would be required at a later date over and above this must be left to subsequent generations.

[*In Mein Kampf Hitler points his finger more precisely on the map. There, he said: "When we speak today of new territory in Europe, we think, in the first place, of Russia and its subject bordering states." At the Nurenberg party rally of 1936 he was even more specific: "If we had at our disposal the incalculable wealth and stores of raw materials of the Ural Mountains and the unending fertile plains of the Ukraine to be exploited under National Socialist leadership, then we would produce, and our German people would swim in plenty." Exactly five years later his armies were in those fertile plains; the Urals he never reached.*]

The development of great world wide national bodies is naturally a slow process and the German people, with its strong racial root, has for this purpose the most

4

favorable foundations in the heart of the European continent. The history of all times—Roman Empire, British Empire—has proved that every space expansion can only be effected by breaking resistence and taking risks. Even setbacks are unavoidable; neither formerly nor today has space been found without an owner; the attacker always comes up against the proprietor.

The question for Germany is where the greatest possible conquest could be made at lowest cost.

German politics must reckon with its two hateful enemies, England and France, to whom a strong German colossus in the center of Europe would be intolerable. Both these states would oppose a further reinforcement of Germany, both in Europe and overseas and in this opposition they would have the support of all parties. [*Thus*] we have to take the following into our political considerations as power factors:

Britain, France, Russia and the adjoining smaller States.

The German question can be solved only by way of force, and this is never without risk. The battles of Frederick the Great for Silesia, and Bismark's wars against Austria and France had been a tremendous risk and the speed of the Russian action in 1870 had prevented Austria from participating in the war. If we place the decision to apply force at the head of the following expositions, then we are left to reply to the questions "when" and "how." In this regard we have to decide upon three different cases.

CASE 1. PERIOD 1943-1945. After this we can only expect a change for the worse. The re-arming of the Army, the Navy and the Air Force, as well as the formation of the Officers' Corps, are practically concluded. Our material equipment and armaments are modern, with further delay the danger of their becoming out-of-date will increase. In particular the secrecy of "special weapons" cannot always be safeguarded. Enlistment of reserves would be limited to the current recruiting age groups and an addition from older untrained groups would no longer be available.

In comparison with the re-armament, which will have to be carried out at that time by other nations, we shall decrease in relative power. Should we not act until 1943/1945, then, depending on the absence of reserves, any year could bring the food crisis, for the countering of which we do NOT possess the necessary currency. This must be considered a "point of weakness in the regime." Over and above that, the world will anticipate our action and will increase counter-measures yearly. Whilst other nations isolate themselves we should be forced on the offensive.

What the actual position would be in the years 1943-1945 no one knows today. It is certain, however, that we can wait no longer.

[*As the Englishman, Martin Wright, has pointed out (The World in March, 1939, edited by Toynbee and Ashton-Gwatkin, 1952, p. 341) "... Hitler's timing was something more than skillful opportunism. It was governed ultimately by his long-term judgment of German strength in relation to the shifting balance of European forces. On 20 February 1933 he enunciated an important principle in a speech at a meeting of industrialists: 'We must first get complete power into our hands, if we want to crush the other side completely to the ground. So long as one is still gaining in power, one should not begin to struggle against the opponent. Only when one knows that one has reached the pinnacle of power, that there is no further upward development, should one attack.'"*]

If the Fuehrer is still living, then it will be his irrevocable decision to solve the German space problem no later than 1943-1945. The necessity for action before 1943-1945 will come under consideration in cases 2 and 3.

CASE 2. Should the social tensions in France lead to an internal political crisis of such dimensions that it absorbs the French Army and thus renders it incapable for employment in war against Germany, then the time for action against Czechoslovakia has come.

Case 3. It would be equally possible to act against Czechoslovakia if France should be so tied up by a war against another State, that it cannot "proceed' against Germany.

For the improvement of our military political position it must be our first aim, in every case of entanglement by war, to conquer Czechoslovakia and Austria simultaneously, in order to remove any threat from the flanks in case of a possible advance Westwards.

The Fuehrer believes personally that in all probability England and perhaps also France have already silently written off Czechoslovakia, and that they have got used to the idea that this question would one day be cleaned up by Germany.

[*Seventeen months later Hitler "cleaned up" the Czechoslovakia question with but verbal protests from London and Paris. It is not without interest to note what one important British statesman, Lord Halifax, thought of Germany's intentions. Two weeks after the November 5 conference, Halifax had a long discussion on international matters with Hitler. In a written report to the British Foreign Office Halifax had this to say: ". . . (our) conversation was quiet and friendly although the Chancellor showed a certain reserve due perhaps to tiredness or perhaps to a feeling that his outlook has so little in common with that of democratic governments. Herr Hitler said that he hoped we might get away from the atmosphere of 'imminent catastrophe.' The situation in Europe was not dangerous and of all nations only Russia might think of war today. The German Chancellor and others gave the impression that they were not likely to embark on adventures involving force or at least war. . . . Lord Halifax formed the view that they would pursue their objectives in Central or Eastern Europe in a fashion that would be perhaps unlikely to give other nations cause or at least the opportunity for intervention."*

*In an oral report to Prime Minister Chamberlain on this same interview Halifax said "that the Germans intended to press their colonial claim, but that they would not press it to the point of war. Unless the claim could be met in some form it would be impossible to improve relations in such a way as to make an advance toward the object which we all had in view. . . . He (Hitler) was not bent on early adventures, partly because they might be unprofitable, and partly because he was busy building up Germany internally. . . . General Goering had assured him that not one drop of German blood would be shed in Europe unless Germany was absolutely forced to do it. The Germans gave him (Lord Halifax) the impression of being convinced that time was on their side and of intending to achieve their aims in orderly fashion." (From Charles C. Tansill, Back Door to War, 1952, pp. 365-366.)]*

# Case Otto

*What Big Teeth You Have,
Adolf!*

July, 1934—February, 1938       2. Document 812-PS

[*The "agriculturally useful" spaces that Hitler ultimately aimed to conquer were not Austria, Czechoslovakia or Poland. Austria he intended to conquer for
ethnic reasons—these Germans he must "bring home to
the Reich." Czechoslovakia was to be smashed and taken
over because it constituted the militarily strategic bastion
which had to be broken and occupied if the drive East ever
was to be successful. Poland owed its position on Hitler's
list of aggression for two reasons, one positive, one
negative: the corridor lands were to be reclaimed and
Germany physically reunited; in all likelihood Poland
would not, without fighting, either give up the corridor
lands nor acquiesce in the establishment of German
hegemony in eastern Europe. Hitler believed that he
could, one way or another, defeat all three of these
opponents. But he was pretty sure the process would,
sooner or later, involve the West, i.e., England and
France; therefore he had to be prepared to defeat these
powers whenever they decided actively to oppose the push
East, a push ultimately to end with the conquest of
Russia.*

*As we have seen, Hitler guessed the time to advance
against Austria and Czechoslovakia would come when a
war broke out between Spain, France and England on the
one hand, and Italy on the other. Here the Fuehrer's*

intuition was working at its worst. Even in those Alice-in-Wonderland days, such a war never had a chance of materializing. By February, 1938, Hitler had improvised a new approach to the Austrian question, an approach which quickly led to the desired Anschluss. Back of this swift moving development lay certain events and circumstances that here need to be reviewed. In the early days of Hitler's chancellorship the chief stumbling-block to Austro-German union was Italy. Mussolini feared Hitler's power, and he feared a Germany on the Brenner pass which Anschluss would effect. Italian troops at the Brenner brought the below mentioned 1934 July coup to nothing. But in between that date and early 1938 Mussolini learned a thing or two. In the Italo-Ethiopian war he learned that Hitler's help was indispensable for the realization of Italian imperial aims. He also understood the meaning of the remilitarization of the Rhineland, begun in March, 1936 and well advanced within the next two years; with this closing the door to easy French ingress into German territory it would take more than a few Alpine battalions along the Brenner to stop Hitler in his next Anschluss attempt. Finally, the joint experiences in the Spanish Civil War clearly demonstrated to Mussolini the efficiency of German arms. Actually, by February 1938 the Duce, without of course admitting any such thing, had become Hitler's lieutenant; as time went on the relationship became obvious to the Italians themselves.

The Fuehrer's new program for Anschluss grew out of increasing confidence generated by past successes, and the self-intoxication of the grandiose schemes set forth in the Hossbach conference, plus an international embarrassment. The removal of Blomberg and Fritsch, undoubtedly decided upon after their disapproving attitude was made clear in the November meeting, came in early February, 1938. But Hitler was deeply chagrined by the circumstances which attended their removal, particularly regarding Blomberg. The latter, with Hitler as a sort of best man, had recently married a woman whose reputation as a prostitute came out soon after the *ceremony. Hitler's anger exceeded even that of the army's; he felt he had been made an international laughing-stock and, with him, Germany. In Austria the German envoy von Papen, who believed the time was ripe to effect Anschluss, considered the situation ideal for persuading Hitler to take action—Anschluss would create the Greater Reich and simultaneously recoup for Hitler and Germany the prestige lost in the Blomberg affair. On February 6, 1938, von Papen had an interview with Hitler, and the next day he flew back to Vienna for a conference with the Austrian Chancellor, von Schuschnigg. Five days later the famous Hitler-Schuschnigg interview took place; within a month, Anschluss had been accomplished—and the world forgot about the affair-Blomberg.*

*The sordid story of Anschluss is told in the following documents. 812-PS is an account of illegal union activities carried on from 1934. The account was written in 1939 by Fritz Rainer, one time gauleiter of Salzburg, upon the request of Seyss-Inquart, who succeeded Schuschnigg briefly as Chancellor. Thus this record comes from a Nazi intimate with the details, written when the Nazi-planned Anschluss seemed, if subsequent enthusiasm among the Austrians themselves and the absence (at least so far uncovered) of internal plans to undo the union are indicative, to be turning out to be a highly successful venture.]*

. . . the first stage of battle . . . ended with the July rising of 1934. The decision for the July rising was right, and the execution of it was faulty. The result was a complete destruction of the organization; the loss of entire groups of fighters through imprisonment or flight into the "Alt-Reich"; and with regard to the political relationship of Germany to Austria, a formal acknowledgement of the existence of the Austrian State by the German Government.

*[This first attempt at Anschluss took place July 25, 1934. The background is as follows. From the very*

*beginning of his tenure as Chancellor, Hitler desired
Austro-German union. Before the advent of Nazi control
in Germany most Austrians desired Anschluss too; but
after 1933 a change took place—apparently the majority
of the Austrian population preferred separation to union
under Hitler. In order to force the issue the German
government, in the Spring of 1933, imposed a 1000 mark
tax on German tourists going into Austria. Since tourist
trade constituted a major item of revenue in Austria's
economy it was felt this pressure might bring her to heel.
But while the ban was felt, no really serious situation
developed, largely because the Austrian government
quickly made arrangements with other foreign countries
which took up the slack. Hence, by mid-1934, German
Nazis came to believe more direct action was needed.
Secondly, Nazi plans to convert Austrian Socialists—
outlawed since February, 1934—to Nazism proved
unrewarding. The blood bath of June, 1934, when Hitler
murdered hundreds of his domestic opponents, served, in
the third place, to drive Austria still further from
Anschluss desires, convincing those Nazis still dubious
about methods, that the direct, violent approach was now
necessary. Finally, Austrian justice, which sentenced a
number of bomb-throwing Nazis to death in late July,
roused Nazi plotters to wrath and immediate action.*

*The plot itself was awkwardly contrived and failed
within a few hours of its attempted execution. Dr.
Dollfuss, Austrian Chancellor, was murdered and Dr.
Rintelen, Nazi-oriented governor of the province of
Styria, was declared the new Chancellor. Other cabinet
members escaped and took counter measures; soon the
Chancery was surrounded by loyal police and guards. By
evening the plotters had surrendered. Hitler, faced with
this failure and Mussolini's hastily assembled troops at
the Brenner, denied any complicity, sent a message of
regret to Austrian President Miklas, removed the
German ambassador and otherwise sought to appease
outraged world opinion. Franz von Papen was appointed
as the new ambassador to Vienna.]*

With the telegram to Papen, instructing him to re-institute normal relationships between the two states, the Fuehrer had liquidated the first stage of the battle; and a new method of political penetration was to begin. By order of the Fuehrer the Landesleitung Munich was dissolved, and the party in Austria left to its own resources.

[*There followed some two years of Nazi factional squabbles in Austria with the result that no real party leadership was felt. The factions tended finally to congeal around the two rivals, Seyss-Inquart and a Captain Leopold. The latter was an exponent of the extremely radical approach while Seyss-Inquart, working very well with von Papen, favored the boring-from-within technique. The Rainer, Globocnik and Hiedler referred to below are of the Seyss-Inquart faction; so too Hinterleitner, though originally he was in the Leopold camp.*]

In May 1936 [Hinterleitner] appointed Rainer, Globocnik and engineer Hiedler to the country leadership in the following spheres of influence:

Rainer to be chief of the political staff; Heidler as chief of the organization; and Globocnik as liaison officer with the Reich and as organizer of all the auxiliary bases outside of Austria.

The principles of the construction of the organization were: the organization is the bearer of the illegal fight and the trustee of the idea to create a secret organization, in a simple manner and without compromise, according to the principle of organizing an elite to be available to the illegal landparty council upon any emergency. Besides all this, all political opportunities should be taken and all legal people and legal chances should be used without revealing any ties with the illegal organization. Therefore, cooperation between the illegal party organization and the legal political aides was anchored at the top of the party leadership. All connections with the party in Germany were kept secret in accordance with the orders of the Fuehrer. They said that the German state should officially be omitted from the creation of an Austrian NSDAP; and that auxiliary centers for propaganda, press, refugees, welfare, etc. should be established in the foreign countries bordering Austria.

Hinterleitner already contacted the lawyer Seyss-Inquart...[He] became a party member when the entire "Styrian Heimatschutz" was incorporated into the NSDAP. Another person who had a good position in the legal field was Col. Glaise-Horstenau who [also] had contacts with both sides. The agreement of 11 July 1936 was strongly influenced by the activities of these two persons. Papen mentioned Glaise-Horstenau to Hitler as being a trusted person.

[*The agreement of July 11, 1936 was a kind of truce arranged between the two states. The agreement publicly stated that a) Germany recognized the full sovereignty of Austria, b) each state would refrain from interfering with the internal affairs of the other and that c) Austria would "conduct its policy in general and in particular towards Germany always on that fundamental line corresponding to the fact that Austria regards herself as a German State." The publicly stated terms represented a victory for Austria. But a secret protocol contained provisions which gave Germany certain advantages. Austria's chancellor Schuschnigg, for example, was to appoint to his cabinet some persons who were friendly to Germany; the outlawed Austrian Nazi party was to be given "a role in the political life of Austria within the framework of the Patriotic Front;" and a general amnesty was to be granted to Nazis imprisoned by Austrian officials. The first and third points of the secret protocol mentioned here were carried out by, respectively, the appointment to the cabinet of Guido Schmidt and Glaise-Horstenau and the releasing of thousands of Nazis from Austrian jails, but practically nothing was done to implement the second point.*]

At that time Hitler wished to see the leaders of the party in Austria in order to tell them his opinion on what

Austrian National-Socialists should do. Meanwhile Hinterleitner was arrested, and Dr. Rainer became his successor and leader of the Austrian party. On 16 July 1936, Dr. Rainer and Globocnik visited the Fuehrer at the "Obersalzberg" where they received a clear explanation of the situation and the wishes of the Fuehrer. On 17 July 1936, all illegal Gauleiters met in Anif near Salzburg, where they received a complete report from Rainer on the statement of the Fuhrer and his political instructions for carrying out the fight. At the same conference the Gauleiters received organizational instructions from Globocnik and Hiedler.

Upon the proposal of Globocnik, the Fuhrer named Lt. Gen. Keppler as chief of the mixed commission which was appointed, in accordance with the state treaty of 11 July 1936, to supervise the correct execution of the agreement. At the same time Keppler was given full authority by the Fuhrer for the party in Austria.

The National Socialist Party became acceptable again in the political field and became a partner with whom one had to negotiate, even when it was not officially incorporated into internal Austrian political developments.

September 1, 1936, Vienna     3. Document 2246-PS

[*This is a letter from von Papen, then German ambassador to Austria, to Hitler. It was written less than two months after the signing of the agreement recognizing Austrian independence.*]

As a guiding principle, I recommend on the tactical side, continued, patient, psychological treatment, with slowly intensified pressure directed at changing the regime. The proposed conference on economic relations, taking place at the end of October, will be a very useful tool for the realization of some of our projects. In discussion with government officials as well as with leaders of the illegal party (Leopold and Schattenfroh) who conform completely with the agreement of July 11, I am trying to direct the next developments in such a manner to aim at corporative representation of the movement in the fatherland front but nevertheless refraining from putting National-Socialists in important positions for the time being. However such positions are to be occupied only by personalities, having the support and confidence of the movement. I have a willing collaborator in this respect in Minister Glaise-Horstenau.

November, 1937, Vienna          4. Document 2994-PS

[*In 1945 former Austrian Chancellor Kurt von Schuschnigg executed an affidavit in which he disclosed a number of the details of the political maneuverings of these times, including those of the so-called Tafs or Tavs Plan. Shortly after the discovery of this plan by the Schuschnigg government, Anschluss was effected.*]

Finally, the most serious violation and disregard for the provisions of the 11 July, 1936 agreement was manifested by the discovery of the Tavs Plan, which plan was captured by Austrian Police at 4 Tienfelstrasse during the month of November, 1937. This plan contained instructions from High Nazi Officials, to wit: the Deputy Leader of the Nazi Party, namely Rudolph Hess, and was as follows:

(1) The overall situation in Germany demonstrates that the time for action has come in Austria. England is occupied with the conflict in the Far East; moreover, she has not yet gotten over the Abyssinian crisis nor the Spanish conflict, which offers a menace to Gibraltar. France is incapable of action due to social conflicts within the country, adverse economic conditions, and the uncertainty of the situation in Spain. Czechoslovakia finds herself in extremely difficult circumstances due to the enormous growth of the Henlein party, the encouragement of the Slovak and Hungarian population occasioned by this growth, and the weakened condition of

France. Yugoslavia fears the restoration of the Hapsburgs in Austria which would revive the old conflict among Croats, Slovenes, and Serbs; she is willing, therefore, to welcome any solution which liquidates the Hapsburg question once and for all. Italy, finally, has been weakened by Abyssinia and the conflict with Spain to such a degree that she is dependent upon the treaty of friendship of Germany and that she will not seriously oppose any action which does not interfere with her direct interests for survival. It is supposed that a strengthened guarantee with regard to the Brenner frontier will suffice to insure Mussolini's neutrality.

(2) It is at this moment that action against Austria will have to be undertaken.

Course to be followed:

(a) For any reason whatever, the details of which will be mentioned later, unrest among National Socialist Party members will break out. This unrest is to provoke the government to employ government forces throughout the country for stringent measures.

(b) The German government, after previously informing her Axis partner, submits an ultimatum to demand the incorporation of National Socialists into the government and with the withdrawal of government forces. In the case of a refusal, the German army would march in.

(c) If the Austrian government accedes to this ultimatum, the incorporation, on a basis of equality, of the illegal party into all government offices, into the Fatherland Front, and professional organizations is to be effected.

(d) It is to be assumed that the government is no more in the position to quelch the unrest in the country.

(e) In this case, the German Army marches into Austria to restore order.

[*Under this increasing pressure and in the circumstances previously mentioned, Schuschnigg finally agreed
to an oft-made von Papen request that the former visit
Hitler and "clear-up the situation." Here is the former
chancellor's account of that famous meeting.*]

. . . at the beginning of the year 1938, Franz von Papen,
the then special Ambassador of Germany in Vienna,
Austria, mentioned for the first time to me, a precise
proposal for me to meet Adolf Hitler at Berchtesgaden.
Subsequently and following this first proposal made to
me by Franz von Papen, we discussed the idea many times
before I definitely made up my mind that I would accept
an invitation to go to Berchtesgaden. I further state and
say, that, during the latter part of January, 1938, I
informed von Papen that I was prepared to go to
Berchtesgaden and discuss the differences and misunder-
standings that had arisen regarding the execution of the
agreement reached by and between our two governments
on July 11, 1936, providing that if I should go, the
following conditions must be guaranteed by Hitler:

1. I must be invited by Hitler.

2. I must prior to going to Berchtesgaden be precisely
informed concerning the matters that would be discussed
between Hitler and me, and I must be assured that the
agreement of July 11, 1936, would be maintained.

3. Hitler must agree with me in advance about the
main points of a communique that each of our two
nations would publish at the end of our meeting, and,
further, that this communique would again reiterate that
the full maintenance of the July 11, 1936, Agreement
would be observed by each of our two nations.

Von Papen informed me that he would go immediately
to Berchtesgaden and discuss with Hitler my demands
and convey to me the reply of Hitler concerning them.

During the first week of February 1938, von Papen again came to me and declared that he had had a discussion with Hitler at Berchtesgaden concerning my demands as set forth above, and that Hitler had authorized him to say—"Hitler invites you to a meeting at Berchtesgaden to discuss all the disagreements that have arisen as a result of the July 11, 1936, Agreement between our two nations." He further authorizes me to inform you that "the whole of the Agreement of July 11, 1936, between Austria and Germany, will be maintained and once more underlined." In regard to your demand concerning the communique, Hitler agrees to meet your request and further agrees that both parties shall issue simultaneously a communique containing the same text which will again affirm and quote the provisions of the July 11, 1936, Agreement. Von Papen then added, "Hitler further anthorizes me to say to you that at any event, the political situation of Austria will in no wise be worse after the conference of Berchtesgaden than it is now."

...on the evening of the 11th of February, 1938, I departed from Vienna accompanied by Secretary of State for Foreign matters, Guido Schmidt, and other members of my staff. During the night of 11 February, 1938, I remained in Salzburg. On the morning of 12 February, 1938, accompanied by Guido Schmidt, I departed from Salzburg for Berchtesgaden, and arrived at the border of Austria and Germany at about 10:30 A.M. According to a former agreement by and between von Papen and my office, I was met at the border by Franz von Papen. Von Papen then and there informed me that I would have a very good speech with the Fuehrer. He further informed me that "the Fuehrer was in a very good mood today." Von Papen had said that the Fuehrer had asked him, von Papen, to enquire of me if I had any objection that by chance some of his, Hitler's, Generals should be present at the Berghof. I enquired of von Papen, who those generals were whom Hitler had present at the Berghof and he, von Papen, replied, Keitel, Sperrle, and Reichenau. Without further conversation of special interest herein, von Papen and my party arrived at the Berghof.

...immediately after the arrival at the Berghof, I commenced a conference with Hitler. Hitler and I were alone for two hours. Hitler attacked in a violent manner the politics of Austria, both of the past and present. He furthermore informed me that he, Hitler, had "decided to bring the Austrian question to a solution so-or-so, even if he had to immediately use military force." At no time during the first two hours of our conversation did Hitler ever make any precise demands or requests of me, but spent the whole of the two hours accusing me and menacing me as a traitor to Austrian politics. Especially he informed me that, according to his knowledge, Austria could no longer reckon with any assistance from other European powers, and Austria now stood alone in the world. He furthermore added—"Schuschnigg, you now have the chance to put your name along side the names of other famous German leaders, such as Goering, Hess, Frick, Epp, Goebbels, and others"—

...at this point there was a pause, or recess in the conversation and we had lunch. After lunch I was allowed to confer with my Foreign Secretary, Guido Schmidt, at which time I informed Schmidt of my experience of the morning with Hitler. While I was conferring with Schmidt, he, Schmidt, informed me that he had learned that Dr. Kajetan Muhlman was present at the Berghof, and was now having a discussion with Hitler.

...I was next called before Joachim von Ribbentrop with my Secretary for Foreign Affairs, Guido Schmidt, and in the presence of von Papen, Ribbentrop exhibited to me a typewritten draft containing the conditions and demands made by Hitler upon me and Austria. He furthermore added that Hitler had informed me, Ribbentrop, "that these demands that I now offer to you are the final demands of the Fuehrer and that he, Hitler, is not prepared to further discuss them." He further stated that "you must accept the whole of these demands herein contained." Ribbentrop then advised me to accept the demands at once. I protested, and referred to my previous agreements with von Papen, made prior to coming to Berchtesgaden, and made it clear to Ribbentrop that I was not prepared to be confronted with such unreasonable demands as he had then and there placed before me. Von Papen, still present, apologized and informed me that he, von Papen, was entirely surprised and not at all informed about the aims of the Fuehrer as here laid. He further assured me that Hitler would take care that, if I signed these demands and acceded to them, that from that time on Germany would remain loyal to this Agreement and that there would be no further difficulties for Austria.

At this point in the conversation I was summoned again before Hitler but before going to him, I requested of my Secretary for Foreign Affairs, Guido Schmidt, that he attempt to reach some amendments of the proposed demands made upon me by Hitler through Ribbentrop—his success was limited to a few unimportant points.

...I then went before Hitler again. Hitler was very excited and informed me that he would make a final test of Austria, and stated further: "that you must fulfill the conditions of the demands made by me on you within three days, or else I will order the march into Austria." I replied: "I am not able to take over the obligations to fulfill your demands, for I am only the Chancellor of Austria, and that obligation you attempt to place upon me is the duty only of the Federal President, Miklas, I am only able to sign the draft and, when I arrive in Vienna, to present it to the Federal President." Hitler then flung open the door and yelled "Keitel." At the same time Hitler asked me to wait outside. Keitel then came in to Hitler. After 20 minutes or more I was again called before Hitler and, when before him, he, Hitler, informed me as follows: "For the first time in my life, I have changed my mind. You must sign the demands that I have made upon you, then report them to the Federal President, Miklas, and within three days from now Austria must fulfill the Agreement, otherwise things will take their natural course." I then agreed to sign the demands and, while waiting in Hitler's private room, he, Hitler, in an entirely changed mood, said to Franz von Papen, who was also present, "Herr von Papen, through your assistance I was appointed Chancellor of Germany and thus the Reich was saved from the abyss of communism. I will never forget that." Papen replied, "Ja, wohl, Mein Fuehrer."

...I, in the presence of Ribbentrop, Guido Schmidt, von Papen, and Hitler, signed the demands and retained a copy for the Austrian Government.

...on the way back to Vienna from Berchtesgaden, Franz von Papen accompanied me and my party. Between the Berghof and Berchtesgaden, von Papen informed me as follows: "Now, you have your own impression of how excited the Fuehrer can get, but that happens very seldom, and I am convinced that the next time you meet him, you will have an amicable conversation with him."

February 26, 1938, Vienna       6. Documents
1544-PS and 1780-PS

[*Von Papen, taking leave of Austria, had a final conference with Schuschnigg on this date. Afterwards he made notes of the meeting. This accunt is from those notes.*]

I introduced into the conversation the widespread opinion that he had acted under "brutal pressure" in Berchtesgaden. I myself had been present and been able to state that he had always and at every point had complete freedom of decision. The Chancellor replied that he had actually been under considerable moral pressure, he could not deny that. He had made notes on the talk which bore that out. I reminded him that despite this talk he had not seen his way clear to make any concessions, and I asked him whether without the pressure he would have been ready to make the concessions he had made late in the evening. He answered: "To be honest, no!" It appears to me of importance to record this statement.

[*The demands to which Schuschnigg reluctantly agreed were essentially these: to appoint Nazi Seyss-Inquart to the Cabinet as Minister of the Interior, to grant further amnesty to Nazi political prisoners in Austria, and to permit Austrian Nazis to be legally recognized as equal*]

*members in the Fatherland Front. To make sure that
Miklas as well as Schuschnigg agreed to and executed the
terms sham military maneuvers were held along the
Austrian border. The following items are from the diary
of Hitler's chief military advisor, General Jodl.*]

## 1938

*11 February:*

In the evening and on 12 February General K[eitel],
with General v. Reichenau and Sperrle, at the Obersalzburg. Schuschnigg together with G. Schmidt are again
being put under heaviest political and military pressure.
At 2300 hours Schuschnigg signs protocol.

*13 February:*

In the afternoon General K. asks Admiral C[anaris]
and myself to come to his apartment. He tells us the
Fuehrer's order is to the effect that military pressure by
shamming military action should be kept up until the
15th. Proposals for these deceptive maneuvers are drafted
and submitted to the Fuehrer by telephone for approval.

*14 February:*

At 2:40 o'clock the agreement of the Fuehrer arrives.
Canaris went to Munich to the Counter-Intelligence
office VII and initiates the different measures.

The effect is quick and strong. In Austria the
impression is created that Germany is undertaking
serious military preparations.

*15 February:*

In the evening an official communique about the
positive results of the conference is issued.

*16 February:*

Changes in the Austrian government and general
poltical amnesty.

March, 1938, Vienna               7. Document 2996-PS

[*Shortly after the coming into the cabinet of the Nazi*

*Seyss-Inquart, Chancellor Schuschnigg decided to thwart Nazi designs by appealing to the country via a plebiscite. This would ask Austrians whether or not they favored an independent, united, social, Christian, German Austria. The Chancellor decided this during "the early days of March" without consultation with his cabinet. The following account of the Chancellor's is from his affidavit.]*

During the first days of March 1938, I was Federal Chancellor of Austria. I then made up my mind that I would hold a plebiscite concerning the independence and sovereignty of Austria, according to the provisions of the Agreement reached with Germany at Berchtesgaden, and, further, according to the Constitution.

*[There was no mention made of such a plebiscite in the Berchtesgaden Agreement.]*

On the evening of the 8th of March, 1938, I informed Dr. Arthur Seyss-Inquart, the then Minister of Interior and Public Security for Austria, of my intention to hold such a plebiscite. I requested that he, Seyss-Inquart, give me his word of honor that he would keep this information secret until after I had published it, which I intended to do on the evening of March 9, 1938, at Innsbruck. He gave me that word of honor. On the evening of the tenth of March, 1938, I had a long conversation with Seyss-Inquart concerning the terms of the plebiscite. He first objected to the procedure which I proposed. However, when we parted on that occasion, Seyss-Inquart expressed his intention to support the plebiscite as proposed, and declared to me there would be no difficulty. He, furthermore, expressed his willingness to broadcast a speech favoring the plebiscite, and directed to his National Socialist followers. On the night of the 10th of March, 1938, I retired firmly convinced that the plebiscite would be a success for Austria, and that the National Socialists would present no formidable obstacle.

At 5:30 A.M. on the morning of the 11th, I received a telephone call from Dr. Skubl, President of Police for Austria. Skubl informed me that the Austrian-German border was closed—the railway traffic between Germany and Austria had been stopped and movements of German military forces had been reported. I hurried to my office. This news that I received from Dr. Skubl was confirmed by the Counsel General of Munich, who stated that the German Army Corps of Munich was mobilized, and that Panzer troops were moving toward the Austrian frontier.

I attempted to contact Seyss-Inquart at once, but every effort to locate him failed until after 10 o'clock the same morning. Sometime after 10 o'clock, Seyss-Inquart, accompanied by Glaise-Horstenau, Minister without Portfolio, appeared in my office. Seyss-Inquart informed me as follows: "I have just come from the airport, where I have met Glaise-Horstenau. Glaise-Horstenau has just now returned from Germany." Glaise-Horstenau then informed me that he had the night before seen Hitler, and that he, Hitler, was very highly excited and in a rage concerning my proposal to hold the plebiscite. "It is my feeling, too, that you should not have done such a thing, it is a big mistake."—Seyss-Inquart was then and there called to the telephone and upon his return, read to me from a scrap of paper which he held in his hand, the contents of a telephone call which he alleged was just then received by him from Goering in Berlin. The contents as he read it to me was as follows: "The Chancellor must revoke the proposed plebiscite within the time of one hour, and after three or four weeks, Austria must oblige herself to carry out a plebiscite concerning the Anschluss according to the Saar status, otherwise the German Army is ordered to pass the Austrian frontier."

After informing the Federal President of this demand made on Austria by Germany, we decided to recall the plebiscite, and thereupon I informed Seyss-Inquart and Glaise-Horstenau of our intentions.

Seyss-Inquart said that he would go to the telephone and inform Goering in Berlin concerning the decision of the Austrian Government at that time made. In a few minutes he, Seyss-Inquart, returned to my office, and informed me further, as follows:

"I have had a telephone conversation with Goering, and Goering has ordered me to inform the Federal Chancellor Schuschnigg, as follows:

'The situation can only be saved for Austria when Schuschnigg resigns as the Chancellor of Austria within two hours and Seyss-Inquart is appointed as the new Chief of the Austrian Government. If Seyss-Inquart does not inform me, Goering, within two hours, I, Goering, will suppose that you are hindered from doing so.'"

March 11, 13, 1938, Berlin, Vienna        8. Document
                                            2949-PS

[*Now follows one of the most remarkable documents, dealing with political affairs, of our time. From the Institute for Research in the German Ministry for Aviation the Allies captured a binder of transcripts of telephone conversations. These transcripts tell us what plans were made and what ideas were behind the plans—for these days.*

*A few cautionary words are in order. The translation is bad, to begin with. Secondly, the monitoring was not of the best with the result that nonsense sentences are not infrequent. In the third place, some of the persons referred to are unidentifiable. The spellings of proper names are not always consistent. Where the hours are given in military style they have here been changed to the customary reading. All but the last of these conversations took place on March 11th; the last took place on March 13th. One other modification from the original is here made; whereas in the first conversation in the original Goering is labelled "F" (for Field-Marshal) here he is designated "G." Names used in the conversations are the following:*

*Dombrowski—an official in the German embassy in Austria*

26

*Ullrich—the same*

*Keppler—a foreign office official sent by Hitler to Vienna March 11th to put pressure on Schuschnigg*

*Fishbock—First Nazi Minister of Commerce and Transport in Reich Cabinet*

*Kaltenbrunner—at this time an Austrian SS leader*

*Bahr—an Austrian Nazi leader*

*Muehlman—the same*

*Muff—German Military Attaché in Vienna*

*Globocnik—Gauleiter of Vienna*

*Dietrich—Reich Press Chief*

*Von Hessen—German Ambassador to Rome*

**Sometimes the first and third persons are both used in the same report.]**

**[2:45 p.m.]**

G:   How do you do, doctor? My brother-in-law, is he with you?

S[eyss-Inquart]:   No.

G:   How are things with you? Have you resigned, or do you have any news?

S:   The Chancellor has cancelled the elections for Sunday, and therefore he has put [himself] and other gentlemen in a difficult situation. Besides having called off the elections, extensive precautionary measures are being ordered, among others curfew at 8 P.M.

G:   Replied that in his opinion the measures taken by Chancellor Schuschnigg were not satisfactory in any respect. At this moment he could not commit himself officially. G will take a clear stand very shortly. In calling off the election, he could see a postponement only, not a change of the present situation which had been brought about by the behavior of the Chancellor Schuschnigg in breaking the Berchtesgadener agreement.

**[3:05 p.m.]**

G:   Told S that Berlin did not agree whatsoever with the decision, made by Chancellor Schuschnigg since he did not enjoy any more the confidence of our government because he had broken the Berchtesgadener agreement, and therefore further confidence in his future actions did not exist. Consequently, the National Minister, S and the others, are being requested to immediately hand in their resignations to the Chancellor, and also to ask the Chancellor to resign. G added that if after a period of one hour no report had come through the assumption would be that S would no more be in the position to phone. That would mean that the gentlemen had handed in their resignations. S was then told to send the telegram to the Fuehrer as agreed upon. As a matter of course, an immediate commission by the Federal President for S to form a new cabinet would follow Schuschnigg's resignation.

[*3:55 p.m.*]

S informed the Field Marshall that the Chancellor Schuschnigg was on his way to Federal President Miklas in order to hand in his resignation, as well as that of the whole cabinet.

Asked by G if, with this, the commission to form a new cabinet intended for S was secure.

S said he would let G know not later than 5:30.

G: Replied emphatically that this, besides the resignation of the Chancellor Schuschnigg was an absolutely firm demand.

[*5:00 p.m.*]

Dombrowski: I have to report the following. Seyss-Inquart has talked to the Austrian Chancellor until 4:30 but he is not in a position to dissolve the Cabinet by 5:30 because it is technically impossible.

Goering: By 7:30 the Cabinet must be formed and several measures must have been taken. Is Seyss-Inquart there?

Dombrowski: He is not here just now. He is in conference. That is why he has sent me here to telephone you.

Goering: What is the message? Repeat exactly.

Dombrowski: His message is that he is not in a position...(Goering interrupts, what does he have to say?) He says that he has no hesitation to allow the party formations to come in now.

Goering: All that is not to the point. I want to know what is going on? Did he tell you that he is now the Chancellor?

Dombrowski: Yes.

Goering: As just transmitted to you?

Dombrowski: Yes.

Goering: Good, go on. What time can he form the Cabinet?

Dombrowski: Possibly by 9:18.

Goering: The Cabinet must be formed by 7:30.

Dombrowski: By 7:30.

Goering: For that purpose Keppler is now going to arrive.

Dombrowski: To continue, the SA and the SS have already been organized as auxilliary police.

Goering: (Goering repeats the last sentence.) The demand of legalizing the Party must also be made.

Dombrowski: All right.

Goering: All right, with all its formations, SA, SS, HJ.

Dombrowski: Yes, Field Marshal, only one thing, that the formations which are now outside the country will not come at this time.

Goering: They will only come during the next few days.

Dombrowski: Yes, he thinks after the plebiscite has been accomplished.

Goering: No, no, what plebiscite.

Dombrowski: Yes. He believes that the program then established will be carried out by Hitler.

Goering: One moment. As to the plebiscite, there are certain special things, aren't there. Anyway, this plebiscite tomorrow is to be cancelled.

Dombrowski: That's already been taken care of. That's now out of the question.

Goering: Good, the cabinet must be entirely National Socialist.

Dombrowski: Good, that also has been settled, by

7:30 that must be...

Goering: (Interrupting) That must be reported by 7:30 and Keppler will bring you several names to be incorporated.

Dombrowski: Very well. One thing Seyss-Inquart requests regarding the organizations now in emigration are to come in later and not now.

Goering: All right, we can talk about that...That will take a few days anyway.

Dombrowski: That is his request.

Goering: Good.

Dombrowski: That is all right then.

Goering: Yes, they will not come immediately. About that we will have a special talk.

Dombrowski: Very well, General Field Marshal.

Goering: Now to go on. The Party has definitely been legalized?

Dombrowski: But that is...it isn't necessary to even discuss that.

Goering: With all of its organizations.

Dombrowski: With all of its organizations within this country.

Goering: In uniform?

Dombrowski: In uniform.

Goering: Good.

Dombrowski: Calls attention to the fact that the SA and SS have already been on duty for one-half hour which means everything is all right.

Goering: Regarding the plebiscite, the Special Envoy will be coming down and will confer with you about the kind of plebiscite that is to be.

Dombrowski: Well then, we have time in that matter.

Goering: Yes, there is time. Seyss-Inquart is of the opinion that the relationship Germany-Austria must be put on a new basis. [*Goering is asking.*]

Dombrowski: What did he mean by that? Well, he means that the independence of Austria should be maintained but that everything else should be ruled on National Socialist basis.

Goering: That will be a natural result. Tell him the units must come down in the next few days. That's in the interest of Seyss-Inquart, namely that he receives first class units which are absolutely at his disposal.

Dombrowski: About that he will talk with you himself.

Goering: All right, he can do that.

Dombrowski: So that he knows who is coming down, but we have a few days for that.

Goering: Yes, and by 7:30 the report about the formed cabinet.

Dombrowski: He'll have that by then.

Goering: And by 7:30 he also must talk with the Fuehrer and as to the cabinet. Keppler will bring you the names. One thing I have forgotten, Fishbock must have the Department of Economy and Commerce.

Dombrowski: That's understood.

Goering: Kaltenbrunner is to have the Department of Security and Bahr is to have the armed forces. The Austrian Army is to be taken by Seyss-Inquart himself and you know all about the Justice Department.

Dombrowski: Yes, yes.

Goering: Give me the name.

Dombrowski: Well, your brother-in-law. Isn't that right?

Goering: Yes?

Dombrowski: Yes.

Goering: That's right and then also Fishbock.

Dombrowski: Yes, that is taken care of.

Goering: Be careful, the daily press must leave immediately and our people.

Dombrowski: Well, as to the man whom you mentioned with regard to the Security Department.

Goering: Kaltenbrunner. Yes, he is to get the security department and then mark this, immediately the press representatives (They both talk at the same time, Dombrowski says several times, "yes.") All right, at 5:30, no at 7:30—Goodby.

M. (Much?): (Much comes to the telephone and calls Goering's attention to the fact that Keppler will not arrive

31

until 5:40. Goering tells Much that he has just given the names to Dombrowski over the telephone.)

M: Requests to be allowed to support the suggestion that the Party formations now abroad would not be let loose until this was called for from "here."

Goering: Yes, no, the Fuehrer wants to...that he will tell to Seyss-Inquart, in person...those are the most disciplined and best units, they will come immediately under the command of Seyss-Inquart so that he has the best possible support.

M: Yes, but as to the foreign political situation...

Goering: (Interrupting) That will be handled. The foreign political situation will be handled exclusively by Germany in this direction. Furthermore, Seyss-Inquart and the Fuehrer will talk about this matter, that will take quite some time anyway, until they can be dispatched. Anyway they won't come today or tomorrow or the day after tomorrow.

*[5:20-5:25 p.m., Goering-Ullrich.]*

G: Look, Franz, you take over the Ministry of Justice, and corresponding to the wish of the Fuhrer, you also take over for the time being the Ministry for Foreign Affairs, later on someone else will replace you in this.

U: Please, there is something else. Fishbock intends, before accepting his appointment, to the Fuehrer—

G: He should not do that at this moment, it won't be necessary at all.

U: Then he will phone you, I am also against it.

G: Yes, let him call me. There is no time for it. Also he cannot afford to get himself special favors, and be responsible now before he has to act history. With the Federal Chancellory, he should still reserve for himself the department of trade, Kaltenbrunner, Security, you the department of Justice, and for the time being the Foreign Office.

U: Does he know about it already?

G: The latter he does not yet know, I shall tell him that myself. He has to form the cabinet immediately, he shall not fly over here, because the cabinet has to be formed till 7:30, otherwise its all for nothing. Otherwise, things will take their own course, and very different decisions will be made then.

U:  That is understood, I shall take care of it immediately.

G:  And then another important factor which I forgot to mention before, but that is rather a matter of course. The Reds, who were given arms yesterday, have to be disarmed in the quickest way and just as well in a ruthless manner, that is rather a matter of course. Also make sure that he gives me a ring immediately, he shall not fly, there is no sense in doing so. Just a moment. He should call me under the following number, 125224. (Here the conversation is interrupted. The conversation was interrupted twice, in the beginning and at the end. It seemed that Vienna was to blame for the interruption.)

[5:26-5:31 p.m., Goering-Seyss-Inquart.]

S:  The situation is like that: The Federal President has accepted the resignation, but his point of view is, that no one but the Chancellor is to be blamed for Berchtesgaden and its consequences, and therefore he'd like . . . but he would like to entrust a man like Ender with the Chancellorship. At this moment our own gentlemen are in conference with him, Globotschnik and so on, and report on the situation.

G:  Yes, now look here: this will change the whole situation. The Federal President or someone else has to be told that this is entirely different from what we were told. Globotschnik said upon your order that you had been given the chancellorship.

S:  I myself? When did he say that?

G:  Just an hour ago. He said that you had the chancellorship and that also the Party had been restored, SA, SS had already taken over police duties, etc.

S:  No, that is not so. I suggested to the Federal President to entrust the chancellorship to me, usually it takes three to four hours. As for the Party, we still do not have the possibility to restore it but we have ordered the SA and SS to take over police duties.

33

G: Well, that won't do! Under no circumstances! The matter is in progress now therefore, please, the Federal President has to be informed immediately that he has to turn the powers of the Federal Chancellor over to you and to accept the cabinet like it was arranged; you as Federal Chancellor and the Army—

S: (Interrupting him) Field Marshall, just now Muehlmann who was there has arrived. May he report to you?

G: Yes.

Dr. Muehlmann (?) takes over the conversation with G—

M: The situation [is] that the Federal President still refuses persistently to give his consent and asks for official diplomatic action by the Reich. Now we three National-Socialists—Rodenstock, Dreila, and I went to speak to him personally in order to make him understand that in this hopeless situation only one thing can be done by him: namely to say yes. He would not even let me see him. So far it looks as if he were not willing to give in.

G: (short conversation) (give me S)

S-I: continues the conversation.

G: Now remember the following: you go immediately together with Lt. General Muff and tell the Federal President that if the conditions which are known to you are not accepted immediately, the troops which are already stationed at and advancing to the frontier will march in tonight along the whole line, and Austria will cease to exist. Lt. General Muff should go with you and demand to be admitted for conference immediately. Please, do inform us of Miklas' position. Tell him, there is no time now for any joke. Just through the false report we received before action was delayed, but now the situation is that tonight action will begin from all the corners of Austria. The invasion will be stopped and the troops will be held at the border only if we are informed that Miklas has entrusted you with the Federal Chancellorship. [*At this point the monitoring becomes comfused.*] M[iklas] does not matter whatever it might be, the immediate restoration of the Party with all its organizations—(again interruption) and then call out all the National Socialists all over the country. They should now be in the streets. So remember, report must be given till 7:30. Lt. General Muff is supposed to come along with you. I shall inform him immediately. If Miklas could not understand it in 4 hours, we shall make him understand it now in 4 minutes.

S:   All right.

[*12:28 (sic)-6:34 p.m. (apparently this is in error; instead of 12:28, 6:28 is meant, so that the time should read 6:28-6:34 p.m.) Goering-Keppler and Muff. Keppler answered the phone first instead of Muff.*]

K:   I just spoke to Muff. The Muff action was going on at the same time as mine was, so I did not know about it. Muff just saw the President, but he also refused. I shall call once more to find out whether or not the President wants to speak to me at this last minute.

G:   Where is Muff now?

K:   Muff just came down, his action was unsuccessful.

G:   But, what does he have to say?

K:   Well, he would not agree with it.

G:   Well, then Seyss-Inquart has to dismiss him; just go upstairs again and just tell him plainly that S-I shall call on the National-Socialist guards and in 5 minutes the troops will march in by my order.

K:   (Muff is called to the phone) Muff (?) does not answer by name.

M:   It is a fact that Schuschnigg tried to prove to the world, that the National Socialists do not have any majority, and only by the threat of German arms—the conversation is interrupted for about 3 minutes, interruption comes from Vienna. G remains at the phone.

Unknown voice (male)

U:   Hello

G:   Is that the Secretary of State Keppler?

U:   No, he is just in conference with the Federal Chancellor.

G:   With the Federal President—

U:   No, with the Federal Chancellor, they are all

together, Federal President and Federal Chancellor.

G: Who is speaking?

U: Fehsemeir (?) Adjutant of—

G: Has he gone upstairs?

U: Yes, just now.

G: Who is with him, upstairs?

U: The Federal President, the Federal Chancellor, and Mayor Schmiz.

G: Yes, I hold on—Fehsemeir. You have to hurry, we have just three minutes left—

U: Yes, I know—

Goering waits a while at the phone.

K: Comes first to the phone, "Well, I just saw the President again, but he has not given his consent."

G: He refused; Well, then Seyss shall call immediately.

K: He came to the phone immediately. [*sic*]

Seyss-Inquart came to the telephone [*sic*]

G: Well, how do we stand?

S: Please, Field Marshall. Yes.

G: Well, what is going on?

S: Yes, ah, the Federal President sticks to his view point. Now the Federal Chancellor (double name, not to be understood clearly—Weserick (?) went to see Schuschnigg in order to change his mind. He himself uses all his influence, but there is no decision made yet.

G: But do you think it is possible that we shall come to a decision in the next few minutes.

S: Well, the conversation cannot take longer than 5 to 10 minutes, it will not take any longer, I guess.

G: Listen, so I shall wait a few more minutes, till he comes back then you inform me via Blitz conversation in the Reich Chancery as usual, but it has to be done fast. I can hardly justify it, as a matter of fact. I am not entitled to do so; if it cannot be done, then you have to take over the power allright?

S: But if he threatens?

G: Yes.

S: Well, I see, then we shall be ready.

G: Call me via Blitz.

S:   Dr. Schuschnigg will give the news over the radio that the Reich Government has given an ultimatum.

G:   I heard about it.

S:   And the Government itself has abdicated, General Schiwaski is in command of the military forces and he will draw the troops back. The gentlemen pointed out that they were waiting for the troops to march in.

G:   Well, they were appointed by you?

S:   No.

G:   Did you dismiss them from their office?

S:   No one was dismissed from his office, but the Government itself has pulled back and let matters take their course.

G:   And you were not commissioned, it was refused?

S:   Not like before it was refused. They expect that they are taking a chance with the invasion and expect that, if the invasion will actually take place the executive power will be transferred to other people.

G:   OK. I shall give the order to march in and then you make sure, that you get the power. Notify the leading people about the following which I shall tell you now: Everyone who offers resistance or organizes resistance, will immediately, be subjected to our courtmartial, of our invading troops. Is that clear?

S:   Yes.

G:   Including leading personalities, it does not make any difference.

S:   Yes, they have given the order, not to offer any resistence.

G:   Yes, it does not matter: the Federal President will not authorize you, and that also can be considered as resistance.

S:   Yes.

G:   Well, now you are officially authorized.

S:   Yes.

G:   Well, good luck, Heil Hitler.

[*No time given, but presumably shortly after the above conversation; Berlin, Vienna. Goering-Muff.*]

G: Tell Seyss-Inquart the following: As we understand it the Government has abdicated but he himself remained. So he should continue to stay in office, and carry out necessary measures in the name of the Government. The invasion is going to happen now, and we shall state that everyone who puts up any resistance has to face the consequences. But the Austrian organizations may join us any time, rather they may seek protection from the German Wehrmacht. I should try to avoid chaos.

M: Seyss, will do so, he is already making a speech.

G: But he should take over now the Government, and should carry things through quietly. The best will be if Miklas resigns.

M: Yes, but he won't. It was very dramatic, I spoke to him almost 15 minutes. He declared that he will under no circumstances yield to force.

G: What does this mean? So he just wants to be kicked out?

M: Yes, he does not want to move.

G: Well, with fourteen children one cannot move as one likes. Well, tell Seyss that he'll take over.

[*8:48-8:54 p.m., Vienna, Berlin. Keppler-Goering.*]

K: I want to inform you shortly. Federal President Miklas has refused to do anything. But, nevertheless, the government has ceased to function. I spoke to Schuschnigg and he said they had laid down their functions and we had to act accordingly. (was the last sentence repeated [*sic*])
They have laid down their functions, and Schuschnigg himself said that we had to act and (consequently?) Buhler (Buhler or Buhle—very unclear) has spoken to Seyss-Inquart over the phone, he (?) who is still in office as Secretary of the Interior, spoke over the radio.

G: (Interrupts) I have read that. Continue.

K: The old Government has ordered the Army not to put any resistance. Therefore, shooting is not allowed.

G: OK, I do not give a darn.

K: Pretty soon Landsleiter Kloose (?) will deliver a

speech over the radio, and now (?) I want to ask you if not a prominent personality in Berlin wants to add a few words for the Austrian people?

G:  Well, I do not know yet. Listen: the main thing is, that Inquart takes over all these powers of the Government, that he keeps the radio stations occupied...

K:  Well, we represent the Government now.

G:  Yes, that's it. You are the Government. Listen carefully: the following telegram should be sent here by Seyss-Inquart: Take the notes

"The provisional Austrian Government which after the dismissal of the Schuschnigg Government, considers it its task to establish peace and order in Austria, sends to the German Government the urgent request, to support it in its task and to help it to prevent bloodshed. For this purpose it asks the German Government to send German troops as soon as possible."

K:  Well, SA and SS are marching through the streets, but everything is quick (*sic; quiet?*]. Everything has collapsed with the professional groups (?).

G:  Now listen: He has to guard the borders, so that they cannot disappear with their fortunes.

K:  Yes, indeed.

G:  And then—above all, he is also responsible for the foreign policy.

K:  Yes, we still do need someone for this post.

G:  Well, that does not matter. Now, Seyss-Inquart has to take it over and he has to appoint a few poeple. He should call upon the people we recommend to him. He should form now a provisional government. It is absolutely unimportant what the Federal President may have to say.

K:  Yes, they are not doing anything.

G:  No, no, he has to form the Government right now like he intended to, and he should inform the people abroad about it.

K:  Yes.

G:  He is the only one who still has power in Austria.

K:  Yes.

G:  Then our troops will cross the border today.

K: Yes.

G: Well. And he should send the telegram as soon as possible.

K: Will send the telegram to S-I in the office of the Federal Chancellery.

G: Please. Show him the text of the telegram and do tell him that we are asking him—well, he does not even have to send the telegram—all he needs to do, is to say: agreed.

K: Yes.

G: Either call me at the Fuehrer's or my place. Well, good luck. Heil Hitler!

*[9:54 p.m. Berlin, Vienna; Dietrich, Keppler.]*

Dietrich: I need the telegram urgently.

Keppler: Tell the General Field Marshal that Seyss-Inquart agrees.

Dietrich: This is marvelous. Thank you.

Keppler: Listen to the radio. News will be given.

Dietrich: Where?

Keppler: From Vienna.

Dietrich: So Seyss-Inquart agrees?

Keppler: Jawohl!

*[10:25-10:29 p.m. Rome, Berlin. Von Hessen, Hitler. The document identifies the former as H, the latter as F. For clarity's sake, here their names shall be used.]*

Hessen: I have just come back from Palazzo Venezia. The Duce accepted the whole thing in a very friendly manner. He sends you his regards. He had been informed from Austria, Schuschnigg gave him the news. He had then said it would be a complete impossibility, it would be a bluff, such a thing could not be done. So he was told that it was unfortunately arranged thus and it could not be changed any more. Then Mussolini said that Austria would be immaterial to him.

Hitler: Then, please, tell Mussolini I will never forget him for this.

Hessen: Yes.

Hitler: Never, never, never, whatever happens. I am still ready to make quite a different agreement with him.

Hessen: Yes, I told him that too.

Hitler: As soon as the Austrian affair has been settled, I shall be ready to go with him through thick and thin, nothing matters.

Hessen: Yes, my Fuhrer.

Hitler: Listen, I shall make any agreement—I am no longer in fear of the terrible position which would have existed militarily in case we had gotten into a conflict. You may tell him that I do thank him so much, never, never shall I forget that.

Hessen: Yes, my Fuehrer.

Hitler: I will never forget it, whatever may happen. If he should ever need any help or be in any danger, he can be convinced that I shall stick to him whatever might happen, even if the whole world were against him.

Hessen: Yes, my Fuehrer.

Hitler: Well.

Hessen: Then, I would like to say that this afternoon the French envoy asked for a conference with Count Ciano, by order of his government on account of the Austrian affair. But Count Ciano refused to see him, and thereupon the envoy stated that they have to disregard any further oral negotiations with Italy.

Hitler: Yes, I thank

Hessen: My Fuehrer, also I wanted to ask you do you want me to stay here, or shall I come back at once, tomorrow?

Hitler: You may still stay there.

Hessen: Shall I send the machine back?

Hitler: No, you may still keep it there.

Hessen: Yes, I shall report again tomorrow.

Hitler: Yes, I thank you.


[*Two days later, after the formal absorption of Austria into Germany two contended German leaders talk it over. Among other interesting matters is the discovery of the ease with which the diplomats slipped into, without very good reason even, rationalization and self-deception. At this time Ribbentrop was German Ambassador to England.*

*March 13, 1938, 9:15-9:55 a.m., Berlin, London.*

G: As you know the Fuehrer has entrusted me with the administration of the current government procedures. And therefore I wanted to inform you. There is overwhelming joy in Austria, that you can hear over the radio.

R: Yes, it is fantastic, isn't it?

G: Yes, the last march into the Rhineland is completely overshadowed. The Fuehrer was deeply moved, when he talked to me last night. You remember it was the first time he saw his homeland again. Now, I mainly want to talk about political things. Well, this story we have given an ultimatum, that is just foolish gossip. From the very beginning the National Socialist ministers and the representatives of the people have presented the ultimatum. Later on, more and more prominent people of the Movement Party participated, and as a natural result, the Austrian National Socialist ministers asked us to back them up, so they would not be completely beaten up again and subjected to terror and civil war. Then we told them we would not allow Schuschnigg to provoke a civil war, under no circumstances. Whether by Schuschnigg's direct order or with consent. The Communists and the Reds had been armed, and were already making demonstrations, which were photographed with "Heil Moskau" and so on. Naturally, all these facts caused some danger for Wiener-Neustadt. Then you have to consider that Schuschnigg made his speeches, telling them the Fatherland Front would fight to its last man, one could not know that they would capitulate like that and therefore Seyss-Inquart who already had taken over the government asked us to march in immediately. Before we had already marched up to the frontier since we could not know whether there would be a civil war or not. These are the actual facts which can be proved by documents. This way the people may_____. The following is interesting: the absolute complete enthusiasm for the National Socialism which is surprising even to us. And the reason for that is: About 80% among the members of the Fatherland Front [were forced to join] otherwise they were subjected to terror, mainly economically, in that everybody who did not belong to the Fatherland Front lost his job so the Fatherland Front really seemed to be something. But actually these were all our people which is just being discovered now, and that explains the whole situation, which did even surpass all our expectations. At least we thought—but with the one exception of the Jews and a part of those deep black ones [*i.e., clericals*], there is no one against us.

R: So it seems that all Austria is on our side.

G: Well, let me tell you, if there were an election tomorrow.—I already told S-I he should invite the representatives of the Democratic powers—they could convince themselves that this was really an election carried through on a democratic basis—and we shall 90% votes in our favor. Absolutely! Only now one gets the reports how these people have been mistreated; I believe it is absolutely necessary that serious people from England and France should be asked to come over here and watch what is actually going on. The biggest trick which ever has been played was done here.

R: I believe that this conversation will grow here. During these last days I had a few conversations not to forget the one I had the day before yesterday. Things are like that: at the moment they had their big surprise were— later on I shall tell you more but generally people act very sensibly.

[*By "sensibly" Ribbentrop means resignedly.*]

The day before yesterday I told Halifax—who was with me quite a long time—that the whole English public opinion knows exactly what is going on in Austria.

G: There is something else I started to say: We cannot afford to have any elections as long as our troops are stationed there, they should be back first. Besides during the next few days our troops will return. No one could stop that, any military man knows that, when such a thing is running, when the order is given to start the matter takes its course, till the troops have reached their

43

destination, and till they are ready to be shipped away and returned. As I was informed yesterday, one figures with 5-6 days. This is now nothing but a friendship march. Nothing has happened, not one shot was fired. Still we have to take over Vienna and Wiener-Neustadt. But I am convinced that will be an easy job—as it was all over. But no one could have expected that. Just remember the speeches of the people. They always shouted these were fanatics, determined—to fight for Austria, for her independence, and so on, that there was nothing behind it, no one could suspect. Officials, for instance, reported and the higher ups just as well as the smaller ones and the ones in the ranks in between, they all told the same story: "You cannot imagine if we only once had mentioned that we were sympathyzing with you we would have been put ruthlessly into the streets with our families." It was such a brutal system! They could only fool the world by covering all their deeds with the word "christianity," they were so slimy. But they were the most brutal days that ever did exist. I have to say I take my hat off to those in Russia, at least they are honest. On top of it, these people here were infamous. There they did not behead people—well, some of them they did behead—but here they killed, they ruined them. One thing I want to say: it is claimed we overpowered the Austrian people and took away their independence, then one should admit at least that just one little part of it was put under pressure—not by us—and that was the government which existed on such a small basis. The Austrian people have only been freed by now. I would suggest to Halifax or to some real serious people whom he trusts to just send them over, so they may have a picture of what is going on here. They shall travel through the country, then they will see everything. Besides, I also want to point out, yesterday, you know, if there—they were saying the most serious things, war, and so on, it made me laugh because where would one find such an unscrupulous statesman who would send again millions of people to death only because 2 German brother-nations—

R:   Yes, this is absolutely ridiculous; one realizes that

over here; I do think one knows pretty well over here what is going on.

G:   Mr. Ribbentrop, I would call attention to one fact particularly: What state in the whole world will get hurt by our union?

[*This sort of logic used to be quite convincing to many people. That Czechoslovakia, with Anschluss, was now pretty thoroughly surrounded was not made a part of the picture by these people. Goering here, of course, is briefing Ribbentrop—just wanting to make sure that the Ambassador knows the right things to tell the British government and public.*]

Do we take anything away from any other state? If the states say: well, that is against our interests! What kind of interest did these states have? They only could have one interest, to create hostile feelings against Germany. The percentage of minorities does not exceed more that 0.1% over all Austria. All the people are German, all the people speak German. Well, not one single state is involved in it. And the states which as the only ones might have an interest. You may say that, Italy and Yugoslavia and Hungary because a few hundred thousand Germans are living there—those who could say that they might feel etc—they actually do not feel that they are threatened. Therefore, if France—Besides I do want to point out that the Czechoslovakian minister came to see me yesterday and he explained, that the rumor Czechoslovakia had mobilized was taken out of the thin air and they would be satisfied with one word from me that I would not undertake the slightest thing against Czechoslovakia.

R:   Of this the embassy was already informed the day before yesterday. He himself called here yesterday and told Woermann so.

G:   Thereupon I said the following: the German troops are supposed to stay away 15-20 Km from the border, on their march through Austria, and north of the Danube in the whole sector only one dissolved battalion was to march merely so that these villages can share in the joy and pleasure. Today the advance does no more take place according to military principles but all over the roads smaller columns are marching because every village wants to see a German soldier.

R: Now let me tell you this: Later on I want to take a plane. I paid my farewell visit to everyone already the day before yesterday. The embassy takes care of all business. I do not have any more authority.

G: But the Fuehrer thought that because you were just there that you could inform the people what is really go on. Above all, that it is absolutely wrong to think Germany had given an ultimatum.

R: I have already spoken very openly with Halifax and Chamberlain. There is no doubt about it. Only the fact that the newspapers—people start to ask questions and it does not seem to be right if I still remain here, it would look strange, somehow.

G: No, no, I think so, too. Only, I did not know if you spoke already to these people. I want that you once more—but no—not at all once more—but generally speaking—tell the following to Halifax and Chamberlain: It is not correct that Germany has given any ultimatum. That is a lie by Schuschnigg, because the ultimatum was presented to him by S-I, Glaise-Horstenau, and Jury. Furthermore, it is not true that we have presented an ultimatum to the Federal President, but it also was given by the others and as far as I know, just a military attache came along, asked by S-I, because of a technical question; he was supposed to ask whether in case S-I would ask for the support of German troops, Germany would grant this request.

[*Goering is referring here to no less a person than Lt. General Muff; it will be recalled that Muff did considerably more than ask Berlin if it cared to send troops to support the Nazi camp.*]

Furthermore I want to state that S-I asked us expressly—by phone as by telegram to send troops because he did not know about the situation in Wiener-

46

Neustadt, Vienna, and so on; because arms had been distributed there. And then he could not know how the Fatherland Front might react since they always had had such a big mouth.

R: Mr. Goering, tell me, how is the situation in Vienna, is everything settled yet?

G: Yes. Yesterday I landed hundreds of airplanes with some companies, in order to secure the airfield and they were received with joy. Today the advance unit of the 17. division marches in, together with the Austrian troops. Also I want to point out that the Austrian troops did not withdraw but that they got together and fraternized immediately with the German troops, wherever they were stationed.

R: That had to be expected.

G: The marching in took place, then, according to this wish. Now we also recognize that further invasion is no more necessary. The whole affair is rolling as it is supposed to roll and it has crystallized into a march of joy; if you want to call it like that, as soon as it will stop—which will be either tomorrow or the day after tomorrow—the transport back shall start. The Austrian Government has informed us that it will then hold a free and secret election, on the basis of democratic principles, so that every Austrian will be able to give his real free vote in a free and secret election. And therefore they want to ask people from abroad so that afterwards no reproach of falsification can be made—like Schuschnigg did—so that they will see that this is a real and secret election. It is also in our interest because we are absolutely convinced that we shall get an overwhelming majority. Therefore it is also in our interest that this election will be handled absolutely correctly. After the election then we shall see the decision the people made and we shall see what is going to happen. But above [*about?*] one thing you must not have any doubt: We will respect the decision, Austria will make in any respect. And, in case she decided for union—of which we have no doubt—then no power on earth will be able to separate us. It may be that a world-league of all states may overpower Germany, but it won't be possible that we will tolerate to be separated again if Austria decides to go together with Germany. And this is no threat for any state whatsoever, I want to make that clear. In no respect are we threatening the CSR [*Czechoslovakian republic*] but the CSR has now the possibility to come to a friendly and reasonable agreement with us.

[*Munich is a bare six months away; and in another six months this CSR shall have been swallowed whole by Germany.*]

They say (the CSR): "We did not mobilize any soldiers in the West. Nothing has been changed in the present situation." Everything under the condition that France remains sensible and does not take any steps. Naturally, if France organizes now a big mobilization close to the border, then it'll not be funny.

R: I believe they will behave all right.

G: We have a clear conscience and that is the decisive factor. Before world history we have a free conscience. Never has it happened in the world that anyone did interfere if two brother nations united. That would be against the sovereign rights of people. That would be absolutely ridiculous.

R:- I had a long intensive conversation with Halifax, and I told him our basic conception also in respect to the German-English understanding—

G: That I wanted to say, you know yourself, Ribbentrop, that I always was in favor of a German-English understanding. No one else would be more glad than I, if the English really wanted it seriously, and if they also recognized that we are also a proud and free nation. After all, we also do represent 2 brother nations.

R: I can tell you one thing, Mr. Goering. The other day I spoke to Chamberlain after that breakfast, and I got a very good impression of him, and he gave me a message, some news for the Fuehrer, which I shall [*sic*]. Will you be in Berlin this afternoon?

G: Yes, I will. We celebrate the "Memorial Day" but

let me tell you this, you'll have to stay in Berlin. The Fuehrer himself gave me the order that every minister— You know, otherwise we would have a great migration— Yesterday not one single minister and official was at home I would have needed 1000 planes. Naturally, they all want to enjoy this ecstasy of joy. Therefore I had to keep the gentlemen back by using draconic measures.

R: I cannot tell you that over the phone. But it is better for me to take off today.

G: Yes, I leave it entirely to you.

R: Otherwise it will not make sense. My conversations are concluded, and if I sit around it might give a funny impression. But I had an excellent impression of Chamberlain.

G: I am glad to hear that.

R: The other day I spoke quite a while to him. I do not want to speak about it over the phone, but I have the impression that Chamberlain also is very serious about an understanding. I told in this conversation that after the Austrian problem had been settled, the understanding between Germany and England will be so much less complicated than before, I believe, he realized that.

G: Look, since the whole problem has been settled down there and no more danger of excitement and disturbance exists—and this was a source of real danger—the people should be thankful for our having eliminated this source of crisis.

R: I told them that, too, and also pointed out that we got rid of a situation, which caused always many troubles. Even if there was some excitement at this moment, the great line for the German-English understanding could only be strengthened by it. I also said to Halifax at the end of our conversation that we honestly do want to come to an understanding and he replied that his only worry was the CSR.

G: No, no, that is out of the question.

R: I told him then that we were not interested and we did not intend to do anything there. On the contrary, if our Fellow-Germans were treated in a sensible way, then we should come to an agreement there, too.

G: Yes, I am also convinced that Halifax is an absolutely reasonable man.

R: I got the best impression of Halifax as well as of Chamberlain. He thought it would be a little difficult with our (Engl.) public opinion, but here it looks like force etc. I have the feeling that the normal Englishman, the man in the street will say, why should England bother with Austria. And therefore I believe that if the English Government will tell Chamberlain today, him as the leader—after all he is the leader; he himself said so during the last few weeks if he really does interfere in this case and if he gives an explanation in the sense in which we worked it out together (3 words unintelligible) that at home, our Fuehrer, as far as he could see that it is proved by the public English opinion which after a few days or weeks on a great problem of world history in the sense of a German-English understanding like we all desire it. (extremely unintelligible)

[*The parenthetical remark is a gratuitous one. But it should be understood that such patches will occur in an account which faces these three hurdles: accurate notation of a telephone conversation; hasty translation from the German (hasty because the Nurenberg prosecutors wanted such documentary evidence as this); and Nazi dialectics.*]

G: This is absolutely clear. (The following unintelligible). There are matters which do concern people, and there are matters which do not concern them at all.

R: I have to say through my last conversation with Halifax I have the impression that he did not react to the arguments I gave him, but at last he said I could be convinced that he also did favor a German-English understanding.

G: More or less everything is in wonderful peace. Two peoples embrace each other and are overjoyed and express their happiness.

R: All the people over here think—

G: Another people which other—the other state

bears the whole responsibility if such misery overcomes the people. Besides I must say, Mussolini behaved wonderfully.

R: Yes, I heard already about it.

G: Wonderful.

R: Very good, indeed. We always thought so!

G: Marvellous! He (M) said Schuschnigg asked him about the election. So he answered Schuschnigg: you cannot do that, you cannot do it, such a kind of an election has never happened before; now we have the material which shows how Schuschnigg wanted to carry out these elections. (Some words unintelligible). Every single vote we found was a yes vote. Only votes which did indicate neither yes nor no were considered as no-votes and on these slips was written "*I say no* Hermann Goering, Innsbruck, Strasse 2."

R: Unbelievable. Any one of the small people would never have dared do that.

G: Listen, if someone took a yes-vote and crossed it out with a pencil and then wrote over it "no," then this was considered as "yes." If you took a yes-vote and you tore it into 2 pieces and you threw both parts in, then it was not considered as one vote, but it counted for 2 yes-votes since it was torn into pieces.

R: Really?

G: As true as I am here! These are the secret matters which we will still publish.

R: By God, you should publish it immediately, this is unbelievable.

G: Well, every torn vote was considered as a yes-vote; so if several were torn, one did not put them together, but every single torn piece was a yes-vote.

R: This is quite unbelievable.

G: Now—but how did one vote!

R: Do we have any material which gives us a clue?

G: Yes, yes, this is how it happened: Well, you went into the voting place and said: I am Mr. Meier! "Yes, Mr. Meier, give me your vote." Now they said that the registry of all the inhabitants was delivered. Well, let's say, this Mr. Meier had this list and he marked it. Then he went into the next voting place in Innsbruck; they had the same lists, every voting had these lists (words unintelligible). Mr. Meier said: "I want to vote." "Please, Mr. Meier." It is being marked again. Now he goes into the third voting-place, where again one has the same list, because every voting-place always had the same list.

R: It is unbelievable.

G: Now, he gives his vote for the third time. The only fear these people had was the following: that one might find more yes-votes than there were people entitled to vote. But even that would not have bothered them, they would just have subtracted them.

R: They just would have subtracted them.

G: S-I believes—and so do I—that he may still find out through interrogation of these employees that they already had fixed beforehand the numbers of the yes and no-votes and also the amount of peoples who had not given their vote at all.

R: Unintelligible.

G: That was the most brazen election which would even have taken place.

R: Immediately when I was informed first I expressed myself very strongly against this election as a pure swindle a few days ago in my conversation with Halifax.

G: Listen: Another swindle was exacted. In spite of the fact that there is a new Minister for foreign affairs, the ambassadors—I believe also the one in London, Frankenstein, (p.h.) went and they have responsibility (unintelligible) toward their old government—they were made to come, changed opinions of their new minister according to their convictions. This is being investigated. S-I informed me about it yesterday. He said, he found out, that there still exist connections between the embassies and underground forces, that is unauthorized people of the old government on behalf of the new one. Do you understand?

R: Yes.

G: And this is supposed to have happened in London.

R: Yes, yes. Frankenstein himself—we have a few

people, I know, they are very unfriendly.

G: How is Frankenstein?

R: Well, toward us—I do not know how he really feels, you see—they borrowed swastika flag for today—

G: That is fine.

R: Yes, that is OK. But I believe he always showed himself loyal and decent toward me, I cannot say differently; I cannot say how he really feels, though. But, as you know, we have a few people here who are most disagreeable.

G: But tell Frankenstein he has to represent the present government.

R: Yes, that is understood.

G: Well, any way, S-I told me yesterday, I do not know whether it was the Austrian Minister in England or in Paris, I believe Paris, who asked. Is it correct that the Austrian government asked for the German troops? So he was told by the new foreign office: Yes, that is correct. Well, we said that the new ministry for foreign affairs did say the government had not asked for them. This matter is being investigated.

[*In the above, the second from last sentence is apparently in error. The gist of the paragraph, however, is doubt in Austrian mind, in Paris about the legality of the change in government.*]

R: There are far more fellows there who just try to mingle in; well, thank you so much, Mr. Goering.

G: Come over here, it is beautiful over here.

R: Well, I shall come this afternoon. Generally speaking, I do believe it is a wonderful thing.

G: I want to tell you, I am happy beyond all description. You do not know how much I suffered under the Austrian question. That was what always made me suffer so immensely, as a German. I never could understand that 4 foreign powers were against us—when just Germans were yearning for Germans. Always this penetrated me to my marrow.

R: I have also, you know, in a very short time—I do

not think I am wrong—one will say here—by God, it is good that finally a problem has been settled in such a peaceful way—isn't it fantastic—

G: Now listen, I do not ask for anything but that the world will respect the election in Austria as we do. If this will happen then I believe that in the next [*near?*] future (unintelligible).

R: And then I believe, we may—

G: Ribbentrop then you have to mention another thing, if you have a chance to—it is very important. The Austrian people is ruined economically. There are many, many unemployed people, a terrific misery. In case Austria will make her decision in favor of Germany, we will be able to help these people with our great economic program. We can continue the Autobahn immediately [*i.e., into Austria*], we can build more highways, we can buy again timber, also some cattle, and imagine, Austria always has lived for tourists. Imagine, if now Austria will make her decision for Germany, then—I am sure—there will not exist a German who will not go to Austria next summer.

R: Well, I believe the unemployment problem will no more exist there, within a short time. I guarantee you, I personally—

G: I believe—within the next 6 weeks—there will be no more un-employed in Austria—but everybody will be working, and they will be put to work in Austria, herself.

R: I want to tell you one more thing: I have not left any doubt whatsoever—that in case of a threat, or if anything would happen—the Fuhrer and the whole nation will stand behind it—100 percent.

G: Let me tell you the following confidentially: the Fuehrer who is usually well controlled—is too much involved in this respect with his heart since it concerns his homeland. I believe if he receives any threat in the Austrian question he will never give in, and I have to make it clear, neither will the 2 nations. That would be a fanatic matter, in Germany as well as in Austria.

R: That is clear.

G: There is no doubt. Who ever threatens, us now,

will strike at both peoples, and both shall put up a fanatic resistance.

R: I believe there is no doubt about that anywhere.

G: Yes, if anyone insists on it, all right—But I always say if there is any statesmen in the world unscrupulous enough—because 2 German people want to get united—ready to threaten with war, or who ever is ready to send millions of people to the battlefield—let him come. I rather want my people eliminated than that they may give in to this.

R: I never left any doubt about that. But I may say, that I am of the opinion that one is rather reasonable, I do believe.

G: In that—I have to say—I'd not see anything reasonable, that would be the most absurd thing. Then the world would have become an insane asylum. It might be different if there was a people over there which might resist with all its force against a German invasion and ask the whole world for help. Then I might understand that. This is just ridiculous.

R: Yes, Mr. Goering—

G: Well, do come! I shall be delighted to see you.

R: I shall see you this afternoon.

G: The weather is wonderful here. Blue sky. I am sitting here on my balcony—all covered with blankets—in the fresh air, drinking my coffee. Later on I have to drive in, I have to make the speech, and the birds are twittering, and here and there I can hear over the radio the enthusiasm, which is wonderful over there.

R: That is marvellous.

G: I do envy all those who could be there yesterday. I have to sit here and have to keep the key position.

R: Just a while ago we also listened in.

G: It is interesting, did you hear the Fuhrer's speech from Linz?

R: No, unfortunately not.

G: To me it was the most interesting one—it was very short—the most interesting speech I ever heard from the Fuehrer. This man who masters the language as hardly anyone—this man could hardly speak. It was not much that he said, but he was deeply moved. Then later he phoned me and said: "Goering, you cannot imagine, how beautiful my homeland is—I had forgotten it." Today he is visiting the grave of his parents where he will deposit a wreath. Linz, imagine, for many years it has been the first time that he is in the city [*sic*], at the grave of his parents—how crazy and grotesque circumstances have been. Imagine, shortly before the Berchtesgadener agreement—when the house of my sister was searched, she is married to the present secretary of Justice—the pictures of the Fuhrer and the one of myself—of her own brother—were taken away. (Next sentence cannot be understood). Nothing was written about that.

R: Was the Fuhrer very much shocked?

G: Yes, very much so. I believe that he goes through very dark days... Well, do Come!

R: Goodby and Heil Hitler.

G: Heil Hitler.

[*On this same day the Fuehrer spoke more succinctly to the Italian dictator.*]

March 13, 1938                    9. Document 2467-PS

To his excellency the Italian minister president and DUCE of Fascist Italy,

Benito Mussolini.

Mussolini, I shall never forget this of you!

signed: ADOLF HITLER

[*The day before, March 12, 1938, the German foreign minister, answering foreign protests against German pressure stated, in a letter to the British Ambassador, Sir Neville Henderson, the official German view of the action just completed.*]

A crisis of the Cabinet occurred in Vienna which, on the 11th of March, resulted in the resignation of the former Chancellor and in the formation of a new Cabinet. It is untrue that the Reich used forceful pressure to bring about this development. Especially the assertion which was spread later by the former Chancellor, that the German Government had presented the Federal President with a conditional ultimatum, is a pure invention; according to the ultimatum he had to appoint a proposed man as Chancellor and to form a Cabinet conforming to the proposals of the German Government, otherwise the invasion of Austria by German troops was held in prospect. The truth of the matter is that the question of sending military or police forces from the Reich was only brought up when the newly formed Austrian Cabinet addressed a telegram, already published by the press, to the German Government, urgently asking for the dispatch of German troops as soon as possible in order to restore peace and order and to avoid bloodshed. Faced with the immediately threatening danger of a bloody civil war in Austria, the German Government then decided to comply with the appeal addressed to it.

Signed:    Freiherr von Neurath

[*Thus ended "Case Otto" and, for the time being, Austria. Now Germany surrounded Czechoslovakia on three fronts. The impact of this event produced, in America, divided opinions. The isolationist front saw nothing in the development which was of consequence to this nation. Said Senator Borah, leading spokesman for this large segment of the American population: ". . . if you begin your study of the event with the signing of the Versailles Treaty, that which happened to Austria would appear natural, logical and inevitable, and a thing which is not of the slightest moment to the Government, as a government, of the United States." (Survey of International Affairs, 1938, Royal Institute of International Affairs, p. 594.) Speaking for the interventionists the New*

*York Herald Tribune admitted that this country could not be expected to underwrite the whole of Anglo-French diplomacy, but "if the democracies were to find themselves at war on clear principles and with a definite purpose, the case would be very different. In such a war they would not call in vain on the support of American factories, American natural resources, and American resources. The Austrian incident has had a profound effect on American opinion. Whether it would add the United States as a reserve of strength to the European democratic front depended on the firmness of Anglo-French policy." (Ibid., 598).*

*Both the New York Times and the Christian Science Monitor failed to understand the meaning of Anschluss viz-a-viz Italo-German relations. Both believed that Hitler's forced union of the German states had played havoc with Mussolini's willingness further to collaborate with the Fuehrer (Ibid., 595). Had they been able to listen in on the Hessen-Hitler telephone conversation, recorded above, they would have been in a better position to assay the situation. The Monitor further believed "that Pan-Germanism had now reached its natural limits ... and ... while deploring that Europe had conceded to force what it had not conceded to reason or justice (believed) that even the German people would back force only as long as it was used to remedy injustices, and that it could therefore never be effectively used against Czecho-slovakia." (Ibid., 597-598.) How unsound this opinion was, was soon to be demonstrated.]*

# III

## Case Green

*Goering Gives His Word of Honor*

March 12, 1938, London          11. Document TC-27

[*After World War I Czechoslovakia commonly came to be regarded as the soundest of the small states of central and eastern Europe. Her leadership, under President Thomas Masaryk and Foreign Minister Benes, was advanced; her people's political know-how in the case of the "Czechia" part of the state at least probably as great as France's and greater than any central or eastern continental people; her economy sound (until, of course, the depression); her literacy rate high and educational program well developed; and her defenses were among the best in Europe. She was regarded as a model succession state. Moreover, American sentimental ties with her were fairly strong (it will be recalled that Czechoslovakia's Declaration of Independence was signed in Independence Hall, Philadelphia, in the closing months of World War I).*

*It is true that a large German minority—formerly a part of the Austro-Hungarian empire, never a part of Germany—clustered along the South Mountains (Sudetenland), numbering some three and one half million. But until the advent of the depression and Hitler there had never been serious trouble between these Germans and the state of which they were a part. Indeed, the prosperity and general happiness of the Sudeten Germans were often cited as an example of what enlightened statecraft could effect in a continent plagued by minorities' strife.*

In spite of these advantaes, Czechoslovakia was not free from potential threats to her security and territorial integrity. It must be remembered that besides the Czechs (Bohemians and Moravians) and the German minority, there were two other ethnic groups included in the state—the Slovakians and the Ruthenians. Ethnically and linguistically the Slovakians were related to the Czechs—but there were still differences. Culturally and politically the two were far apart. For many centuries Slovakia had been Hungary-dominated and influenced, while the Czechs were oriented towards the teutonic Austrian part of the Austro-Hungarian empire. These differences led in our own times to the formation of a minority group in Slovakia, led by Mgr. A. Hlinka (later by Father Joseph Tiso) desiring a complete separation from the Czechs. The third ethnic group, the Ruthenians, are really Ukranians. Before World War I they were a part of the Austro-Hungarian empire; after the war they were incorporated into Czechoslovakia. Their language and religion are distinctly different from both the Czechs' and the Slovakians'.

Religious differences in Czechoslovakia were not without significance. Although the majority of the Czechs were Roman Catholic, there existed a very strong anti-clerical party, besides a strong minority Protestant bloc. In Slovakia these latter groups were practically non-existent. Hence tension from this source was felt from time to time.

A further difficulty rooted in the Treaty of Trianon, signed after World War I, which, unfortunately, assigned close to a million Hungarians to the Slovakian part of Czechoslovakia. The Hungarians, a proud and energetic people, never really accepted this verdict. Agitation for treaty revision therefore continually plagued relations between Hungary and the Prague government. Hitler later made use of these tensions, as the documents presented below demonstrate.

Under Hitler, Germany pursued a seemingly complicated but actually very simple policy toward this newly created state. The Sudeten Germans were to be "brought home;" the military bastion of "Czechia" was to be conquered and annexed; Slovakia was to be made into a puppet state; Ruthenia was to be given to Hungary provided the latter played ball with the Fuehrer. In carrying out this policy Hitler stressed publicly the ethnic identity of the Sudeten-deutsch and the Germans, played up the incongruity of the Czech-Slovak Trianon "marriage," encouraged Slovakian dissidents to secede from the state by now secretly promising help and now covertly encouraging the Hungarians to demand large slices of Slovakia in order better to soften up the latter when the decisions seemed hard to make. Continually he played Hungary against Slovakia for the purpose of weakening the whole state and thus bringing nearer the day when he could dominate both the Czechs and the Slovakians. In the Ruthenians he was uninterested, save as bait to encourage Hungary to play his game against Slovakia.

Toward the Balkan states, Yugoslovia, Rumania, and Bulgaria, his aims, again, were quite simple. Yugoslavia was an important trade area, nothing was to be allowed to retard commercial development here. But politically, Hitler did not mind if Mussolini called the turn in this Balkan nation. The Duce had long cast eyes towards the Dalmation coast and beyond; if Italy could come to dominate Yugoslavia without it in any way penalizing Yugoslav-German economic relations, such would be acceptable to the German leader. The one thing above all others not to be countenanced was infiltration into Yugoslav political life of Russian influence. As things turned out, Hitler took over the role of conqueror here too, when Mussolini proved weaker than was thought, and the Russians somewhat stronger. Rumania was needed in the German orbit for two reasons—to keep it from being used as a springboard by the Russians, and to guarantee needed oil deliveries. As for Bulgaria, Hitler looked upon it as a wedge to foster his drive against Russia.

Among the Balkan states themselves friction was great and chronic. Boundary questions constituted a perennial *problem. For centuries Greece, Bulgaria, Rumania and Serbia—or the peoples representing these nation-names—have drawn and redrawn map lines; and this boundary uncertainty exists down to the present day. For reasons the telling of which is beyond the scope of this brief introduction, Bulgaria has more or less found itself lined up against the other Balkan states. Consequently now this great power and that one has used Bulgaria to further its own Balkan designs. Religion plays an important part in keeping the Balkan pot boiling. Three religions vie for dominance in this small area—Roman Catholic, Greek Orthodox, and Mohammedan. In Yugoslavia all three uneasily rub elbows. Moreover, linguistic differences are sharp. In Belgrade, for example, street signs during the period between World Wars I and II used three different languages and two alphabets; a feeling of unity and concord can hardly exist in such a situation.*

*For these and other reasons the Balkans have long been known as the powder keg of Europe. In the 1930's the main fuse leading to this keg stemmed from Czechoslovakia, not itself a Balkan nation but inextricably connected with the complex of Balkan problems. After Anschluss Hitler turned his attention to this state. The following documents tell the story of German expansion in this area. The first is a declaration reported by Jan Masaryk, son of the first president, and then Czech ambassador to London—a declaration received by Czechoslovakia from Germany.]*

Yesterday evening (the 11th March) Field Marshal Goering made two separate statements to M. Mastny, the Czechoslovak Minister in Berlin, assuring him that the developments in Austria will in no way have any detrimental influence on the relations between the German Reich and Czechoslovakia, and emphasizing the continued earnest endeavor on the part of Germany to improve those mutual relations.

In the first statement the field-marshal used the

expression: "Ich gebe Ihnen mein Ehrewort" [*I give you my word of honor.*]

In the second statement Field-Marshal Goering asserted that, having given his own word previously, he was now able to give the word of the head of State, who had authorized him to take over temporarily his official duties. He then repeated the above assurances.

Today (the 12th March) Field Marshal Goering asked M. Mastny to call on him, repeated yesterday's assurances and added that the German troops, marching into Austria, have strictest orders to keep at least 15 kilom. from the Czechoslovak frontier; at the same time he expressed the hope that no mobilization of the Czechoslovak army would take place.


March 17, 1938                    12. Document 2789-PS

[*Konrad Henlein wrote a congratulatory note, after Anschluss, to Ribbentrop. Henlein was the leader of the Nazi party in the Sudetenland of Czechoslovakia.*]

Most honored Minister of Foreign Affairs:
In our deeply felt joy over the fortunate turn of events in Austria we feel it our duty to express our gratitude to all those who had a share in this new grand achievement of our Fuhrer.

I beg you, most honored Minister, to accept accordingly the sincere thanks of the Sudeten Germans herewith.

We shall show our appreciation to the Fuhrer by doubled efforts in the service of the Greater German Policy.

The new situation requires a re-examination of the Sudeten German policy. For this purpose I beg to ask you for the opportunity for a very early personal talk.

In view of the necessity of such a clarification I have postponed the Nation-wide Party Congress, originally scheduled for 26th and 27th of March, 1938, for 4 weeks.

I would appreciate if the Ambassador, Dr. Eisenlohr,

and two of my closest associates would be allowed to participate in the requested talks.

Heil Hitler
Loyally yours
Konrad Henlein

March 29, 1938, 12:00 noon,
Reich Foreign Office          13. Document 2788-PS

[*This document is made of notes of a conference called by Ribbentrop to discuss "the new situation." Besides Ribbentrop, present were Henlein himself, Karl Haushofer, the geopolitician, Karl Frank, later deputy-governor of the "Protectorate," Ambassador Eisenlohr and Weissaecker, an offical in the German foreign office.*]

The Reichminister started out by emphasizing the necessity to keep the conference which had been scheduled strictly a secret; he then explained, in view of the directives which the Fuhrer himself had given to Konrad Henlein personally yesterday afternoon, that there were two questions which were of outstanding importance for the conduct of the policy of the Sudeten German Party:

1. The Sudeten Germans must realize that they are backed up by a nation of 75 million which will not tolerate a continued suppression of the Sudeten Germans by the Czechoslovak Government.

[2. ?] It is the task of the Sudeten German Party to formulate such demands from the Czechoslovak Government as it deems necessary in order to obtain the privileges desired by it.

The Foreign Minister explained in this connection that it could not be the task of the Reich Government to give Konrad Henlein, whose position as the leader of the Sudeten Germans has been acknowledged and again confirmed by the Fuhrer, detailed suggestions about what to demand from the Czechoslovak Government. It is essential to propose a maximum program, which as its final aim grants full freedom to the Sudeten Germans. It appears dangerous to be satisfied prematurely with the consent of the Czechoslovakian Government; this on the one hand would give the impression abroad that a solution has been found, and on the other hand would only partially satisfy the Sudeten Germans. In any case, caution is the proper thing, because one cannot have any confidences in the assurances of Benes and Hodza according to past experiences. The aim of the negotiations to be carried out by the Sudeten German party with the Czechoslovakian Government is finally this: to avoid entry into the Government by the extension and gradual specification of the demands to be made.

[*In other words Ribbentrop is instructing the Sudeten Germans to thwart a peaceful settlement of the Sudeten question. If the Czech government consented to a list of Sudeten demands, the list was to be lengthened; if this new list were agreed to, new demands were to be made.*]

Konrad Henlein was instructed to keep in the closest possible touch with the Reichminister and the Head of the Central Office for Racial Germans, as well as the German Minister in Prague, as the local representative of the Foreign Minister.

April 22, 1938, Reichchancellery     14. Document 388
PS-item 2

[*On this day Hitler and Keitel discussed Czechoslovakia. Hitler's adjutant, Schmundt, was present and prepared the notes which comprise this part of the document. In number B. 1 below "Gruen" refers to Fall Gruen—Case Green—which was the German code name for action against Czechoslovakia; the later reference to "Rot" signifies the German army's plans in case war broke out between Germany and France—i.e., "Case Red." A word about Case Green is necessary here. Originally (shortly after 1935) Case Green was prepared in the more or less formal way that military plans are prepared during peacetime by all countries, for use in a possible contingency the elements of which were not at the time foreseen. In like manner the United States has, presumably, in its War Department files a plan of action for a Mexican war should one ever break out. But it is of the essence, here, to understand that the more or less formal planning of Case Green gradually turned into the deliberate pattern of aggression which it later obtained. At the Nuremberg trials the Defense consistently sought to prove that these "Cases" were merely formal military matters unconnected with current politics. In the case of Fall Gruen, let the reader judge for himself.*]

## A.   Political Aspect

1. Strategic surprise attack out of a clear sky without any cause or possibility of justification has been turned down. As result would be: hostile world opinion which can lead to a critical situation. Such a measure is justified only for the elimination of the *last* opponent on the mainland.

2. Action after a time of diplomatic clashes, which gradually come to a crisis and lead to war.

3. Lightning swift action as the result of an incident (*e.g.*, assassination of German ambassador in connection with an anti-German demonstration.)

## B.   Military Conclusions

1. The preparations are to be made for the political possibilities 2 and 3. Case 2 is the undesired one since "Gruen" [*i.e.*, *Czechoslovakia*] will have taken security measures.

2. The loss of time caused by transporting the bulk of the divisions by rail—which is unavoidable but should be cut down as far as possible—must not impede a lightning-swift blow at the time of action.

3. "Separate thrusts" are to be carried out immediately with a view to penetrating the enemy fortification lines at

numerous points and in a strategically favorable direction. The thrusts are to be worked out to the smallest detail (knowledge of roads, of targets, composition of the columns according to their individual tasks). Simultaneous attacks by the Army and Air Force.

4. Politically, the first 4 days of military action are the decisive ones. If there are no effective military successes, a European crisis will certainly arise. Accomplished facts must prove the senselessness of foreign military intervention, draw Allies into the scheme (division of spoils!) and demoralize "Gruen."

5. If possible, separation of transport movement "Rot" from "Gruen." A simultaneous strategic concentration "Rot" can lead "Rot" to undesired measures. On the other hand it must be possible to put "Fall Rot" into operation at any time.

## C.  *Propaganda*

1. Leaflets on the conduct of Germans in Czechoslovakia.

2. Leaflets with threats for intimidation of the Czechs.

May 20th and 30th, 1938,
Reichschancellery                *Ibid.,* items 5 and 11

[*Shortly after the discussion above, Keitel set down a revised "Case Green" and submitted it to Hitler for his approval. In a letter to Hitler accompanying the new plan Keitel said: "It has not yet been discussed with the Commanders-in-Chief. I intend to do this only after this draft in its fundamental ideas has been approved by you my Fuehrer, so that it can then be resubmitted to be signed." Ten days later the Hitler revision, signed by him, was distributed. Both the Keitel preliminary and Hitler final drafts are here presented. In between the two, Czechoslovakia partially mobilized against what she considered a German threat in the third week in May.*]

| [*Keitel*] | [*Hitler*] |
|---|---|
| 1. *Political Prerequisites:* It is not my intention to smash Czechoslovakia without provocation, in the near future through military action. Therefore inevitable political developments *within* Czechoslovakia must force the issue, or political events in Europe create an especially favorable opportunity and one which may never come again. | 1. *Political Prerequisites:* It is my unalterable decision to smash Czechoslovakia by military action in the near future. It is the job of the political leaders to await or bring about the politically and militarily suitable moment. |

An inevitable development of conditions inside Czechoslovakia or other political events in Europe creating a surprisingly favorable opportunity and one which may never come again may cause me to take early action.

The proper choice and determined and full utilization of a favorable moment is the surest guarantee of success. Accordingly the preparations are to be made at once.

2. Political Possibilities for the Commencement of the Action: An invasion without suitable obvious cause and without political justification cannot be considered with reference to the possible consequences of such an action in the

2. Political Possibilities for the Commencement of the Action: The following are necessary prerequisites for the intended invasion:

a. suitable obvious cause and, with it

b. sufficient political justification,

present situation.

Rather will the action be initiated either:

a. after a period of increasing diplomatic clashes and tension, which is coupled with military preparations and is made use of to push the war-guilt onto the enemy. Even such a period of tension preceding the war however will terminate in sudden military action on our part, which must come with all possible surprise as to time and extent, or

b. by lightning-swift action as the result of a serious incident through which Germany is provoked in an unbearable way and for which at least part of the world opinion will grant the moral justification of military action.

"b" is militarily and politically the more favorable.

c. action unexpected by the enemy, which will find him prepared to the least possible degree.

From a military as well as a political standpoint the most favorable course is a lightning-swift action through which Germany is provoked in an unbearable way for which at least part of the world opinion will grant the justification of military action.

But even a period of tension, more or less preceding a war, must terminate in sudden action on our part—which must have the elements of surprise as regards time and extent—before the enemy is so advanced in military preparedness that he cannot be surpassed.

3. *Conclusions for the Preparations of "Fall Gruen";* which must take into account the possibilities mentioned in 2a and 2b.

a. For *Armed War* it is essential to create—

3. *Conclusions for the Preparation of "Fall Gruen."*

a. For the *Armed War* it is essential that the surprise element as the most important factor contributing to success be

already in the first 4 days—a military situation which plainly proves to hostile nations eager to intervene, the hopelessness of the Czechoslovakian military situation, and gives the nations with territorial claims on Czechoslovakia an incentive to immediate intervention against Czechoslovakia. In such a case the intervention of Poland and Hungary against Czechoslovakia can be expected, especially if France, due to Italy's clearly pro-German attitude fears or at least hesitates, to unleash a European war by her intervention against Germany.

It is very probable that attempts by Russia to give military support to Czechoslovakia are to be expected. If concrete successes are not achieved as a result of the ground operations during the first few days, a European crisis will certainly arise.

b. The *Propaganda War* must, on the one hand, intimidate Czechoslovakia by threats and reduce her power of resistance, on the other

made full use of by appropriate preparatory measures, already in peace-time and by an unexpectedly rapid course of the action. Thus it is essential to create a situation within the first four days which plainly demonstrates, to hostile nations eager to intervene, the hopelessness of the Czechoslovakian military situation and which at the same time will give nations with territorial claims on Czechoslovakia an incentive to intervene immediately against Czechoslovakia. In such a case, intervention by Poland and Hungary against Czechoslovakia may be expected, especially if France—due to the obviously pro-German attitude of Italy—fears, or at least hesitates, to unleash a European war by intervening against Germany. Attempts by Russia to give military support to Czechoslovakia mainly by the Air Force are to be expected. If concrete successes are not achieved by the land operations within the first few days, a European crisis will certainly result. This knowl-

hand, give instructions to the national minorities for supporting the Armed War and influence the neutrals into our way of thinking.

c. The Economic War has the task of employing all means at the disposal of economy to hasten the final collapse of Czechoslovakia.

The opening of the Economic and Propaganda war can precede the Armed war. I myself will determine the date.

edge must give commanders of all ranks the impetus to decided and bold action.

b. The *Propaganda War* must on the one hand intimidate Czechoslovakia by threats and soften her power of resistance, on the other hand issue directions to national groups for support in the Armed War and influence the neutrals into our way of thinking. I reserve further directions and determination of the date.

May 28, 1938, Reichschancellery

15. Document 3037-PS

[*The following is an affidavit sworn to by Fritz Wiedemann, one of Hitler's adjutants in the period 1935-1939. On this day he himself attended the meeting he described.*]

I recall that on the afternoon of May 28, 1938 Hitler called a conference in the winter garden of the Reichs Chancellory of all the people who were important, from the Foreign Office, the Army, and the Command Staffs. Those at this conference, as I recall, included Goering, Ribbentrop, von Neurath, General Beck, Admiral Raeder, General Keitel, and General von Brauchitsch. On this occasion Hitler made the following statement: "It is my unshakable will that Czechoslovakia shall be wiped off the map." Hitler then revealed the outlines of the plan to attack Czechoslovakia. Hitler addressed himself to the Generals, saying: "So, we will first tackle the situation in the East. Then I will give you three to four years time, and then we will settle the situation in the West." The situation in the West was meant to be war against England and France.

I was considerably shaken by these statements, and on leaving the Reichs Chancellory I said to Herr von Neurath: "Well, what do you say to these revelations?" Neurath thought that the situation was not so serious as it appeared and that nothing would happen before the spring of 1939.

Undated entry in General Jodl's Diary, entered in the latter part of May, 1938    16. Document 1780-PS

[*General Jodl, chief of Hitler's Armed Forces Staff's Operations Division and perhaps closer to Hitler in this and later periods than any other military figure, even including Keitel, kept a diary which has several entries regarding "Case Green."*]

After the annexation of Austria, the Fuehrer mentions that there is no hurry to solve the Czech question because Austria has to be digested first. Nevertheless, preparations for case Green will have to be carried out energetically; they will have to be newly prepared on the basis of the changed strategic position because of the annexation of Austria.

[*In between the preceding sentence and the next occurred the Czech demonstration previously mentioned. The Czechs, alarmed at Hitler's absorption of Austria and fearful of being an immediately next victim partially mobilized in the frontier areas May 21, 1938. That action prompted the decision mentioned in the next entry.*]

The intention of the Fuehrer not to touch the Czech problem as yet is changed because of the Czech strategic troop concentration of 21 May, which occurs without any German threat and without the slightest cause for it.

[*The reader may not find it possible, in view of the above documents, to subscribe wholeheartedly to this Jodl item.*]

Because of Germany's self restraint, its consequences lead to a loss of prestige of the Fuhrer, which he is not willing to take once more. Therefore, the new order is issued for "Green" on 30 May.

[*And the May 30th entry in the Jodl Diary reads:*]

*30 May:*

The Fuhrer signs directive Green, where he states his final decision to destroy Czechoslovakia soon and thereby initiates military preparation all along the line. The previous intentions of the Army must be changed considerably in the direction of an immediate break-through into Czechoslovakia right on D-Day, combined with aerial penetration by the Air Force. Further details are derived from directive for strategic concentration of the army. The whole contrast becomes acute once more between the Fuehrer's intuition that we *must* do it this year and the opinion of the army that we cannot do it as yet, as most certainly the Western Powers will interfere and we are not as yet equal to them.

[*In between May and September Germany continued to put the heat on the harassed Czech state. The spearhead of the attack was Henlein's Sudeten party. Negotiations between this party and the Czech government went on throughout a good part of this period, with Henlein and his subordinates, egged on by Hitler, uping the ante in well calculated efforts to drive Benes and the Czechs to some desperate move. Beyond the harassment from the Sudeten Germans, the Czechs were beset by Hungarian demands for boundary changes, also encouraged by Hitler.*

*It was in this period that England began to fear war unless Czechoslovakia made drastic concessions. Out of this fear Chamberlain sent Lord Runciman to Prague, ostensibly to look over the situation and make such suggestions as he could, but actually to prepare the way for substantial appeasement of Hitler. (Some insight concerning Chamberlian's faith in the democratic way may be gained by reading a portion of a letter the Prime Minister wrote, in this year of crisis, to Dino Grandi, Italian ambassador to England. Said Chamberlain: "... I consider the Rome-Berlin Axis as a reality which might represent the most valuable pillar of European peace.... I want the Duce himself to know that while my immediate aim is a strong and permanent treaty with the Duce and Fascist Italy, my long range ... aim is a permanent and as strong as possible a treaty with the Fuehrer and National Socialist Germany." Quoted in Tansil, op. cit., pp. 381-382.) The following documents tell of the military and quasi military preparations made in the pre-Munich period, of the Balkan complications, the generals' plot to change the course of German history, its fiasco, the capitulation at Munich, and the final dismemberment of Czechoslovakia.*

September 18, 1938                    17. Document 388-PS,
                                                     item 25

[*German and Sudeten Nazis formed at this time a quasi-military organization called the Free Corps. It worked closely with the Sudeten German Party. The following telegram, found in adjutant Schmundt's files, bespeaks its importance.*]

LAST NIGHT CONFERENCE TOOK PLACE BETWEEN FUERHER AND OBERSTLEUTNANT KOECHLING. DURATION OF CONFERENCE SEVEN MINUTES. LT. COL. KOECHLING REMAINS DIRECTLY RESPONSIBLE TO OKW. HE WILL BE ASSIGNED TO KONRAD HENLEIN IN AN ADVISORY CAPACITY. HE RECEIVED FAR-

REACHING PLENARY POWERS FROM THE
FUERHER. THE SUDETEN GERMAN FREE
CORPS REMAINS RESPONSIBLE TO KONRAD
HENLEIN ALONE. PURPOSE: PROTECTION OF
THE SUDETEN GERMANS AND MAINTENANCE
OF DISTURBANCES AND CLASHES. THE FREE
CORPS WILL BE ESTABLISHED IN GERMANY.
ARMAMENT ONLY WITH AUSTRIA WEAPONS.
ACTIVITIES OF FREE CORPS TO BEGIN AS SOON
AS POSSIBLE.

September 26, 1938, Bayreuth    18. Document 388-PS,
item 30

[*This note, intended for Henlein but, according to a
pencilled notation by Schmundt, never sent off, was
written when the Munich crisis was reaching its climax.*]

Herr Benesch has dissolved the Sudeten-German
Party and believes that he will thus be able to destroy the
unity of the Sudeten-German racial group and to deal the
death blow to the Sudeten-Germans. Konrad Henlein
knew the answer to this. He issued a call on 17.9.38 for the
formation of a Sudeten-German Free Corps. Within a
few hours, thousands of Sudeten-Germans had already
[*flocked*] to the colors all along the border. Thousands
who were burning to fight for their tortured homeland
were forced, to their great disappointment, to remain at
their places of work, because it was impossible, in such a
short period of time, to induct, equip and arm the masses
of enthusiastic volunteers.

Since 19 Sept.—in more than 30 missions—the Free
Corps has executed its task with an amazing spirit of
*attack* [*here an inked correction is written in: "defense"*]
and with a willingness often reaching a degree of
unqualified self-sacrifice. The result of the first phase of
its activities: more than 1500 prisoners, 25 MG's and a
large amount of other weapons and equipment, aside

from serious losses in dead and wounded suffered by the *enemy [again an inked correction is written in: "The Czech Terrorists."]*

Thousands of members of the Sudeten-German Free Corps stand shoulder to shoulder on the frontiers of Germany. They are inspired by but one desire: The freedom of the homeland within Adolf Hitler's Greater Germany.

September, 1938          19. Document 3036-PS

*[This is an affidavit sworn out by Gottlob Berger, a member of the SS.]*

1. In the fall of 1938 I held the rank and title of Oberfuehrer in the SS. In mid-September I was assigned as SS Liaison Officer with Konrad Henlein's Sudeten German Free Corps at their headquarters in the castle at Dondorf outside Bayreuth. In this position I was responsible for all liaison between the Reichsfuehrer Himmler and Henlein.

2. In the course of my official duties at Henlein's Headquarters I became familiar with the composition and activities of the Free Corps. Three groups were being formed under Henlein's direction: One in the Eisenstein area, Bavaria; one in the Bayreuth area; one in the Dresden area; and possibly a fourth group in Silesia. These groups were supposedly composed of refugees from the Sudetenland who had crossed the border into Germany, but they actually contained Germans with previous service in the SA and NSKK (Nazi Motor Corps) as well. These Germans formed the skeleton of the Free Corps. On paper the Free Corps had a strength of 40,000. I do not know its actual strength, but I believe it to be considerably smaller than the paper figure.

3. In the days preceding the conclusion of the four-power pact at Munich I heard of numerous occasions on which the Henlein Free Corps was engaged in skirmishes

with Czech patrols along the border of the Sudetenland. These operations were under the direction of Henlein, who went forward from his Headquarters repeatedly in order to take direct command of his men.

August 24, 1938, Berlin      20. Document 388-PS, item 17

[*Meantime military preparations within Germany and diplomatic negotiations with Italy and Hungary (as well as others) were going on. The following is a memorandum sent by Hitler's military adviser, Jodl, to Hitler on this date requesting his opinion on a number of things, among them a difference between the army and air force which needed to be straightened out.*]

The *Luftwaffe's* endeavor to take the enemy air forces by surprise at their peace-time air ports justifiably leads them to oppose measures taken in advance of the X-order and to the demand that the X-order itself be given sufficiently late on X minus 1 to prevent the fact of Germany's mobilization becoming known to Czechoslovakia on that day.

The *Army's* efforts are tending in the opposite direction. It intends to let OKW initiate all advance measures between X minus 3 and X minus 1 which will contribute to the smoothness and rapid working of the mobilization.

To this the following must be said:

Operation Gruen will be set in motion by means of an "incident" in Czechoslovakia which will give Germany provocation for military intervention. The fixing of the *exact time* for this incident is of the utmost importance.

It must come at a time when weather conditions are favorable for our superior air force to go into action and at an hour which will enable authentic news of it to reach us on the afternoon of X minus 1.

[*This is a report by a Major D.G.H. Moericke who was
assigned to special work in Czechoslovakia. Later he was
charged with bungling his work. This report is in the
nature of a defense and was sent to Goering's office. At
the time of his "mission" he was air attaché at the German
legation in Prague.*]

I was ordered by the General Staff of the Air Force to
reconnoiter the land in the region of Freudenthal/Frei-
hermersdorf for landing possibilities.

For this purpose I obtained lodgings in Freudenthal
with the manufacturer Machdolt, through one of my
trusted men in Prague.

I had specifically ordered this man to give no details
about me to M, particularly about my official position.

I used my official car for the journey to Fr. taking
precautions against being observed.

The manufacturer M. is head of the Sudeten German
Glider Pilots in Fr. and said to be absolutely reliable by
my trusted man. My personal impression fully confirmed
this judgment. No hint of my identity was made known to
him, although I had the impression that M. knew who I
was.

At my request with which he complied without
question M. travelled with me over the country in
question. We used M.'s private car for the trip.

As M. did not know the country around Beneschau
sufficiently well, he took with him the local leader of the
F.S., a Czech reservist of the Sudeten German Racial
Group, at that time on leave. He was in uniform. For
reasons of camouflage I was entirely in agreement with
this—without actually saying so.

As M., during the course of the drive, observed that I
photographed large open spaces out of the car, he said
"Aha, so you're looking for airfields!" I answered that we
supposed that, in the case of any serious trouble, the

Czechs would put their airfields immediately behind the lines of fortifications. I had the intention of looking over the country from that point of view.

To my question as to when the farmers in this part were generally in the habit of ploughing up the fields he answered: "Always immediately after the harvest."

Before leaving Fr. I bound M. to absolute secrecy as regards what he had seen.

September 3, 1938,
the Berghof                     22. Document 388-PS, item 18

[*A portion of a report in Schumndt's handwriting giving details of a conversation between Hitler and von Brauchitsch, Commander-in-Chief of the German Army, is here given.*]

*Gen. Ob.v. Brauchitsch*
Reports on the exact time of the transfer of the troops to "exercise areas" for "Gruen." Field units to be transferred on 28 Sept. From here will then be ready for action. When X day becomes known, field units carry out exercises in opposite directions.

*Fuehrer*
Has objection. Troops assemble; field units a two-day march away. Carry out camouflage exercises everywhere.

?
OKH [*Army Headquarters*] must know when X day is by 1200 noon, 27 September.

September 28, 1938, Berlin          Document 388-PS,
                                                    item 33

[*This is a pencilled note by Schmundt entitled "Most Secret Memorandum."*]

At 1300 September 27 the Fuehrer and Supreme Commander of the Armed Forces ordered the movement of the assault units from their exercise areas to their jumping-off points.

The assault units (about 21 reinforced regiments, or 7 divisions) must be ready to begin action against "Gruen" on September 30, the decision having been made one day previously by 1200 noon.

This order was conveyed to General Keitel at 1320 through Major Schmundt.

August 23 and 27, 1938          23. Documents 2791-PS
                                                  and 2792-PS

[*Mussolini tried to get exact information regarding the German attack on Czechoslovakia but Germany was cagey in replying to such feelers. These two notes are initialed by Ribbentrop.*]

On the voyage of the *Patria* Ambassador Attolico explained to me that he had instructions to request the notification of the contemplated time for German action against Czechoslovakia from the German Government.

In case the Czechs should again cause a provocation against Germany, Germany would march. This would be tomorrow, in six months or perhaps in a year. However, I could promise him that the German government, in case of an increasing gravity of the situation or as soon as the Fuehrer made his decision, would notify the Italian Chief of government as rapidly as possible. In any case, the Italian government will be the first one who will receive such a notification.

[*And on the 27th*]

Ambassador Attolico paid me a visit today at 12 o'clock to communicate the following:

He had received another written instruction from

Mussolini asking that Germany communicate in time the probable date of action against Czechoslovakia. Mussolini asked for such notification, as Mr. Attolico assured me, in order "to be able to take in due time the necessary measures on the French frontier."

August 23rd and 25th, 1938    24. Documents 2796-PS
and 2797-PS

[*The Fuehrer wanted to count Hungary in, for this would increase Czechoslovakia's difficulties. Since 1919 Hungary had been demanding a substantial share of Czechoslovakian territory, as rightfully hers.*

*On the first date Hitler had a discussion with von Imredy, an Hungarian official. Two days later Ribbentrop talked to a colleague of Imredy's, von Kanya. Both of these documents were found in the files of the German Under-Secretary-of-State, Herr Woerman.*]

When Von Imredy had a discussion with the Fuehrer in the afternoon, he was very relieved when *the Fuehrer explained to him, that, in regard to the situation in question, he demanded nothing of Hungary.* He [*i.e., Hitler*] himself would not know the time. Whoever wanted to join the meal would have to participate in the cooking as well. Should Hungary wish conferences with the General Staffs, he would have no objections.

[*And on the 25th.*]

Concerning Hungary's military preparedness in case of a German-Czech conflict, von Kanya mentioned several days ago that his country would need a period of one to two years in order to develop adequately the armed strength of Hungary. During today's conversation von Kanya corrected this remark and said that Hungary's military situation was much better. His country would be ready as far as armaments were concerned, to take part in the conflict by October 1st of this year.

September 19, 1938, Berlin     25. Document 2858-PS

[*Slovakia was not forgotten, as the following telegram testifies. Altenburg was a foreign office official; "deputy Kundt" was a Slovakian member of the Czechoslovakian parliament.*]

Please inform deputy Kundt, at Konrad Henlein's request, to get into touch with the Slovaks at once and induce them to start *their* demands for autonomy tomorrow.

ALTENBURG

[*September 14th Henlein fled to Germany. The 26th Hitler made his famous Sportspalast speech saying the Sudetenland was his last territorial demand but it was a righteous one and would be carried through come what may. As a result, Chamberlian came to Munich. The Munich story is well known. Much less well known is a dramatic plot designed by the German opposition to dispose of Hitler and his regime, at the time of Munich. The plot involved some of the most important personages in the Reich. The account here given is by Hans Gisevius, a former official in the Ministry of the Interior, and by General Halder, Army Chief of Staff at the time of Munich and the man who was to have supervised the execution of the plot. An editorial statement shall show where Gisevius' account leaves off and Halder's takes up. The story as here told by Gisevius is taken from his testimony during the Nurenberg Trials, TRIAL OF THE MAJOR WAR CRIMINALS, 42 volumes, published by the Secretariat of the International Military Tribunal, 1946-1949, Vol. 12, pp. 213 et seq.; as told by Halder, from his interrogation as printed in NAZI CONSPIRACY AND AGGRESSION, United States Government Printing Office, Washington, D.C., 1946-1947, Supple-*]

*ment B, pp. 1557-58. Reference is made to Goerdeler, Witzleben, Schacht and Oster. Carl Goerdeler was a one time mayor of Leipzig who, in 1936, resigned as a means of protesting anti-Jewish measures; from 1931 to 1936 he was Reich Price Control Commissioner; he was one of the leading civilian members of the German resistance movement. Had the Generals' Plot of 1944 succeeded in doing away with Hitler and his government, Goerdeler would probably have been made Chancellor by the conspirators. Witzleben was a Field Marshal who, in 1938, was Commander of the Berlin Military District. Schacht was one-time Minister of Economics and president of the Reichsbank. Major General Hans Oster was one time Chief of the Central Division of the Bureau of Foreign Intelligence.]*

[*During the last days of July, 1938*] Halder once again declared his firm intention of effecting a revolt; but again he wished to wait until the German nation had received proof of Hitler's war-like intentions by means of a definite order for war. Schacht pointed out to Halder the tremendous danger of such an experiment. He made it clear to Halder that a war could not be started simply to destroy the Hitler legend in the eyes of the German people.

In a detailed and very excited conversation Halder then declared that he was prepared to start the revolt, not after the official outbreak of the war, but at the very moment that Hitler gave the army the final order to march.

We asked Halder whether he would then still be able to control the situation or whether Hitler might not surprise him with some lightning stroke. Halder replied literally, "No, he cannot deceive me. I have designed my General Staff plans in such a way that I am bound to know it 48 hours in advance." I think that is important, because during the subsequent course of events the period of time between the order to march and the actual march itself was considerably shortened.

Halder assured us that besides the preparations in

Berlin he had an armoured division ready in Thuringia under the command of General Von Hoeppner, which might possibly have to halt the Leibstandarte, which was in Munich, on the march to Berlin.

Although Halder had, told us all this, Schacht and I had a somewhat bitter aftertaste of that conference. Halder had told Schacht that he, Schacht, seemed to be urging him to effect this revolt prematurely; and Schacht and I were of the opinion that Halder might abandon us at the last moment. We informed Oster immediately of the bad impression we had had, and we told Oster that something absolutely must be done to win over another general in case Halder should not act at the last minute. Oster agreed and these are the preliminary events which led to the later General Field Marshal Von Witzleben first coming into our circle of conspirators.

Schacht won Witzleben over. Oster visited Witzleben and told him everything that had happened. Thereupon Witzleben sent for me, and I told him that in my opinion the police situation was such that he, as commanding General of the Berlin Army Corps, could confidently risk a revolt. Witzleben asked me the question which every general put to us at that time: Whether a diplomatic incident in the East [*i.e., Czechoslovakia*] would really lead to war or whether it was not true, as Hitler and Ribbentrop repeatedly told the generals in confidence, that there was a tacit agreement with the Western Powers giving Germany a free hand in the East. Witzleben said that if such an agreement really existed, then, of course, he could not revolt. I told Witzleben that Schacht with his excellent knowledge of the Anglo-Saxon mentality could no doubt give him comprehensive information about that.

A meeting between Schacht and Witzleben was arranged. Witzleben brought with him his division general, Von Brockdorff, who was to carry out the revolt in detail. Witzleben, Brockdorff, and I drove together to Schacht's country house for a conference which lasted for hours. The final result was that Witzleben was convinced by Schacht that the Western Powers would under no circumstances allow Germany into the Eastern territories and that now Hitler's policy of surprise had come to an end. Witzleben decided that he, on his part and independently of Halder, would make all preparations which would be necessary if he should have to act.

He issued me false papers and gave me a position at his district headquarters so that there, under his personal protection, I could make all the necessary police and political preparations. He delegated General Von Brockdorff and he and I visited all the points in Berlin which Brockdorff was to occupy with his Potsdam Division.

Immediately after Hitler announced his intention to invade Czechoslovakia [*i.e., in the Spring of 1938*], friends tried to keep the British Government informed, from the first intention to the final decision. The chain of events began with the journey of Goerdeler in the Spring of 1938 to London, where he gave information concerning the existence of an opposition group which was resolved to go to any lengths. In the name of this group the British Government was continuously informed of what was happening and that it was absolutely necessary to make it clear, to the German people and to the generals, that every step across the Czech border would constitute for the Western Powers a reason for war. When the crisis neared its climax and when our preparations for a revolt had been completed to the last detail, we took a step unusual in form and substance. We informed the British Government that the pending diplomatic negotiations would not, as Hitler asserted, deal with the question of the Sudeten countries but that Hitler's intention was to invade the whole of Czechoslovakia and that, if the British Government on its side were to remain firm, we could give the assurance that there would be no war.

The more the crisis moved toward the Munich conference, the more we tried to convince Halder that he should start the revolt at once. As Halder was somewhat uncertain, Witzleben prepared everything in detail. On 27 September it was clear that Hitler wanted to go to the utmost extremity. In order to make the German people war-minded he ordered a parade of the Berlin army through Berlin. Witzleben had to execute the order. The parade had entirely the opposite effect. The population, which assumed that the troops were marching to war, showed their open displeasure. The troops, instead of jubilation, saw clenched fists; and Hitler, who was watching the parade from the window of the Reich Chancellery, had a fit of rage. He stepped back from the window and said, "With such a people I cannot wage war." Witzleben came home indignant and said that he would have liked to have had the guns unlimbered in front of the Reich Chancellery.

The following morning—that was the 28th—we believed that the opportunity had now come to carry out the revolt. That morning we also learned that Hitler had rejected the final offer from the British Prime Minister, Chamberlain, and had sent the intermediary, Wilson, back with a refusal. Witzleben got the letter and took it to Halder. He believed that proof of Hitler's desire for war had now been produced, and Halder agreed. Halder went to see Brauchitsch while Witzleben waited in Halder's room. After a few moments Halder came back and said that Brauchitsch had now also realized that the moment for action had arrived and that he merely wanted to go over to the Reich Chancellery to make quite sure that Witzleben and Halder's account was correct. Brauchitsch went to the Reich Chancellery after Witzleben had told him over the telephone that everything was prepared; and it was that noon hour of 28 September when suddenly, and contrary to expectations, Mussolini's intervention in the Reich Chancellery took place, and Hitler, impressed by Mussolini's step, agreed to go to Munich.

[*Now General Halder's story concludes the incident.*]

Adolf Hitler was at the Berghof at the time when Schacht was with me. Von Witzleben was ready with his preparations. But they could be put into action only after Hitler had come back to Berlin. On the day when

Schacht—in the evening—had been to see me, I learned that Hitler had come back to Berlin. I communicated with von Witzleben at once. He came to see me in my office during the noon hours. We discussed the matters. He requested that I give the order of execution. We discussed other details—how much time he needed for the other preparation, etc. During this discussion, the news came that the British Prime Minister and the French Premier had come to Hitler for a discussion. This was in the presence of von Witzleben and therefore I took back the order of execution because, owing to this fact, the entire basis for action had been taken away.

Now came Mr. Chamberlain, and with one stroke the danger of war was avoided. Hitler returned from Munich as an unbloody victor glorified by Mr. Chamberlain and M. Daladier. Thus, it was a matter of course that the German people greeted and enjoyed his successes. Even in the circles of Hitler's opponents—the senior officers' corps—those successes of Hitler's made an enormous impression. I do not know if a non-military man can understand what it means to have the Czechoslovak army eliminted by the stroke of the pen, and Czechoslovakia, being stripped of all her fortifications, stood as a newly born child, all naked. With the stroke of a pen, an open victory was attained. The critical hour for force was avoided. One could only wait in case any chance should come up again. I want to emphasize once more what extreme importance must be attributed to this Munich Agreement.

[*And in answer to this question of the American interrogator, Captain Sam Harris: "Do I understand you to say that if Chamberlain had not come to Munich, your plan would have been executed, and Hitler would have been deposed?" Halder replied: "I can only say the plan would have been executed, I do not know if it would have been successful."*]

[*Chamberlain, addressing the House of Commons on this day, interrupted himself to announce:*]

I have something further to say to the house yet. I have now been informed by Herr Hitler that he invites me to meet him at Munich tomorrow morning. He has also invited Signor Mussolini and M. Daladier. Signor Mussolini has accepted, and I have no doubt M. Daladier will also accept. I need not say what my answer will be.

September 29, 1938, Munich                          *Ibid.*

[*On this day the Sudeten question was "settled." The essential items of the agreement follow.*]

Germany, the United Kingdom, France and Italy, taking into consideration the agreement, which has been already reached in principle for the concession to Germany of the Sudeten German territory, have agreed on the following terms and conditions governing the said concession and the measures consequent thereon, and by this agreement they each hold themselves responsible for the steps necessary to secure fulfillment:

1. The evacuation will begin on the 1st October.

2. The United Kingdom, France and Italy agree that the evacuation of the territory shall be completed by the 10th October, without any existing installations having been destroyed and that the Czechoslovak Government will be held responsible for carrying out the evacuation without damage to the said installations.

8. The Czechoslovak Government will within a period of four weeks from the date of this agreement release from their military and police forces any Sudeten Germans who may wish to be released, and the Czechoslovak Government will, within the same period release Sudeten German prisoners who are serving terms of imprisonment for political offenses.

[*In the famous September 12 party rally speech
attacking Czechoslovakia and, personally, Dr. Benes,
Hitler took time off to announce innocence of any desire
to dismember that unhappy country, or to incorporate
any Czechs into the Reich. Later, at Berchtesgaden, the
Fuehrer repeated this policy to Chamberlain and then, at
Godesberg a few days later, stated it yet a third time.*
   *Less than two weeks after the signing of the Munich
agreement Hitler's Chief-of-Staff, Keitel, sent the
following telegram to army and air force officials.*]

1: WHAT REINFORCEMENTS ARE NECES-
SARY IN THE PRESENT SITUATION TO BREAK
ALL CZECH RESISTANCE IN BOHEMIA AND
MORAVIA?
2: HOW MUCH TIME IS REQUIRED FOR THE
REGROUPING OR MOVING UP OF NEW FORCES?
4: HOW MUCH TIME WOULD BE REQUIRED
TO ACHIEVE THE STATE OF READINESS OF [*last*]
OCT. 1ST?

[*This document, found in OKW (Ober Kommand
Wehrmacht—Supreme Command of the Armed Forces)
files, was signed by both Hitler and Keitel.*]

The future tasks for the Armed Forces and the
preparations for the conduct of the war resulting from
these tasks will be laid down by me in a later Directive.
   Until this Directive comes into force the Armed Forces
must be prepared at all times for the following eventualities:
   1. The securing of the frontiers of Germany and the
protection against surprise air attacks.

2. The liquidation of the remainder of Czechoslovakia.

3. The occupation of the Memelland.


December 17, 1938, Berlin          29. Document C-138

[*This is a Keitel reference to the above document.*]

Reference "Liquidation of the Rest of Czechoslovakia" The Fuehrer has given the following additional order:

The preparations for this eventuality are to continue on the assumption that no resistance worth mentioning is to be expected.

To the outside world too it must clearly appear that it is merely an action of pacification and not a warlike undertaking.

The action must therefore be carried out by the peace time Armed Forces *only,* without reinforcements from mobilization. The necessary readiness for action, especially the ensuring that the most necessary supplies are brought up, must be effected by adjustment within the units.

Similarly the units of the Army detailed for the march must, as a general rule, leave their stations only during the night prior to the crossing of the frontier, and will not previously form up systematically on the frontier.

The Air Force should take action in accordance with the similar general directives.


January 21, 1939,
Reichschancellery          30. Document 2906-PS

[*After the cession of the Sudetenland Dr. Benes, M. Hodza and other like-minded officials left office in favor of those who could talk the language of Hitler. Emil Hacha became president of Czechoslovakia and a rather weak-willed individual by the name of Chvalkowsky— variously spelled in the documents—became minister for*]

The foreign policy of a people is shaped by its domestic policy. It is impossible to conduct a foreign policy A and a domestic policy B. That would work for a short time only. From the beginning the development in Czechoslovakia was leading toward a catastrophe. This catastrophe was prevented by Germany's moderate attitude. If Germany had not been prevented by its National Socialistic principles from annexing foreign nationalities, fate would have had an entirely different course. What is left of Czechoslovakia has been saved by the National Socialistic tendencies and not by Mr. Benes. But he believes that the consequences arising from this situation have not yet been drawn.

February 12, 1938, 5-6:15 p.m.,
Reichschancellery                     31. Document 2790-PS

[*Hitler thus warned the Czechs. But he did not satisfy himself with this, what might be called, "softening-up" process. He knew that many Slovaks wanted an independent Slovakia; with an "independent" Slovakia, Czechia would be rather easy to handle. Thus Hitler talked with Slovakian leaders. Professor Tuca, a fanatic Slovakian nationalist, and Secretary of State Karmasin, leader of the Germans in Hungary, on this day visited Hitler and Ribbentrop for a conversation. This document, found in the foreign office files, reports a part of that conversation.*]

After a brief welcome Tuca thanks the Fuehrer for granting this meeting. He addresses the Fuehrer with "My Fuehrer" and he voices the opinion that he, though only a modest man himself, might well claim to speak for the Slovak nation. The Czech courts and prisons gave him the right to make such a statement. He states that the Fuehrer had not only opened the Slovak question but that he had been also the first one to acknowledge the dignity of the Slovak nation. The Slovakian people will gladly fight under the leadership of the Fuehrer for the maintenance of European-civilization. Obviously future association with the Czechs had become an impossibility for the Slovaks from a moral as well as an economic point of view. The fact that they still belonged to the Czech state was only possible because of the thought that the present government was only transitory, but he and his colleagues were determined to give in to the pressure of the Slovak people and to bring about an independent Slovakia. The destiny of Slovakia rested with the Fuehrer. Just as he had suffered imprisonment for his convictions, he was equally prepared to sacrifice his life for his ideals. Should there be a rising, the Czechs would immediately try to surpass it with bloodshed, but the mere word of the Fuehrer sufficed to halt these attempts. The same applied to the aspirations of Hungary and Poland, who would be stopped by a single word of the Fuehrer. "I entrust the fate of my people to your care."

Early March, 1939                    32. Document 3030-PS

[*Alfred H. Naujocks, a member of the "S.D."— security police—was used to facilitate the development of "fate." In a deposition sworn out at Nurenberg after the war, Naujocks told of his activities. The following is the deposition. The Pressburg referred to is the German name for Bratislava, in Slovakia.*]

1. From 1934 to 1941 I was a member of the SD. Early in March, four or five days before Slovakia declared its independence, Heydrich, who was chief of the SD, ordered me to report to Nebe, the Chief of the Reich

Criminal Police. Nebe had been told by Heydrich to accelerate the production of explosives which his department was manufacturing for the use of certain Slovak groups.

2. As soon as forty or fifty of these explosives had been finished, I carried them by automobile to a small village called Engeran, just across the border from Pressburg in Slovakia. The Security Police had a Service Department in this village for the handling of SD activities. I turned over the explosives to this office and found there a group of Slovaks including Karmasin, Mach, Tuca and Durcansky. In fact, three of these people then present later became ministers in the new Slovak government. I was informed that the explosives were to be turned over to the Hlinka Guards [*a Slovakian counterpart of the Nazi SA*] across the border in Slovakia and were to be used in incidents designed to create the proper atmosphere for a revolution.

3. I stayed in Engeran for a day and a half and then returned to Berlin.

4. One or two weeks later I met in Berlin the Slovak delegation, including Nach, Tuca, Durcansky and Karmasin, which I had seen in Engeran. They had flown to Berlin for a conference with Goering. Heydrich asked me to look after them and to report to him what developed during the conference with Goering. I reported this conversation in detail to Heydrich. It dealt principally with the organization of the new Slovak state. My principal recollection of the conference is that Slovaks hardly got a word in because Goering was talking all the time.

Spring (probably March), 1939, Berlin    33. Document 2801-PS

[*In this undated document a report is made, presumably by some one from the Air Force Ministry, of a conversation between, among others Durcansky—*

*Slovakian Deputy Prime Minister in the new set-up after
Munich—and Goering.*]

To begin with Durkansky [*variously spelled in
different documents*] reads out declaration. Contents:
"Friendship for the Fuehrer; gratitude that through the
Fuehrer autonomy [*but to be distinguished from
independence*] has become possible for the Slovaks." The
Slovaks never want to belong to Hungary. The Slovaks
want *full independence* with strongest political, economic
and military ties to Germany. Bratislava to be capital. The
execution of the plan only possible if the army and police
are Slovak.

An independent Slovakia to be proclaimed at the
meeting of the first Slovak Diet. In case of a plebiscite the
majority would favor a separation from Prague. Jews will
vote for Hungary. The area of the plebiscite to be up to
March, where a large Slovak population lives.

The *Jewish problem* will be solved similarly to that in
Germany. The Communist party to be prohibited.

The Field Marshall considers: that the Slovak negotiations towards independence are to be supported in a
suitable manner. Czechoslovakia without Slovakia is still
more at our mercy.

Air bases in Slovakia are of great importance for the
German Air Force for use against the East.


March 13, 1939, Budapest        34. Document 2816-PS

[*Hitler and his colleagues were playing diplomatic ball
with Hungary, as we have seen, as well as Slovakia. As a
matter of fact Germany played off the two against each
other for her own advantage. The following letter is from
Horthy, Hungary's dictator, to Hitler. The "big blow"
referred to is the occupation of Ruthenia, then a part of
Czecho-Slovakia. The Slovaks, ever suspicious of the
Hungarians, who used to rule them in the days of the old
Austro-Hungarian empire, believed that unless they were
very careful Hungary would end up master again of*

*Slovakia. To the Slovaks Hitler presented himself as a
buffer between them and Hungary; to the Hungarians, he
presented himself the other way around.*]

Your Execllency,
My sincere thanks.
I can hardly tell you how happy I am...
In spite of the fact that our recruits have only been
serving for 5 weeks we are going into this affair with eager
enthusiasm. The dispositions have already been made. On
Thursday, the 16th of this month, a frontier incident will
take place which will be followed by the big blow on
Saturday.
I shall never forget this proof of friendship and your
Excellency may rely on my unshakable gratitude at all
times.

Your devoted friend,
(signed) Horthy

March 13, 1939, 6:40-7:15 p.m.,
Reichschancellery    35. Document 2802-PS

[*On the same day that Horthy wrote thus to Hitler the
latter was meeting with Slovakian Prime Minister Tiso
and Minister Durcansky to persuade them the time had
come to separate from "Czechia;" otherwise he felt they
ran a grave risk, after he, Hitler, had dealt with the
Czechs, of themselves being swallowed up by the
Hungarians. Did or did not they want this to happen?
This meeting was attended by Ribbentrop and Keitel,
among others. The report is signèd "Hewell," who was
Ribbentrop's liaison man with Hitler.*]

The Fuehrer greets Prime Minister Tiso and describes
to him in a long detailed account the developments in
Czechoslovakia.
The Germans [*in Czecho-Slovakia*] had been subject
to constant surveillance so that their situation was now
worse than before the September crisis. This development

was not in accordance with the agreements. Until the day before yesterday Germany had striven for an absolutely loyal attitude in the press.... During this time the Czech press had repeatedly published unfavorable things about Germany; certain organs had not ceased their systematic agitation. The Fuehrer had already spoken... to Chvalkowsky and reproached him that oil had continuously been thrown on to the fire. Central Europe was a fixed, closed economic area which could only live when fully pacified. It needed pacification. Geographically the situation was made clear by the fact that Bohemia and Moravia were enclosed by Germany, and Germany could never tolerate in her own territory a hot-bed of unrest.

In recent weeks the circumstances had become unbearable. The old spirit of Benes had again been revived. The Czech people had been incited to resistance. Conditions were insecure and tumultuous. Yesterday incidents in Bruenen and Iglau occurred.

We had solved the Czech question [*in the Fall of 1938*] according to our world interpretation. If, however, this solution leads to no results, then we have decided absolutely to pursue it to its conclusion, without consideration for this ideological principle.

The second disappointment for us was the attitude of Slovakia. In the past year the Fuehrer had had to face a difficult decision, whether or not to permit Hungary to occupy Slovakia. The Fuehrer had been under a wrong impression as he had, of course, believed that Slovakia wished to be annexed to Hungary. It was only in the crisis that the Fuehrer was dissuaded from this opinion. It was then that he first heard and noted that Slovakia wished to conduct her own affairs.

Now he had permitted Minister Tiso to come here in order to make this question clear in a very short time. Germany had no interests east of the Carpathian mountains. It was indifferent to him what happened there. He did not wish anything from Slovakia. He would not pledge his people or even a single soldier to something which was not in anyway desired by the Slovak people. He would like to secure final confirmation as to what

Slovakia really wished. He did not wish that reproaches should come from Hungary that he was preserving something which did not wish to be preserved at all. He took a liberal view of unrest and demonstration in general, but in this connection unrest was only an outward indication of interior instability. He would not tolerate it and he had for that reason permitted Tiso to come in order to hear his decision. It was not a question of days, but of hours. He had stated at that time that if Slovakia wished to make herself independent he would support this endeavor and even guarantee it. He would stand by his word as long as Slovakia would make it clear that she wished for independence. If she hesitated or did not wish to dissolve the connection with Prague, he would leave the destiny of Slovakia to the mercy of events.

The Fuehrer asked the Reich Foreign Minister if he had any remarks to add. He showed the Fuehrer a message he had just received which reported Hungarian troop movements on the Slovak frontiers. The Fuehrer read this report, mentioned it to Tiso, and expressed the hope that Slovakia would soon decide clearly for herself.

Tiso thanked the Fuehrer for his words. He had for sometime longed to hear from the Fuehrer himself how he (the Fuehrer) stood in relation to his (Tiso's) people and country and how he regarded the problems. He took note of the statement, and gave the assurance that the Fuehrer could rely on Slovakia. He wished to be excused for the fact that under the impression made by the Fuehrer's words he could not clearly express his opinion at that moment or could hardly make a decision. He wished to withdraw with his friend and to think the whole question over at his ease; they would, however, show that they were worthy of the Fuehrer's care and interest for their country. With that the conversation was ended.


March 14, 1939, French Embassy,
Berlin                          36. Document 2943-PS, No. 65

[*Three days before Tiso's visit to the Fuehrer a decisive*

*event had taken place. The Prague government—even the
pliable one under Hacha—had decided to dismiss the
Slovakian government under Tiso because it, the latter,
had done nothing to stop the secessionist activities of the
Slovakian extremists led by such men as Mach,
Karmasin, and Tuca. `With this Czech action Hitler
decided to act. He denounced the move and continued to
recognize Tiso's government. It was in these circumstances that he summoned Tiso—who was pretty
confused himself—to Berlin on the 13th. The following
summary is one made by the French Ambassador to
Germany, M. Coulondre, and sent to his chief, M.
Bonnet, French Minister for Foreign Affairs.*]

With regard to the visit which Mgr. Tiso, accompanied
by M. Durcansky, made to Berlin yesterday, I have
gathered the following information.

A telegram from Berlin inviting Mgr. Tiso to go to the
Fuehrer without delay was received at Bratislava at ten
o'clock yesterday morning. After conferring with the
principal leaders of the Slovak People's Party, Mgr. Tiso
decided to obey this summons. In the course of the
interview which he had with Herr Hitler towards the end
of the afternoon, the latter declared that he desired to see
a completely free Slovakia, and that in other respects it
rested with the Slovak people to choose their own destiny.
Mgr. Tiso and M. Durcansky conferred from nine p.m.
until three a.m. with Herr von Ribbentrop and various
Nazi high officials and dignitaries, in particular with Herr
Keppler [*who, it will be recalled, had gained experience in
this sort of thing just a year before in Austria*], who
appears to have played an important part in the whole
affair.

They are said to have examined every aspect of the
situation and any further developments which might
result from it, and the conclusions arrived at through
these discussions appears to be that the salvation for the
Slovaks can only lie in complete separation from Prague.

It is announced that the Slovak Diet, whose sitting was
to take place today but had been postponed until the 28th,

will now sit this morning; it is anticipated that it will vote for complete independence of the country. The Slovak Ministers are said to have received from the Nazi leaders an assurance that Germany's friendship will be given to an independent Slovakia.

March 15, 1939, 1:15-2:15 a.m., Reichschancellery
37. Document 2798-PS

[*With the Slovaks thus declaring their independence and with Hungary ready to pour troops into Ruthenia— events which took place March 14th—the Fuehrer had one more loose end to tie into the web. He must prevail upon the Czech leaders to ask for protection, a la Seyss-Inquart the year before. To this end Hitler called Hacha and the Czech Foreign Minister, Chvalkowsky, to Berlin late on the night of March 14th; delays here and there prevented the doomed delegation from getting into Berlin until after midnight. The following document, written by Hewell, Ribbentrop's liaison man with Hitler, reveals what took place at this meeting. Ribbentrop, Keitel, Hitler, Chvalkowsky, Goering and Hacha were the principals. From the document it is evident that Hitler would have sent his troops into Czechoslovakia whatever attitudes had prevailed that night.*]

State President Hacha greets the Fuehrer and expresses his thanks for being received by him. For a long time he had been desirous of meeting the man whose wonderful ideas he had often read and followed. (Everyone sits down.)

Hacha: He was an unknown person until recently. He had never dabbled in politics. He had been just a judicial official in the Viennese civil service, and as such he had deliberately taken no part in politics in order to be unbiased toward the Parties, with which he had to deal as a judge. In 1918 he had been called to Prague, and in 1925 he was appointed president of the *Verwaltungsgericht-shaf* (Supreme Court for Administrative Law). In this

99

capacity he had had no relations to the politicians, or, as he preferred to say, with the so-called politicians; and it was only rarely that he had come into contact with them. He must mention at the outset that he had also had hardly any relations with the Government and that he had confined his intercourse with the members of the Government to the minimum. He had never been persona grata. He used to meet President Masaryk only once a year at a dinner of the judges. Benes [he met] even less frequently. The only time he had met the latter, misunderstanding's had occurred. For the rest the whole regime had been alien to him, in fact, so much so that immediately after the sudden change [*i.e., after Munich*] he had asked himself whether it was really a good thing for Czechoslovakia to be an independent state. This autumn the task had been allotted to him of becoming head of the state. He was an old man. He had overcome his doubts when it was shown him that it was his patriotic duty to take over the office. By accepting it the most difficult task of his life had fallen to him, and, therefore, he had dared to ask the Fuehrer to receive him.

[*Actually, it must be pointed out, the idea of the visit did not originate with Hacha; why he makes this remark it is difficult to know; or perhaps Hewell thought it would read better this way.*]

He was convinced that the fate of Czechoslovakia lay in the hands of the Fuehrer, and he believed that her fate was safe in the Fuehrer's hands. He had no grounds of complaint over what had happened in Slovakia recently. He had been convinced for a long time that it was impossible for the various peoples to live together in this [*single*] body politic. Although their languages resembled each other to a certain extent, they had developed along very different lines. Czechoslovakia was more closely related to Germany than it was to Slovakia, which showed a stronger inclination toward the Magyars. The Czechs had maintained relations only with the Evangelical Slovaks, whilst the Catholic Slovaks had been rejected by the Czechs.

These were the reasons why a good understanding could never be achieved, and he was glad that the development had followed this path. He was not alone in holding this view, but was sure that 80 percent of the population shared it with him. Half an hour ago he had received reports that the Carpatho-Ukraine had proclaimed its independence.

[*Carpatho-Ukraine is the name sometimes given to that region more commonly called Ruthenia.*]

He was of the opinion that the Fuehrer's experiences with regard to the Slovaks would be none too good. During these last few days rumors about a violation of the constitution in Prague had doubtless reached the Fuehrer's ears. This breach of the constitution would doubtless be laid to his (Hacha's) charge. But being a lawyer he knew that the dismissal of the government had been based on sound legal foundations. Moreover, the constitution itself had not been respected by part of the Czech government. Unfortunately incidents had occurred in this connection which he regretted; they had, however, taken place as a consequence of measures connected with the maintenance of order. These incidents had not been intended. Otherwise he did not shed any tears over Slovakia.

Now he came to the point which concerned him most, the fate of his people. He believed that the Fuehrer, especially, would understand him when he expressed his opinion that Czechoslovakia had the right to wish to live her own national life. Naturally, the geographical position of Czechoslovakia made the existence of the friendliest terms with Germany necessary. This must be the foundation of a distinct national life. The greater part of the Czech people shared this conviction. There were, of course, some exceptions, but the fact that the new Czechoslovakia had only been in existence for six months had to be kept in mind. The charge had been made that there were still many followers of the Benes system in Czechoslovakia. But the persons who were named are not the ones. This system only had friends in journalistic circles. The government with all the means at its disposal was resolved to reduce them to silence. This was practically all he wanted to say.

The Fuehrer answered and expressed his regret for having had to ask the President to undertake this journey. This morning, however, after careful consideration he had reached the conclusion that, in spite of the advanced age of the President, this journey might prove of great service to his country, since Germany's attack was only a matter of hours. The German Reich had, in principle, no animosity against any other nations. Nations which do not wrong us are dear to us, or at least uninteresting to us. The German people harbor no hatred against Czechoslovakia. Czechoslovakia, however, had adopted an entirely different attitude toward us. The Fuehrer quoted several occasions when, during great political events, this attitude had manifested itself, e.g., during the occupation of the Rhineland. Czechoslovakia had then sent a memorandum to France declaring that, if that country would take military measures against Germany, Czechoslovakia would be prepared to assist her. Czechoslovakia had done this in spite of the fact that the territory in question was purely German. The same attitude was shown by her on many other occasions, e.g., against Italy during the Abyssinian conflict, etc. The situation had become unbearable by 1938. On May 28th, therefore, he had decided to face the consequences. He had no animosity against any nation, but he was the most ruthless defender of the rights of his own people, and in that struggle he was determined to take any step. In this regard he would be the frontline soldier who stands and fights for his conviction, ruthlessly and without any scruples. For the rest of the existence of the remainder of Czechoslovakia was only due to his loyal attitude. At the risk of incurring the hostility of a friendly Hungary he had stopped her political ambitions and had forced her to solve the problem, like Germany, only according to ethnographical principles, although the craziest situation, both [from the point of view] of economics and customs duties, resulted from it. He had accepted these restrictions not because he could not have acted differently, but because he was convinced that this was the correct way. For the other countries Czechoslovakia had merely been a means to an end. London and Paris had shown themselves in no position to do anything for Czechoslovakia.

Slovakia was a matter of complete indifference to him. Had Slovakia established closer connections with Germany, this would have been a committment for Germany, and he was, therefore, glad not to be under any obligation now. East of the Lower Carpathian Mountains he had no interest at all. Last autumn he had not wanted to push things to an extreme because he then still thought it possible to live together. At that time, and also later on in his discussion with Chvalkowsky, he did not leave any doubt that he would ruthlessly break up this state unless the Benes tendencies disappeared altogether. Chvalkowsky had then understood this, and had asked the Fuehrer to be patient. The Fuehrer agreed, but months elapsed without any change being brought about. The new regime did not succeed in uprooting the old one psychologically. This could be seen from the press, the whispering propaganda, the dismissal of Germans, and from many other facts symbolical to him of the whole situation. At first he had not realized this, but when he became fully aware of it, he had definitely drawn his conclusions since, if matters continued to develop in this way, the [German] situation towards Czechoslovakia would have become the same as it was six months ago. Why did not Czechoslovakia immediately reduce her army to a reasonable strength? Such an army represented an enormous burden to such a State, since its only significance was to support the State's foreign policy. Czechoslovakia's foreign policy, however, had no mission to fulfill so there was no point in retaining such an army. He quoted several instances which had shown him that the spirit of the army had not changed. From this particular symptom he gained the conviction that for the future the army would be a serious liability in a political respect. In addition, there was the inevitable development arising from economic necessity and, furthermore, the protests of the national groups, who could no longer endure such a life.

"Last Sunday, therefore, for me the die was cast. I summoned the Hungarian envoy and notified him that I was going to withdraw my [restraining] hands from this country." *Now we were facing this pact. He had issued the order for German troops to march into Czechoslovakia, and to incorporate this country into the German Reich.* He intended to grant Czechoslovakia the fullest autonomy and a distinct life, more than she had ever enjoyed under the Austrian regime.

[*But of course the Fuehrer did not compare his "fullest autonomy" with the freedom Czechoslovakia enjoyed under the Czechoslovakian regime.*]

Germany's attitude toward Czechoslovakia would be defined tomorrow and the day after, and would be dependent on the behavior shown by the Czech people and army towards the German troops. He had no longer confidence in the Government. Though believing in Hacha's and Chvalkowsky's sincerity and honesty, he doubted whether the Government would be able to exert an effective control over the whole population. To-day the Germany army was already marching, and resistance offered at one barracks had been ruthlessly crushed whilst another was said to have given in when the heavy artillery was ordered out.

This morning at 6 a.m. the German Army would invade Czechoslovakia at all points, and the German Air Force would occupy all Czech airports. There were two possibilities. The first was that the invasion of the German troops might develop into a battle. This resistance would then be broken down with all available means. The other was that the entry of the German troops should take place in a peaceable manner, and then it would be easy for the *Fuehrer,* in the course of the new development of Czech life, to give to Czechoslovakia an individual existence on a generous scale, autonomy and a certain amount of national freedom.

We were living, at this moment, through a great turning point in history. He did not wish to torment or to denationalize the Czechs. He was doing all of this, not out of hate, but in order to protect Germany. If, in the autumn of the preceding year, Czechoslovakia had not yielded, the Czech people would have been utterly destroyed. Nobody could have prevented him from doing it then. It was his will that the Czech people should develop on their own national lines, and he believed firmly that a form for this could be found, in which it would be possible to meet, to a great extent, Czech wishes. If, tomorrow, it came to a fight, any pressure would produce counterpressure, and it would no longer be possible for him to give the promised alleviations. In two days the Czech army would cease to exist. Some Germans would, also, be killed, and this would produce a feeling of hatred which would compel him, from motives of self-preservation, to refuse any longer to grant autonomy. The world would not care a jot about this. He felt sorry for the Czech people when he read the foreign press. It gave him the sort of impression expressed by the German proverb: "The Moor has done, the Moor may go."

That was the state of affairs. There were two courses open to Germany: a stern one offering no concessions, and bearing the past in mind, desiring that Czechoslovakia should be crushed with bloodshed; and the other in accordance with his proposals stated above.

That was the reason he had asked Hacha to come here. This invitation was the last good deed he would be able to render the Czech people. If it came to fighting, then the bloodshed would compel us to hate also. But perhaps Hacha's visit might avert the worst. Perhaps he could contribute to the finding of a plan which would be much more far-reaching for Czechoslovakia than any they could ever have hoped for in the old Austrian Empire. His sole aim was to procure the essential security for the German nation.

The hours were passing. At 6 o'clock the troops would march in. He felt almost ashamed to say that, for every Czech battalion, a German division would come. The military operation was not a trifling one, but had been planned on a most generous scale. He would advise him to withdraw now with Chvalkowsky in order to discuss what should be done.

Hacha says that the situation is completely clear to him and that any resistance to this would be foolish. But he would ask the Fuehrer how it could be arranged, within four hours, to hold back the entire Czech nation from offering resistance. The Fuehrer says that he is at liberty to consult his advisers. The military machine now in motion cannot be stopped. He should appeal to his authorities in Prague. It might be a great decision, but he could see the possibility dawning of a long period of peace between the two nations. Should the decision be otherwise, he could foresee the annihilation of Czechoslovakia.

Hacha asks whether the whole purpose of the invasion is to disarm the Czech army. This might, perhaps, be done in some other way.

The Fuehrer says that his decision is irrevocable. Everyone knows what a decision by the Fuehrer means. He could see no other practical method of disarmament, and asks the others present if they agree with him, which they confirm. The only possibility of disarming the Czech army would be by the German army.

For Hacha the path he was taking today was the most difficult in his life, but he believed that in a few years' time this decision would be regarded as understandable and in 50 years probably as a fortunate one. [*This is Hitler still speaking, not Hacha.*]

At this point both Czechs withdrew.

After the discussion between Hacha and Chvalkowsky and our representatives, at the conclusion of which the wording of the agreement had been settled, the representatives mentioned at the beginning of the report meet again for a concluding discussion in the Fuehrer's study. The military situation is reviewed fully again, and the Field Marshal [Goering] gives a detailed description of the situation.

[*In other words, further softening up seemed to be required.*]

The Fuehrer considers that possibly here and there Hacha's message might not have gotten through and this might lead to clashes, but by and large, one might count on an entry without opposition.

The Fuehrer goes on to say that he believes that, in spite of any bitterness that might be caused by the entry and occupation by the German Reich, the conviction will slowly dawn of the benefit to be derived by a century-long common life of the two nations. The idea that the two people were compelled to fight one another would disappear. Czechoslovakia was an integral part of the German Reich, and every reasonable person must admit that closest cooperation must be the watchword. In addition, the problem of de-nationalization is of no significance as this is quite remote from the German people themselves and also from the National-Socialist ideology. We do not desire nor do we intend de-nationalization. They, on the one hand, still live as Czechs, and we wish to live contentedly as Germans. The German Reich could be enormously magnanimous in this sphere.

Hacha replied that this statement of the Fuehrer's is of the greatest importance to him:

The Fuehrer continues that only in the economic, military and political spheres could we brook no opposition. Czechia should keep her own Head of State, and his principles, which he would put into force, would form the basis for the appeasement of this area for centuries to come.

Hacha interjects that, in other words, there is no "soul

107

buying" on the program, as there had been during the Austrian period, and asks whether in the economic sphere a customs union is planned.

The first point the Fuehrer denied with a smile. The Field Marshal answers the second question in the affirmative, saying that Germany and Czechoslovakia were one economic unit. In addition, Czechoslovakia would get orders which would certainly double her production.

The Fuehrer says that the Czechoslovak people would gain economically from the annexation to Germany, since it would participate in the Greater German economic sphere. He did not wish to destroy the Czech economy, but to enliven it tremendously.

Hacha asks if any definite directives to this effect have already been laid down.

The Fuehrer replies that this question is one for an Economic Commission, because for him, also, the whole thing came as a surprise. A few weeks ago he knew nothing of the whole affair. He referred once again to the past and to Benes' tactics, and finally mentioned May 28th, the date on which he confided his decision to take action to a small circle.

The Fuehrer concludes with the remarks that the settlement now formulated must be final, supportable and unequivocal. In any case, the Czechs would obtain more rights than they had ever granted to the Germans in their territory.

Thereupon the agreement was signed by the Fuehrer, the Reich Foreign Minister, Hacha and Chvalkowsky.

March 15, 1939, Berlin                    38. Document TC-49

[*And the Agreement:*]

The Fuehrer and Reich's Chancellor today received in Berlin, at their own request, the President of the Czecho-Slovak State, Dr. Hacha, and the Czecho-Slovak Foreign

Minister, Dr. Chvalkowsky, in the presence of Herr von Ribbentrop, the Foreign Minister of the Reich. At this meeting the serious situation which had arisen within the previous territory of Czecho-Slovakia, owing to the events of recent weeks, was subjected to a completely open examination. The conviction was unanimously expressed on both sides that the object of all their efforts must be to assure quiet, order and peace in this part of Central Europe. The President of the Czecho-Slovak State declared that, in order to serve this end and to reach a final pacification, he confidently placed the fate of the Czech people and of their country in the hands of the Fuehrer of the German Reich. The Fuehrer accepted this declaration and expressed his decision to assure to the Czech people, under the protection of the German Reich, the autonomous development of their national life in accordance with their special characteristics. In witness whereof this document is signed in duplicate.

ADOLF HITLER     DR. HACHA
VON RIBBENTROP     DR. CHWALKOWSKY

[*What Hitler meant by "protection of the German Reich," and Czech "autonomous development" is illustrated in the next document.*]

March 25, 1939,
Reichschancellery            39. Document R-100

[*This document is headed: "Information given to the Supreme Commander of the Army [von Brauchitsch] by the Fuehrer on 25 March 1939." It deals with Danzig, Poland, Slovakia, and then passes on to the Czech question. The reference to "when Neurath takes over" signifies Hitler's intention to appoint his former Minister of Foreign Affairs, Constantine von Neurath as "Protector" of Bohemia-Moravia. Thus he voided his promise to Hacha to permit a Czech to execute the laws of the "autonomous region."*]

We take all the war material of former Czechoslovakia *without* paying for it. The guns bought by contract before 15 February though shall be paid for.

Officers of the Czech army shall be cared for. This has to be done in accordance with the discussions between General Reinecke, Colonels Wagner and Burgsdorf of the Supreme Command of the Army. The pensions shall warrant a good standard of life, so as to prevent discontent. Maybe we shall take over payment of the pensions or a part of them—so to speak as installment on the captured war loot. Negotiations should be conducted on this basis.

H. [*translator's note: Hacha*] shall be requested to change his residence, to a place where he can do no harm. The respective request, though, is to come from Hacha.

If the Czechs intend to establish a labor service, the problem should be dealt with in a dilatory manner. The Czech people should not be strengthened by such concentrations.

A certain financial sovereignty shall be granted to the Czech State; maybe similar to that of Bavaria in former times.

[*Before 1918 Bavaria was permitted to establish and maintain her own system of coinage and taxation.*]

Fuehrer does not yet see way clear with regard to adjustment of debts. Conversion into mark will be made in due time.

Bohemia and Moravia have to make annual contributions to the German treasury. [*This*] amount shall be fixed on the basis of expenses earmarked formerly for the Czech Army.

At the time when Neurath takes over, there should be a few more troops than shall remain permanently.

March 18, 1939, Berlin          40. Document 1439-PS

[*A few days after the occupation of Bohemia and*

*Moravia, Germany and the "independent" state of Slovakia signed a treaty the major terms of which follow.*]

ARTICLE 1. The German Reich undertakes to protect the political independence of the State of Slovakia and the integrity of its territory.

ARTICLE 2. For the purpose of making effective the protection undertaken by the German Reich, the German armed forces shall have the right, at all times, to construct military installations and to keep them garrisoned in the strength they deem necessary.

Military sovereignty will be assumed by the German armed forces in the zone [*elsewhere delimited.*]

ARTICLE 3. The Government of Slovakia will organize its military forces in close agreement with the German armed forces.

ARTICLE 4. In accordance with the relationship of protection agreed upon, the Government of Slovakia will at all times conduct its foreign affairs in close agreement with the German Government.

December 1, 1939,
Berlin                    41. Document 2794-PS,
                    item dated December 1, 1939

[*Before the year was out the protection of the Reich became indeed an intimate thing. In the foreign office files of Germany was found this document signed by Ernest Woerman, a foreign affairs official.*]

Today the Reich Foreign Minister received [*Slovak*] State Secretary Karmasin on the latter's request in the presence of [*German*] Minister Bernard and myself.

After Mr. Karmasin had discussed briefly the communist, Czech and other anti-German influence which were strongly felt in Slovakia, the Reich Foreign Minister issued the following directives:

1. An attempt should be made to place German advisors with further branches of the Slovak administration and economic agencies. Minister Bernard was to draw up and submit a plan. In this matter, one had to proceed with caution, avoiding hurting Slovak feelings. If possible the cards should be played in such a way that the request for advisors is submitted by the Slovaks themselves.

The funds which might be needed for this task must be requested from Minister Bernard. No effort to influence the interior structure of Slovakia should be undertaken from our side.

2. The cultural influence of Germany shall be increased with the cooperation of the German minority.

State Secretary Karmasin promised the Reich Foreign Minister on his request that Germany's intention to exercise this influence would be kept secret from the outer world.

The Reich Foreign Minister then requested Mr. Karmasin to establish liaison with Minister Bernard or, in especially important cases, to report to him in person if he had any requests to make.

April 15, 1939, Rome        42. Document 1874-PS

[*Shortly after the absorption of Bohemia-Moravia Goering visited the Duce to bring him abreast of developments, as it were. The following is an extract from German notes on a conference Goering had with Mussolini and Ciano.*]

[*The*] action taken by Germany in Czechoslovakia is to be viewed as an advantage for the axis in case Poland should finally join the enemies of the axis powers. Germany could then attack this country from 2 flanks and be within only 25 minutes flying distance from the new Polish industrial center which had been moved further into the interior of the country, nearer to the other Polish industrial districts, because of its proximity to the border. Now by the turn of events it is located again in the proximity of the border.

[*Now that "Green" was finished, "White" was possible.*]

# Case White

*How to Start a World War*

January 5, 1939, Berlin          43. Document TC-73
                                          No. 48

[*This document is taken from the Polish White Book. It is made up of minutes of a conversation held on this day between Hitler and Polish Foreign Minister Beck in the presence of Ribbentrop and Lipski, Polish Ambassador in Berlin. Beck came because Poland was now apprehensive about German intentions. The reference to the "Declaration of 1934" deals with the agreement of that year, between Poland and Germany (i.e., Pilsudski and Hitler) providing for a renunciation of force as a weapon to settle quarrels between the two states and a determination to overcome differences by means of negotiation.*]

The Chancellor then discussed the Danzig question, and emphasized that, as it was a German city, sooner or later it must return to the Reich. He stated that, in his opinion, by way of mutual agreement it would be possible to find some way out and achieve a form of guarantee to the legitimate interests of both Poland and Germany. If an agreement was reached on this question, all difficulties between the two States could quite definitely be settled and cleared out of the way. He emphasized that he was ready in that case to give an assurance, similar to that which he had given France with respect to Alsace and Lorraine, and to Italy with respect to the Brenner. Finally he drew attention, without stressing the matter, to the necessity for greater freedom of communication between Germany and East Prussia.

[*In other words, something should be done about the Polish Corridor which separated East Prussia from the rest of Germany.*]

M. Beck replied that the Danzig question was a very difficult problem. He added that in the Chancellor's suggestion he did not see any equivalent for Poland, and that the whole Polish opinion, and not only people thinking politically but the widest spheres of Polish society, were particularly sensitive on this matter.

In answer to this the Chancellor stated that in order to solve this problem it would be necessary to try to find something quite new, some new form, for which he used the term "Koerperschaft," which on the one hand would safeguard the interests of the German population, and on the other the Polish interests. In addition, the Chancellor declared that the Minister could be quite at ease, there would be no faits accomplis in Danzig and nothing would be done to render difficult the situation of the Polish Government.

January 6, 1939, Berlin      44. Document TC-73
No. 49

[*The next day Ribbentrop added the assurances of the Reich Foreign Office. The minutes are from the Polish White Book.*]

M. Beck asked M. von Ribbentrop to inform the Chancellor that whereas previously, after all his conversations and contacts with German statesmen, he had been feeling optimistic, today for the first time he was in a pessimistic mood. Particularly in regard to the Danzig question, as it had been raised by the

Chancellor, he saw no possibility whatever of agreement.

In answer M. von Ribbentrop once more emphasized that Germany was not seeking any violent solution. The basis of their policy toward Poland was still a desire for the further building up friendly relations. It was necessary to seek such a method of clearing away the difficulties as would respect the rights and interests of the two parties concerned.

January 30, 1939, Berlin          45. Document TC-73
                                             No. 57

[*Hitler himself publicly underlined his peaceful intentions vis a vis Poland when, in an address to the Reichstag on this day, he proclaimed the following.*]

We have just celebrated the fifth anniversary of the conclusion of our non-aggression pact with Poland. There can scarcely be any difference of opinion today among the true friends of peace as to the value of this agreement. In signing it, the great Polish marshal and patriot [Pilsudski] rendered his people just as great a service as the leaders of the National-Socialist State rendered the German people. During the troubled month of the past year the friendship between Germany and Poland has been one of the reassuring factors in the political life of Europe.

January 25, 1939, Warsaw          46. Document 2530-PS

[*A few days before, Ribbentrop, then in the Polish capital, expressed the same sentiment. The question is from the Voelkischer Beobachter for February 1, 1939.*]

In accordance with the resolute will of the German National Leader, the continual progress and consolidation of friendly relations between Germany and Poland, based upon the existing Agreement between us, constitute an essential element in German policy.


February 20, 1938                    47. Document 2357-PS

[*A year earlier Hitler, before the Reichstag, specifically approved the course of events as it dealt with Danzig. The source of this excerpt is the Nazi "Documents of German Politics."*]

In the fifth year, following the first great foreign political agreement of the Reich, it fills us with sincere gratification to be able to state that in our relations with the State with which we had had perhaps the greatest difference, not only has there been a detente [*lessening of strained relations*], but in the course of these years there has been a constant improvement in relations.

Relying on her friendships, Germany will not leave a stone unturned to save that ideal which provides the foundation for the task which is ahead of us—peace.


1938-1939                           48. Document L-172

[*On November 7, 1943 General Jodl, Hitler's chief military advisor, was requested to deliver a lecture to the Nazi gau or district leaders on the general war situation. The lecture was a long, involved one including much background material. The following statement is taken from that lecture, included in the documents captured by the Allies.*]

The bloodless solution of the Czech conflict in the autumn of 1938 and spring of 1939 and the annexation of Slovakia [*sic*] rounded off the territory of Greater Germany in such a way that it now became possible to consider the Polish problem on the basis of more or less favorable strategic premises.

[*The following is taken from the Polish White Book, and is a communication from Ambassador Lipski to Foreign Minister Beck.*]

I saw M. von Ribbentrop today. He began by saying he had asked me to call on him in order to discuss Polish-German relations in their entirety.

He complained about our Press, and the Warsaw students' demonstrations during Count Ciano's visit. He said the Chancellor was convinced that the poster in Danzig had been the work of Polish students themselves. [Some days prior to the date of this conversation a poster had been put up in a cafe at Danzig, bearing the inscription: "Entry forbidden to Poles and Dogs." This had caused protest demonstrations by Polish students.] I reacted vigorously, asserting that this was a clear attempt to influence the Chancellor unfavorably to Poland.

Further, M. von Ribbentrop referred to the conversation at Berchtesgaden between you and the Chancellor, in which M. Hitler put forward the idea of guaranteeing Poland's frontiers in exchange for a motor road and the incorporation of Danzig in the Reich. He said that there had been further conversations between you and him in Warsaw on the subject, and that you had pointed out the great difficulties in the way of accepting these suggestions. He gave me to understand that all this had made an unfavorable impression on the Chancellor, since so far he had received no positive reaction whatever on our part to his suggestions.

It must also be remembered that Danzig and Pomorze had belonged to the Second Reich [*i.e., the Germany of Bismarck's creation*] and that only through Germany's breakdown had Poland obtained these territories.

At this point I remarked that it was not to be

forgotten that before the Partitions [*1778-1795*] these territories had belonged to Poland.

M. von Ribbentrop replied that it was difficult to appeal to purely historical conceptions, and he stressed that the ethnic factor was today of prime importance.

I remarked that Pomorze certainly was Polish, and alluded to the fact that in regard to the annexation of Bohemia and Moravia the Germans had used historical arguments.

M. von Ribbentrop recalled that after all Danzig was a German city, but he realized that in regard to the Danzig question Poland also was actuated by sentiment.

I corrected him by pointing out that in addition it was a vital necessity to Poland, to which M. von Ribbentrop remarked that that could be settled by way of a guarantee.

In connection with Danzig, the motor road and the guarantee, M. von Ribbentrop also mentioned the question of Slovakia, indicating that conversations would be possible on this subject.

[*That is, Ribbentrop is suggesting a piece of Slovakia might be given to Poland if the latter played ball with Hitler.*]

I promised to refer to you the subject of a conversation between you and the Chancellor. M. von Ribbentrop remarked that I might go to Warsaw during the next few days to talk over this matter. He advised that the talk should not be delayed, lest the Chancellor should come to the conclusion that Poland was rejecting all his offers.

Finally, I asked whether he could tell me anything about his conversation with the Foreign Minister of Lithuania [*as to whether or not, i.e., Germany intended to take Memel.*]

M. von Ribbentrop answered vaguely that he had seen M. Urbszys on the latter's return from Rome, and they had discussed the Memel question, which called for a solution.

In view of the importance of this conversation I am sending this report through Prince Lubormirski.

Arising out of the conversation, I am prompted to make the following remarks:

The fact that M. von Ribbentrop said nothing on his own initiative about Memel suggests that his conversation with me today, proposing a fundamental exchange of views between you and the Chancellor, is perhaps aimed at securing our neutrality during the Memel crisis.

M. von Ribbentrop's suggestion of a conversation and his emphasis on the urgency are a proof that Germany has resolved to carry out her Eastern program quickly, and so desires to have Poland's attitude clearly defined.

In these circumstances the conversation acquires very real importance, and must be carefully considered in all its aspects.

I assume that you will be desiring to summon me to Warsaw in a day or two in regard to this matter.

End of March, 1939, Berlin     50. Document 1796-PS

[*On March 26, 1939, German naval and military forces took over Memelland which had a quasi-independent status in Lithuania. The Polish reaction was, as the diplomats would express it, negative. The following excerpt is from "Notes to the War Diary" made up by the Army General Staff.*]

End of March 1939:

The Fuehrer decides to make military preparations for the gradual, seemingly unavoidable conflict with *Poland*, in such manner that these can be executed in late summer 1939. Thereby the Fuehrer hopes only to wage war on one front.

[*To the regular, formal war plans Hitler added, at this time, some specific directives regarding Poland. This document was made up by the High Command of the Armed Forces (OKW).*]

The Fuehrer has added the following Directives to "Fall Weiss":

1. Preparations must be made in such a way that the operation can be carried out at any time from *1.9.39* onwards.

2. The High Command of the Armed Forces has been directed to draw up a precise time-table for "Fall Weiss" and to arrange by conferences the synchronized timings between the 3 branches of the Armed Forces.

3. The plans of the branches of the Armed Forces and the details for the time-table must be submitted by the OKW by 1.5.39.

[*Shortly after the absorption of Czechoslovakia and the consequent threat to Poland it implied, the latter thankfully accepted an offer of protection from Great Britain. In a speech to the Reichstag on this day Hitler publicly changed his Polish tune and denounced the 1934 pact with Poland, the pact which two months before he had hailed as a "great political agreement" which had made a detente between the two peoples possible.*]

After the problem of Danzig had already been discussed several times some months ago, I made a concrete offer to the Polish Government. [*Hitler asked for a "corridor across the Corridor," and for Danzig. In return he promised to respect Poland's then boundaries in perpetuity.*] I now make known this offer to you, Gentlemen, and you yourselves will judge whether this offer did not represent the greatest imaginable concession to the interests of European peace. As I have already pointed out, I have always seen the necessity of an access to the sea for this country, and have consequently taken this necessity into consideration. I am no democratic statesman, but a National Socialist and a realist.

I consider it, however, necessary to make it clear to the Government in Warsaw that just as they desire access to the sea, so Germany needs access to her province in the east. Now these are all difficult problems. It is not Germany who is responsible for them, however, but rather the jugglers of Versailles, who either in their maliciousness or their thoughtlessness placed 100 powder barrels round about in Europe, all equipped with hardly extinguishable lighted fuses. The problems cannot be solved according to old fashioned ideas; I think, rather, that we should adopt new methods. Poland's access to the sea by way of the Corridor, and, on the other hand, a German route through the Corridor have, for example, no kind of military importance whatsoever. Their importance is exclusively psychological and economic.

[*Perhaps it ought to be pointed out that the suggestion of a "corridor through the Corridor" had more seeming than real merit. The new corridor, if granted, would have, according to Hitler's terms, given Germany extra-territorial rights throughout. That is, German law, German police, German fiat would all be effective exclusively. It is not difficult to imagine the countless opportunities for "pushing" such a situation would have afforded Hitler. The Chinese long since discovered, in the case of Japanese extra-territorial rights in Korea and certain parts of Manchuria, that the granting of them was but preliminary to a loss of the surrounding territory.*]

Consequently, I have had the following proposal

submitted to the Polish Government:

(1) Danzig returns as a Free State into the framework of the German Reich.

(2) Germany receives a route through the Corridor and a railway line at her own disposal possessing the same extra-territorial status for Germany as the Corridor itself has for Poland.

In return, Germany is prepared:

(1) To recognize all Polish economic rights in Danzig.

(2) To insure for Poland a free habour in Danzig of any size desired which would have completely free access to the sea.

(3) To accept at the same time the present boundaries between Germany and Poland and to regard them as ultimate.

(4) To conclude a twenty-five year non-aggression treaty with Poland, a treaty therefore which would extend far beyond the duration of my own life.

(5) To guarantee the independence of the Slovak State by Germany, Poland and Hungary jointly—which means in practice the renunciation of any unilateral German hegemony in this territory.

The Polish Government have rejected my offer and have only declared that they are prepared (1) to negotiate concerning the question of a substitute for the Commissioner of the League of Nations and (2) to consider facilities for the transit traffic through the Corridor.

I have regretted greatly this incomprehensible attitude of the Polish Government, but that alone is not the decisive fact; the worst is that now Poland, like Czechoslovakia a year ago believes, under the pressure of an international lying campaign, that it must call up troops, although Germany on her part has not called up a single man and had not thought of proceeding in any way against Poland. As I have said, this is in itself very regretable and posterity will one day decide whether it was really right to refuse this suggestion made this once by me. The intention to attack on the part of Germany which was merely invented by the international press, led as you know to the so-called guarantee offer and to an obligation on the part of the Polish Government for mutual assistance, which would also, under certain circumstances, compel Poland to take military action against Germany in the event of a conflict between Germany and any other Power and in which England, in her turn, would be involved.

I therefore look upon the agreement which Marshal Pilsudski and I at one time concluded as having been unilaterally infringed by Poland and therefore no longer in existence!

May 16, 1939, Berlin            53. Document C-126

[*In the captured Germany navy files was found a copy of the following directive.*]

1. *Directive by the Fuehrer:* the Fuehrer has issued the following directive:

"*Fall Weiss*"

Poland's present attitude necessitates military preparations being made over and above the protection of the Eastern Frontiers already dealt with, in order if necessary to eliminate all threats from this side for ever.

2. *Conclusions in the military field:* the Major aims in building up the German army continue to be determined by the hostility of the Western democracies. "Fall Weiss" constitutes merely a completion, by way of precaution, of preparations, and should on no account be regarded as the fore-runner of a settlement with our opponents in the West by force of arms.

The isolation of Poland will be maintained the more readily even after the outbreak of war, if we succeed in opening the war with heavy blows struck by surprise and followed up by rapid successes.

8. (a) It can be expected that Y-hour will be a time

in the early hours of the morning, two hours before it grows light (three hours before sunrise). This time of day is required by the Navy to carry out the measures she has to take, and is recognized by the Supreme Command of the Armed Forces.

(b) With a view to maintaining, on a large scale, the routine of peacetime training, and to avoid a premature exposure of the measures it is intended to take, a warning (preparation) period of 48 hours may be expected.

V. *Date fixed for completion of preparations.* According to the instructions of the Fuehrer, "Fall Weiss" should be so worked on that it can be carried out at any time from 1 September 1939 onwards.

May 23, 1939, Berlin                    54. Document L-79

*[In spite of seemingly definitive arrangements for attack in the East, Hitler was still not absolutely sure of the sequence of steps to be taken to gain mastery of Europe. He was plagued, in the Spring of 1939, with the question of where his next major move should take place—East or West. There seemed to be good reasons for each alternative. Consequently the important speech he delivered to high officials in May of 1939, notes of which constitute this document, reflected this dichotomy. Those present included Goering, Raeder, Colonel-General von Brauchitsch (successor to Fritsch), Colonel-General (later Field Marshal) Keitel and other military personages. The meeting was held in the Fuehrer's study in the new Reich Chancellery. Lieutenant Colonel Schmundt, then acting as Hitler's adjutant, took the minutes which are now commonly known as "the little Schmundt notes." Schmundt decided to write up the minutes in the first person. The reader is cautioned of the jumbled condition of the notes. A Hitler discourse reported verbatim usually is difficult to follow, for the Fuehrer did not know what succinct and disciplined speech was; when the covering*

*notes are fuzzy, of course the confusion is confounded. The importance of the document, however, warrants the added effort needed to understand it. Allied prosecutors at Nurenberg called it part of the "Common Plan."*]

[After the first world war] Germany had dropped from the circle of Great Powers. The balance of power had been effected without the participation of Germany.

This equilibrium is disturbed when Germany's demands for the necessities of life make themselves felt, and Germany re-emerges as a Great Power. All demands are regarded as "Encroachments." The English are more afraid of dangers in the economic sphere than of the simple threat of force.

A mass of 80 million people has solved the ideological problems. So, too, must the economic problems be solved. No German can evade the creation of the necessary economic conditions for this. The solution of the problems demands courage. The principle, by which one evades solving the problems by adapting one-self to circumstances, is inadmissable. Circumstances must rather be adapted to aims. This is impossible without invasion of foreign states or attacks upon foreign property.

Living space, in proportion to the magnitude of the state, is the basis of all power. One may refuse for a time to face the problem, but finally it is solved one way or another. The choice is between advancement or decline. In 15 or 20 years time we shall be compelled to find a solution. No German statesman can evade the question longer than that.

[*It will be recalled that in the Hossbach notes 1943-1945 was set as the period of latest action. But perhaps the Fuehrer here means that living space "in proportion to the magnitude of the state," i.e., the complete and final boundaries of Germany; in which case, 15 or 20 years might represent the maximum latest time. Or he may have meant in 15 or 20 years, as the notes say, Germany would, willy-nilly, be "compelled" to find a solution; and she ought not wait until she was forced, for circumstances then might not be so favorable as earlier.*]

We are at present in a state of patriotic fervor, which is shared by two other nations: Italy and Japan.

After 6 years, the situation is today as follows:

The national-political unity of the Germans has been achieved, apart from minor exceptions. Further success cannot be achieved without the shedding of blood.

The demarcation of frontiers is of military importance.

The Pole is no "supplementary enemy." Poland will always be on the side of our adversaries. In spite of treaties of friendship, Poland has always had the secret intention of exploiting every opportunity to do us harm.

Danzig is not the subject of the dispute at all. It is a question of expanding our living space in the East and of securing our food supplies, of a settlement of the Baltic problems.

[*In a word the problem was this, how should living space in the East be achieved—by conquering first in the West, for the West would never consent, in the long run, to Germany's getting all the "Lebensraum" she wanted? Or should Germany strike East first and let the sequence develop naturally?*]

If fate brings us into conflict with the West, possession of extensive areas in the East will be advantageous. Upon [German] record harvests we shall be able to rely even less in time of war than in peace.

The population of non-German areas will perform no military service, and will be available as a source of labor.

The Polish problem is inseparable from conflict with the West.

It is questionable whether military success in the West can be achieved by a quick decision, questionable too is the attitude of Poland.

The Polish government will not resist pressure from Russia. Poland sees danger in a German victory in the West, and will attempt to rob us of the victory.

There is therefore no question of sparing Poland, and we are left with the decision:

*To attack Poland at the first suitable opportunity.*

We cannot expect a repetition of the Czech affair. There will be war. Our task is to isolate Poland. The success of the isolation will be decisive.

[*The crux of the problem of isolating Poland was England. If, whenever it was that Germany was to attack Poland, she could keep England out of it, France would, it would seem, remain neutral also, with the result that only Russia was left as a possible champion of Poland. Hitler believed, for a number of reasons, that Russia would not, by herself, defend Poland against Germany.*]

Therefore, the Fuhrer must reserve the right to give the final order to attack. There must be no simultaneous conflict with the Western Powers.

If it is not certain that a German-Polish conflict will not lead to war in the West [*i.e., if it should*], then the fight must be primarily against England and France.

Fundamentally therefore: Conflict with Poland—beginning with an attack on Poland—will only be successful if the Western Powers keep out of it. If this is impossible, then it will be better to attack in the West and to settle Poland at the same time.

The isolation of Poland is a matter of skillful politics.

[*It also was a matter of peculiar dialectics. The above paragraphs say, in this order—the attack on Poland must not lead to German involvement in a war with the West; but if it does, Germany must primarily attend to the West. The attack on Poland can only be*

*successful if the Western Powers keep out; but if they
don't, Germany must not fail to "settle" with both at
the same time. What the rather befuddled Fuehrer is
saying, however, is quite simple: He would like to
attack Poland without anyone helping her; this would
result in a decisive German victory. But if the West
helps Poland the conflict will no longer be a German-
Polish one; hence there can be no successful (or any
other) termination of it. For it will then be a general
conflict in which Germany will throw her predominant
strength against the West without, however, being
satisfied with a mere holding action against Poland.]*

Japan is a weighty problem. Even if at first for
various reasons her collaboration with us appears to be
somewhat cool and restricted, it is nevertheless in
Japan's own interest to take the initiative in attacking
Russia in good time.

Economic relations with Russia are possible only if
political relations have improved. A cautious trend is
apparent in Press comment. It is not impossible that
Russia will show herself to be disinterested in the
destruction of Poland. Should Russia take steps to
oppose us, our relations with Japan may become closer.

[*Thus Hitler already was wondering about a pact
with Russia, but banking on Japan if a pact proved
impossible.*]

[I doubt] the possibility of a peaceful settlement with
England. We must prepare ourselves for the conflict.
England sees in our development the foundation of a
hegemony which would weaken England. England is
therefore our enemy, and the conflict with England will
be a life and death struggle.

The possession of the Ruhr basin will determine the
duration of our resistance.

The Dutch and Belgian air bases must be occupied
by armed force. Declarations of neutrality must be
ignored. If England and France intend the war between

129

Germany and Poland to lead to a conflict, they will support Holland and Belgium in their neutrality, and make them build fortifications, in order finally to force them into cooperation.

Albeit under protest, Belgium and Holland will yield to pressure.

Therefore, if England intends to intervene in the Polish war, we must occupy Holland with lightning speed. We must aim at securing a new defence line on Dutch soil up to the Zuider Zee.

[*Typically, Hitler justifies his actions, when he needs to, by assumption.*]

The idea that we can get off cheaply is dangerous; there is no such possibility. We must burn our boats, and it is no longer a question of justice or injustice, but life and death for 80 million human beings.

Every country's armed forces or government must aim at a short war. The government, however, must also be prepared for a war of 10-15 years' duration.

History has always shown that the people have believed that wars would be short. In 1914, the opinion still prevailed that it was impossible to finance a long war. Even today this idea still persists in many minds. But on the contrary, every state will hold out as long as possible, unless it immediately suffers some grave weakening (*e.g.,* Ruhr Basin). England has similar weaknesses.

England knows that to lose a war will mean the end of her world power.

England is the driving force against Germany. Her strength lies in the following:

1. The British themselves are proud, courageous, tenacious, firm in resistance and gifted as organizers. They know how to exploit every new development. They have the love of adventure and bravery of the Nordic race.

2. World power in itself. It has been constant for 300 years. Extended by the acquisition of allies, this

power is not merely something concrete, but must also be considered as a psychological force, embracing the entire world. Add to immeasurable wealth, with consequential financial credit.

3. Geopolitical safety and protection by strong sea power and a courageous air force.

*England's weaknesses:*

If in the World War I we had had two battleships and two cruisers more, and if the battle of Jutland had begun in the morning, the British fleet would have been defeated and England brought to her knees. It would have meant the end of World War. It was formerly not sufficient to defeat the fleet, landings had to be made in order to defeat England. England could provide her own food supplies. Today that is no longer possible.

The moment England's food supply routes are cut she is forced to capitulate. The import of food and fuel depends upon the fleet's protection.

If the German Air Force attacks English territory, England will not be forced to capitulate in one day. But if the fleet is destroyed, immediate capitulation will be the result.

There is no doubt that a surprise attack can lead to a quick decision. It would be criminal, however, for the government to rely entirely on the element of surprise.

Experience has shown that surprise may be nullified by:

1. Betrayal from the wider circle of military experts.
2. Mere chance, which may cause the collapse of the whole enterprise.
3. Human incompetence.
4. Weather conditions.

The final date for striking must be fixed well in advance. Beyond that time the tension cannot be endured for long. . . .

1. An effort must be made to deal the enemy a significant or the final decisive blow right at the start. Considerations of right and wrong, or treaties, do not enter into the matter. This will be only possible if we

are not involved in a war with England on account of Poland.

[*I.e., if Poland fights alone against Germany.*]

2. In addition to the surprise attack, preparations for a long war must be made, while opportunities on the Continent for England are eliminated.

The army will have to hold positions essential to the Navy and Air Force. If Holland and Belgium are successfully occupied and held, and if France is also defeated, the fundamental conditions for a successful war against England will have been secured.

England can then be blockaded from Western France at close quarters and by the Air Force, while the Navy with its submarines can extend the range of the blockade.

*Consequences:*

England will not be able to fight on the Continent.

Daily attacks by the Air Force and Navy will cut all her life lines;

Time will not be on England's side;

Germany will not bleed to death on land.

...World War I is responsible for the following strategic considerations which are imperative:

1. With a more powerful Navy at the outbreak of the War, or a wheeling movement by the Army towards the channel ports, the end would have been different.

2. A country cannot be brought to defeat by an Air Force. It is impossible to attack all objectives simultaneously and the lapse of time of a few minutes would evoke defensive counter-measures.

3. The unrestricted use of all resources is essential.

4. Once the army, in cooperation with the Air Force and Navy, has taken the important positions, industrial production will cease to flow into the bottomless pit of the Army's battles and can be diverted to benefit the Air Force and Navy.

The Army must therefore be capable of taking these

positions. Systematic preparation must be made for the attack.

Study to this end is of the utmost importance.

The aim will always be to force England to her knees.

The Fuehrer has therefore decided to order the formation of a small planning staff at OKW. It will keep the Fuehrer informed and report to him.

Secrecy is the decisive requirement for success. Our object must be kept secret even from Italy or Japan.

The close combination of the services, for the study of the problem in its entirety, is important.

*The object:*
1. Study of the problem in its entirety.
2. Study of the procedure.
3. Study of the necessary training.

The staff must include men of great imaginative power and the best technical knowledge, as well as officers of sober and sceptical judgment. Working principles:

1. No one must be admitted who is not concerned.

2. No one must know more than is necessary for him to know.

3. When must the person concerned know, at latest? No one may know of a matter earlier than is necessary for him to know it.

[*But Poland remained the immediate problem.*]


June 14, 1939, Dresden        55. Document 2327-PS

[*The following document is an order signed by the commander of the German Army Group 3, General Blaskowitz.*]

1. The commander-in-chief of the army has ordered the working out of a *plan of deployment against Poland* which takes in account the demands of the

political leadership for the opening of war by surprise and for quick success.

4. The order of deployment "Fall Weiss" will be put into operation on 20 August 1939; all preparations have to be concluded by this date.

7. The whole correspondence on "Fall Weiss" has to be conducted under the classification Top Secret. This is to be disregarded only if the content of a document, in the judgment of the chief of the responsible command is harmless in every way— even in connection with other documents.

8. For the middle of July a conference is planned where details on the execution will be discussed. Time and place will be ordered later on.

9. I declare it the duty of the commanding Generals, the divisional commanders and the commandants to limit as much as possible the number of persons who will be informed, and to limit the extent of the information, and ask that all suitable measures be taken to prevent persons not concerned, from getting information.


July 3, 1939          56. Document TC-71
                                      No. 1


[*The British Consul-General at Danzig reported to Foreign Minister Halifax some things he had recently learned.*]


Yesterday four German army officers in mufti arrived here by night express from Berlin to organize Danzig Heimwehr [*Home guard.*]

2. All approaches to hills and dismantled fort, which constitute a popular promenade on Western fringe of city, have been closed with barbed wire and "verboten" notices.

3. The walls surrounding the shipyards bear placards: "Comrades keep your mouths shut lest you

regret consequences."

4. Master of British steamer "High Commissioner Wood," whilst he was roving Koenigsburg from 28th June to 30th June, observed considerable military activity including extensive shipment of camouflaged covered lorries and similar material by small coasting vessels. On 28th June four medium-sized steamers loaded with troops, lorries, field kitchens, etc., left Koenigsburg, ostensibly returning to Hamburg after manoeuvres, but actually proceeding to Stettin.

July 27, 1939                    57. Document C-30

[*This is from the German Navy files.*]

I. The Fuehrer and Supreme Commander of the Armed Forces has ordered the reunion of the German Free State of Danzig with the Greater German Reich. The Armed Forces must occupy the Danzig Free State immediately in order to protect the German population. There will be no hostile intention on the part of Poland so long as the occupation takes place without the force of arms.

II. *How the occupation is to be effected.*

a. The Army will enter the Danzig Free State with troop units from East Prussia, in order to occupy and defend the Polish frontiers.

Until the town of Danzig is reached the advance, unhindered, is expected about—o'clock (Y + 16 hours),—the Danzig police, supported by the population, will hold and defend the town.

b. *The Air Force*, will support the army by the employment of air-borne troops in Danzig and will defend Danzig territory against the Polish air-force.

c. *The Navy* will defend the bay of Danzig against Polish forces. . . . It will afford protection and support to the German population, by entering the Neufahr waters and Danzig and defend the westerplatte which belongs to the Polish armed forces installation.

August 22, 1939                    58. Document 798-PS

[*On this day Hitler faced his military commanders to
tell them the time had come to act. Now he is no longer
uncertain as to where to strike—it is to be in the East.*

*The following document is remarkable in several
respects. It constitutes the minutes of a meeting Hitler
held with his commanders just a few days before World
War II began. Compelling reasons for the invasion are
frankly related. It is further remarkable as one of four
versions of this meeting; allied authorities have been
able to come upon, one way or another, three other
accounts. All save one of these—as is this one—are
unsigned and undated. German defendants at Nurenberg tried to make much of this, but their objections
seem hardly sustainable. For one thing, a signed copy,
introduced by one of the defendant's witnesses,
substantially agrees with this version. Also, the present
document was captured in German files by invading
Americans. Finally, internal evidence strongly suggests
its validity. Apart from the text itself the only notation
reads, "The Fuehrer's Speech to the Commanders in
Chief on 22 August 1939." In it Hitler makes two
points, why Germany must make war now and
secondly, why and how Germany will be successful.*]

I have called you together to give you a picture of
the political situation, in order that you might have
insight into the individual elements on which I have
based my decision to act and in order to strengthen
your confidence.

After this we will discuss military details.

It was clear to me that a conflict with Poland had to
come sooner or later. I had already made this decision
in spring, but I thought that I would first turn against
the West in a few years, and only afterwards against the

East. But the sequence cannot be fixed. One cannot close one's eyes ever before a threatening situation. I wanted to establish an acceptable relationship with Poland in order to fight first against the West. But this plan, which was agreeable to me, could not be executed, since essential points have changed. It became clear to me, that Poland would attack us in case of a conflict with the West. Poland wants access to the sea. The further development became obvious after the occupation of the Memel region, and it became clear to me that under circumstances a conflict could arise at an inopportune moment. [*Or, succinctly, it is well to attack Poland now.*] I enumerate as reasons for this reflection:

1. First of all two personal constitutions:

My own personality and that of Mussolini.

Essentially it depends upon me, my existence, because of my political activities. Furthermore the fact that probably no one will ever again have the confidence of the whole German people as I do. There will probably never again be a man in the future with more authority than I have. My existence is therefore a factor of great value. But I can be eliminated at any time by a criminal or an idiot.

The second personal factor is the Duce. His existence is also decisive. If something happens to him, Italy's loyalty to the alliance will no longer be certain. The basic attitude of the Italian court is against the Duce. Above all, the court sees in the expansion of the empire a burden. The Duce is the man with the strongest nerves in Italy.

The third factor favorable for us is Franco. We can ask only benevolent neutrality from Spain. But this depends upon Franco's personality. He guarantees a certain uniformity and steadiness of the present system in Spain. We must take into account the fact that Spain does not as yet have a Fascist party of our internal unity.

On the other side a negative picture as far as decisive personalities are concerned. There is no outstanding personality in England or France.

For us it is easy to make decisions. We have nothing to lose, we can only gain. Our economic situation is such, because of our restrictions, that we cannot hold out more than a few years. Goering can confirm this. We have no other choice, we must act. Our opponents risk much and gain only a little. England's stake in a war is unimaginably great. Our enemies have men who are below average. No personalities. No masters, no men of action.

Besides the personal factor, the political situation is favorable for us; in the Mediterranean rivalry among Italy, France and England, in the Orient tension, which leads to the alarming of the Mohammedan world.

The English empire did not emerge from the last war strengthened. From a maritime point of view, nothing was achieved. Conflict between England and Ireland. The South African Union became more independent. Concessions had to be made to India. England is in great danger. Unhealthy industries. A British statesman can look into the future only with concern.

Franco's position also has deteriorated particularly in the Mediterranean.

Further favorable factors for us are these:

Since Albania there is an equilibrium of power in the Balkans. [*A month before Italy had taken over this country.*] Yugoslavia carries the germ of collapse because of her internal situation.

Rumania did not grow stronger. She is liable to attack and vulnerable. She is threatened by Hungary and Bulgaria. Since Kemel's death, Turkey has been ruled by small minds, unsteady, weak men.

All these fortunate circumstances will no longer prevail in 2 to 3 years. No one knows how long I will live. Therefore conflict better now.

The creation of Greater Germany was a great achievement politically, but militarily it was questionable, since it was achieved through a bluff of the political leaders. It is necessary to test the military. If at all possible, not by general settlement, but by solving individual tasks.

The relation to Poland has become unbearable. My Polish policy hitherto was in contrast to the ideas of the people. [*Hitler is affirming that he was more lenient toward Poland than the Germans wanted him to be.*] My propositions to Poland (Danzig corridor) were disturbed by England's intervention. Poland changed her tone toward us. The initiative cannot be allowed to pass to others. This moment is more favorable than in 2 to 3 years. An attempt on my life or Mussolini's can change the situation to our disadvantage. One cannot eternally stand opposite one another with cocked rifle. A suggested compromise would have demanded that we change our convictions and make agreeable gestures. They talked to us again in the language of Versailles. There was danger of losing prestige. Now the probability is still great that the West will not interfere. We must accept the risk with reckless resolution. A politician must accept a risk as much as a military leader. We are facing the alternative to strike or to be destroyed with certainty sooner or later.

Reference to previous risks. [*Typically, Hitler reviewed his phenomenal rise.*]

I would have been stoned if I had not carried my point. [*The notes do not make clear the specific case here referred to.*] The most dangerous step was the invasion of the neutral zone. Only a week before, I got a warning through France. I have always accepted a great risk in the conviction that it may succeed. [*In 1936 Hitler had ignored his own military advisors and had marched into the Rhineland area that, under the Versailles treaty, was to have remained demilitarized in perpetuity.*]

Now is also a great risk. Iron nerves, iron resolution.

The following special reasons strengthen my idea. England and France are obligated, neither is in a position for it. There is no actual rearmament in England, just propaganda. It has done much damage

139

that many reluctant Germans said and write to Englishmen after the solution of the Czech question: The Fuehrer carried his point because you lost your nerve, because you capitulated too soon. This explains the present propaganda war. The English speak of a war of nerves. It is one element of this war of nerves to present the increase of armament. But how is British rearmament in actual fact? The construction program for the Navy of 1938 has not yet been filled. Only mobilization of the reserve fleet. Purchase of fishing steamers. Considerable strengthening of the Navy, not before 1941 or 1942.

Little has been done on land. England will be able to send a maximum of 3 divisions to the continent. A little has been done for the air force, but it is only a beginning. AA defense is in its beginning stages. At the moment England has only 150 AA guns. The new AA gun has been ordered. It will take a long time until enough have been produced. Fire directors are lacking. England is still vulnerable from the air. This can change in 2 to 3 years. At the moment the English air force has only 130,000 men, France 72,000 men, Poland 15,000 men. England does not want the conflict to break out for two or three years.

The following is characteristic for England. Poland wanted a loan from England for rearmament. England, however, only gave credit to make sure that Poland buys in England, although England cannot deliver. This means that England does not really want to support Poland. She does not risk 8 million pounds in Poland, although she put half a billion into China. England's position in the world is very precarious. She will not accept any risks.

[*Hitler, it seems, did expect to bluff England out again. His plans called for the invasion of Poland the early morning of August 26, just four days hence. On August 25th England published the announcement of her guarantee treaty with Poland, causing Hitler to make a frantic second effort to keep Britain out of the war.*]

France lacks men (decline of birth rate). Little has been done for rearmament. The artillery is antiquated. France did not want to enter upon this adventure. The West has only two possibilities to fight against us:

1. Blockade: It will not be effective because of our autarchy and because we have sources of aid in the East.

2. Attack from the West from the Maginot line: I consider this impossible.

Another possibility is violation of Dutch, Belgian and Swiss neutrality. I have no doubts that all these states as well as Scandinavia will defend their neutrality by all available means. England and France will not violate the neutrality of those countries. Actually England cannot help Poland. There remains an attack on Italy. A military attack is out of the question. No one is counting on a long war. If Mr. [*sic*] von Brauchitsch had told me that I would need 4 years to conquer Poland I would have replied: then it cannot be done. It is nonsense to say that England wants to wage a long war.

We will hold our position in the West until we have conquered Poland. We must be conscious of our great production. It is much bigger than in 1914-1918.

The enemy had another hope, that Russia would become our enemy after the conquest of Poland. The enemy did not count on my great power of resolution. Our enemies are little worms. I saw them in Munich.

I was convinced that Stalin would never accept the England offer. Russia has no interest in maintaining Poland and Stalin knows that it is the end of his regime no matter whether his soldiers come out of a war victoriously or beaten.

[*I.e., Stalin realized, Hitler believed, that war per*

*se—involving Russia—would mean the end of Stalin's rule. Why Hitler should say this is quite clear—he is assuring his generals that there isn't too much to fear— but why he should consider it plausible enough to say is not clear. After all, history records few examples of regimes emerging from victorious wars and falling as a result of the victory.]*

Litvinov's replacement was decisive. I brought about the change. In connection with the commercial treaty we got into political conversation. Proposal of a non-aggression pact. Then came a general proposal from Russia. Four days ago I took a special step, which brought it about that Russia answered yesterday that she is ready to sign. The personal contract [*sic*] with Stalin is established. The day after tomorrow von Ribbentrop will conclude the treaty. Now Poland is in the position in which I wanted her.

We need not be afraid of a blockade. The East will supply us with grain, cattle, coal, lead and zinc. It is a big arm which demands great efforts. I am only afraid that at the last minute some Schweinhund ... will make a proposal for mediation.

The political arm is set farther. A beginning has been made for the destruction of England's hegemony. The way is open for the soldier, after I have made the political preparations.

To-day's publication of the non-aggression pact with Russia hit like a shell. The consequences cannot be overlooked. Stalin also said that this course will be of benefit to both countries. The effect on Poland will be tremendous.

Georing answers with thanks to the Fuehrer and the assurance that the armed forces will do their duty.


August 22, 1939               59. Document 1014-PS

[*Apart from the context the only notation on this document is "Second Speech by the Fuehrer on 22 Aug.*

It may also turn out differently regarding England and France. One cannot predict it with certainty. I figure on a trade barrier, not on blockade, and with severance of relations. Most iron determination on our side. Retreat before nothing. Everybody shall have to make a point of it that we are determined from the beginning to fight the Western powers. Struggle for life or death. Germany has won every war as long as she was united. Iron, unflinching attitude of all superiors, greatest confidence, faith in victory, overcoming of the past by getting used to heaviest strain. A long period of peace will not do us any good. Therefore it is necessary to expect everything. Manly bearing. It is not machines that fight each other. We have the better quality of men. Mental factors are decisive. The opposite camp has weaker people. In 1918, the Nation fell down because the mental prerequisites were not sufficient. Fredric the Great secured final success only through his mental power.

Destruction of Poland in the foreground. The aim is elimination of living forces, not the arrival at a certain line: even if war should break out in the West, the destruction of Poland shall be the primary objective. Quick decision because of the season.

I shall give a propagandistic cause for starting the war—never mind whether it be plausible or not. In starting and making a war, not the Right is what matters but Victory.

Have no pity. Brutal attitude. 80 million people shall get what is their right. Their existence has to be secured. The strongest has the Right. Greatest severity.

Quick decision necessary. Unshakable faith in the German soldier. A crisis may happen only if the nerves of the leaders give way.

First aim, advance to the Vistula and Narew. Our

technical superiority will break the nerves of the Poles. Every newly created Polish force shall again be broken at once. Constant war of attrition.

New German frontier according to healthy principles. Possibly a protectorate as a buffer. Military operations shall not be influenced by these reflections. Complete destruction of Poland is the military aim. To be fast is the main thing. Pursuit until complete elimination.

Conviction that the German Wehrmacht is up to the requirements. The start shall be ordered, probably by Saturday morning.

[*Two other documents bear upon this August 22nd meeting. Document L-3 was not used by the prosecution at Nurenberg because it seemed to be the work of a newspaper man rather than the notes of one who attended the meeting; how a reporter could have gotten access to material permitting him to compose such a report is not known. The other version, by far the longest, is the only signed report. Its author was Admiral Hermann Boehm, who was a colleague of Raeder. His notes were full; from them he composed, on the night of August 22, 1939, a thirteen page transcript account of the meeting. This account was introduced by the defense (Raeder) at Nurenberg as counter evidence purportedly showing the harmlessness of the Fuehrer's speech. This was a most curious move on the defense's part since the Admiral's version is, in substance, the same as that given above.*]

August 12, 1939, Obersalzburg 60. Document TC-77

[*Now follows a memorandum of a conversation between Hitler, Ribbentrop and Ciano. It is unsigned; probably Hitler's adjutant, again, is responsible for these notes. Hitler is speaking.*]

Since the Poles through their whole attitude had made it clear that in any case in the event of a conflict they would stand on the side of the enemies of Germany and Italy, a quick war at the present moment could only be of advantage for the unavoidable conflict with the Western Democracies. If a hostile Poland remained on Germany's Eastern frontier, not only would the eleven East Prussian divisions be tied down, but also further contingents would be kept in Pomerania and Silesia. This would not be necessary in the event of a previous liquidation. Generally speaking, the best thing to happen would be for the neutrals to be liquidated one after the other. This process could be carried out more easily if on every occasion one partner of the Axis covered the other, while it was dealing with an uncertain neutral.

Coming back to the Danzig question, the Fuehrer said it was impossible for him now to go back. He had made an agreement with Italy for the withdrawal of the Germans from South Tyrol, but for this reason he must take the greatest care to avoid giving the impression that this Tyrolese withdrawal could be taken as a precedent for other areas. Furthermore, he had justified the withdrawal by pointing to a generally easterly and northeasterly direction of a German policy. The East and North-East, that is to say the Baltic countries, had been Germany's undisputed sphere since time immemorial, as the Mediterranean had been an appropriate sphere for Italy. For economic reasons also, Germany needed the foodstuffs and timber from these Eastern regions. In the case of Danzig, German interests were not only material, although the city had the greatest harbor in the Baltic. Danzig was a Nurenberg of the north, an ancient German City awakening sentimental feelings for every German and the Fuehrer was bound to take account of this psychological element in public opinion. To make a comparison with Italy, Count Ciano [was asked to suppose] that Triest was in Yugoslav hands and that a large Italian minority was being brutally treated on Yugoslav soil.

Count Ciano in replying to the Fuehrer's statement first expressed the great surprise on the Italian side over the completely unexpected seriousness of the position. Neither in the conversation in Milan nor in those which took place during his Berlin visit had there been any sign from the German side that the position with regard to Poland was so serious. On the contrary, Ribbentrop had said that in his opinion, the Danzig question would be settled in the course of time. On these grounds the Duce, in view of his conviction that a conflict with the Western Powers was unavoidable, had assumed that he should make his preparations for this event, he had made plans for a period of two or three years. If immediate conflict were unavoidable, the Duce as he had told Ciano, would certainly stand on the German side but for various reasons he would welcome the postponement of a general conflict until a later time. Ciano then showed, with the aid of a map, the position of Italy in the event of a general war.

[*The Fuehrer believed that for a*] solution of the Polish problem no time should be lost; the longer one waited until the autumn, the more difficult would military operations in Eastern Europe become. From the middle of September, weather conditions made air operations hardly possible in these areas, while the conditions of the roads, which were quickly turned into a morass by the autumn rains, would be such as to make them impossible for motorized forces. From September to May, Poland was a great marsh and entirely unsuited for any kind of military operations. Poland could, however, occupy Danzig in September and Germany would not be able to do anything about it since they obviously could not bombard or destroy the place.

Ciano asked how soon, according to the Fuehrer's view, the Danzig question must be settled. The Fuehrer answered that this settlement must be made one way or another by the end of August.

During this exchange of conversation the Fuehrer was given a telegram from Tokio. The conversation was interrupted for a short time and Ciano was then told the text of the Moscow telegram. The Russians agreed to the dispatch of a German political negotiator to Moscow. Ribbentrop added that the Russians were fully informed of the intentions of Germany with regard to Poland. He himself at the Fuehrer's order had informed the Russian Charge d'Affaires, the Fuehrer added that according to his opinion Russia would not be ready to take the chestnuts out of the fire for the Western Powers.

After a further consideration over the communique proposal the Fuehrer said that he would consider this proposal and Ciano's news about the general situation for inter-aid. He therefore proposed that the discussion should be continued on the following day.


August 13, 1939                                    *Ibid.*


[*The conversation was concluded on this day. Again, Hitler did most of the talking. Typically, he went over ground already covered. Probably a remark should be made concerning the two stipulations under which he considered "taking" Poland: the Polish provocation repeatedly referred to by Hitler is historically a myth; the desire to have Poland "state her intentions clearly" is Hitlerese for "voluntarily give up Danzig and the Corridor to Germany."*]


The Fuehrer said that since the last conversation, he had been considering the whole position. Ribbentrop had meanwhile told him that in the circumstances Ciano had decided not to conclude the conversations with a communique. The Fuehrer had agreed with that decision. The door was therefore open, no one was committed and no course was blocked.

The Fuehrer had also come to the conclusion, as he had said in a previous conversation, that the danger of delaying too long into the autumn was that Poland would be able to carry out its relatively limited aims.

Danzig could be made to submit by slow pressure and the treaty position was extremely favorable to Poland. It was therefore necessary that within the shortest time, Poland should clearly state her intentions, and no further provocation should be endured by Germany. If these provocations were allowed to pass, the affair would be prolonged until October when tanks and aircraft could not be used. The Polish General Staff knew these climatic conditions and their effect upon the German forces and therefore Poland was playing for time. The Fuehrer had therefore come to two definite conclusions, 1) in the event of any further provocation, he would immediately attack, 2) if Poland did not clearly and plainly state her political intention, she must be forced to do so. It should not be forgotten that the test of nerves which the Poles had begun by means of continual instances of provocation had not [*sic; now?*] lasted for three months. Any signs of giving way would, in view of the Slav mentality, bring a violent reaction of over-confidence on the part of the Poles. Surrender would not, in any way strengthen the German position but would be regarded by every other country as a sign of weakness. If the Western Democracies had already decided to move against the Axis, they would not in any case wait for three or four years before carrying out their plan and attack only at a time when the Axis Powers had completed their necessary preparations, but they would pass the earlier conflict [*sic*]. If, however, they had not yet come to a decision in the matter (and the Fuehrer thought that in the state of their armaments they had not come to this decision), the best way of preventing them would be to deal with the Polish matter quickly. In general, however, success by one of the Axis partners, not only strategical but also psychological strengthening of the other partner and also of the whole Axis would ensue. Italy carried through a number of successful operations in Abyssinia, Spain and Albania and each time against the wishes of the Democratic Entente. These individual actions have not only strengthened Italian local interests but had also reinforced her general position, the same was the case with German actions in Austria and Czechoslovakia. Here also not only had German local interest been strengthened but the general position had been re-inforced. The Axis had thereby won considerable victories. If one were to consider what would have happened if these individual operations had not been successful and to ask what the position of Germany would then have been, one reached a similar conclusion [?]. The strengthening of the Axis by these individual operations was of the greatest importance for the unavoidable clash with the Western Powers. As matters now stand, Germany and Italy would simply not exist further in the world through lack of space, not only was there no more space but existing space was completely blockaded by its present possessors, they sat like misers with their heaps of gold and deluded themselves about their riches. The Western Democracies were dominated by the desire to rule the world and would not regard Germany and Italy as their class. This psychological element of contempt was perhaps the worst thing about the whole business. It could only be settled by a life and death struggle which the two Axis partners could meet more easily because their interests did not clash on any point. The Mediterranean was obviously the most ancient domain for which Italy had a claim to predominance. The Duce himself had summed up the position to him in the words that Italy already was the dominant power in the Mediterranean. On the other hand, the Fuehrer said that Germany must take the old German road eastwards and that this road was also desirable for economic reasons, and that Italy had geographical and historical claims to permanency in the Mediterranean. Bismarck had recognized it and had said as much in his well known letter to Mazzini. The interests of Germany and Italy were in quite different directions and there never could be a conflict between them. Ribbentrop added that if the two problems mentioned in yesterday's conversations were settled, Italy and Germany would have their backs free for work against the West. The Fuehrer said that Poland must be struck down so that for (50?) years she would be incapable of fighting. In such a case, matters in the west could be settled. Ciano thanked the Fuehrer for his extremely clear explanation of the situation. He had, on his side, nothing to add and would give the Duce full details. He asked for more definite information on one point in order that the Duce might have all the facts before him. The Duce might indeed have to make no decision because the Fuehrer believed that the conflict with Poland could be localized on the basis of long experience. He (Ciano) quite saw that so far the Fuehrer had always been right in his judgment of the position. If, however, Mussolini had no decision to make, he had to take certain measures of precaution and therefore Ciano would put the following question:

The Fuehrer had mentioned two conditions under which he would take Poland—1, if Poland were guilty of serious provocation and, 2, if Poland did not make her political position clear. The first of these decisions depended upon the decision of the Fuehrer and German reaction would follow it in a moment. The second condition required certain decisions as to times. Ciano therefore asked what was the date by which Poland must have satisfied Germany about her political condition. He realized that this date depended upon climatic conditions.

The Fuehrer answered that the decision of Poland must be made clear by the end of August. Since, however, the decisive part of military operations against Poland could be carried out within a period of 14 days and the final liquidation would need another 4 weeks it could be finished at the end of September or the beginning of October these could be regarded as the dates. It followed therefore that the last dates on which he could begin to take action was the last of August. Finally Fuehrer assured Ciano that since his youth he had favored German-Italian co-operation and that no other view was expressed in his books. He had always thought that Germany and Italy were naturally suited for collaboration since there were no conflicts of interest between them. He was personally fortunate to live at a time in which, apart from himself, there was one other great statesman who would stand out great and unique in history; that he could be this man's friend was for him a matter of great personal satisfaction and if the hour of common battle struck, he would always be found at the side of the Duce.

Late August, 1939                                   61. Affidavit A

*[Ciano, of course, was not taken in by Hitler's oft repeated references to "Polish provocations." It is quite possible that a number of Germans were; and perhaps today, after a lapse of almost two decades, the argument might possibly carry weight with those who have forgotten or were too young to remember now. It may be in order, therefore, to interpolate here some first hand testimony by Germans who were in a position to report the actual facts. The following document is from an affidavit of Major General Erwin Lahausen, a high ranking officer in the German Intelligence unit called Abwehr.]*

Some time prior to the start of the Polish campaign, the Abwehr office was ordered to deliver a number of Polish uniforms, Polish army equipment, forged papers, and other articles to the SD *[security police]* which it did. After the beginning of the Polish campaign, it became known officially that the broadcasting station at Cattovici had been seized. This was propagandized as the incident leading to hostilities with Poland. This was an incident which had been deliberately engineered and directed by the SD and it was executed by prisoners from concentration camps dressed up in Polish uniforms, and using Polish weapons and equipment. These prisoners were later murdered by the SD in order to eliminate any possibility of their giving testimony about the incident. Immediately after receiving information of this incident, Canaris stated to me that it was now apparent to what use the uniforms and equipment which had been furnished to the SD had been put.

I learned through official channels that the incident had been deliberately staged and executed by the SD as set forth above and this was later admitted to me by a member of the SS, a man by the name of Birkel.

Same time,
Gleiwitz on the Polish border          62. Document
                                                          2751-PS

[*This document is another affidavit giving more details of Polish "provocation." The affiant is Alfred Helmut Naujocks.*]

1. I was a member of the SS from 1931 to 19 October 1944 and a member of the SD from its creation in 1934 to January 1941. I served as a member of the Waffen-SS [*the "party army," as it were*] from February 1941 until the middle of 1942. Thereafter I served in the economic department of the military administration of Belgium from September 1942 to September 1944. I surrendered to the Allies on 19 October, 1944.

2. On or about 10 August 1939, the chief of the Sipo [*criminal police*] and SD, Heydrich, personally ordered me to simulate an attack on the radio station near Gleiwitz, near the Polish border, and to make it appear that the attacking force consisted of Poles. Heydrich said, "Practical proof is needed for these attacks of the Poles for the foreign press as well as for German propaganda purposes." I was directed to go to Gleiwitz with five or six other SD-men and wait there until I received a code word from Heydrich indicating that the attack should take place. My instructions were to seize the radio station and to hold it long enough to permit a

Polish speaking German who would be put at my disposal to broadcast a speech in Polish. Heydrich told me that this speech should state that the time had come for conflict between Germans and Poles and that Poles should get together and smash down any Germans from whom they met resistance. Heydrich also told me at this time that he expected an attack on Poland by Germany.

3. I went to Gleiwitz and waited there fourteen days. Then I requested permission of Heydrich to return to Berlin but was told to stay in Gleiwitz. Between the 25th and the 31st of August I went to see Heinrich Mueller, head of the Gestapo, who was then nearby at Oppeln. In my presence, Mueller discussed with a man named Mehlhorn plans for another border incident, in which it should be made to appear that Polish soldiers were attacking German troops. Germans in the approximate strength of a company were to be used. Mueller stated that he had 12 or 13 condemned criminals who were to be dressed in Polish uniforms and left dead on the ground of the scene of the incident, to show that they had been killed while attacking. For this purpose they were to be given fatal injections by a doctor employed by Heydrich. Then they were also to be given gunshot wounds. After the incident members of the press and other persons were to be taken to the spot of the incident. A police report was subsequently to be prepared.

4. Mueller told me that he had an order from Heydrich to make one of those criminals available to me for the action at Gleiwitz. The code name by which he referred to those criminals was "Canned Goods."

5. The incident at Gleiwitz in which I participated was carried out on the evening preceding the German attack on Poland. As I recall, war broke out on the 1st of September 1939. At noon of the 31st August I received by telephone from Heydrich the code word for the attack which was to take place at 8 o'cock that evening. Heydrich said, "In order to carry out this attack report to Mueller for Canned Goods." I did this and gave Mueller instructions to deliver the man near

the radio station. He was alive but completely unconscious. I tried to open his eyes. I could not recognize by his eyes that he was alive, only by his breathing. I did not see the shot wounds but a lot of blood was smeared across his face. He was in civilian clothes.

6. We seized the radio station as ordered, broadcast a speech of three to four minutes over an emergency transmitter, fired some pistol shots and left.


August 27, 1939, Warsaw      63. Document TC-72
                                             No. 55

[*The British Blue Book includes the following telegraphic communication from Sir H. Kennard to Viscount Halifax. Kennard was the British Ambassador to Warsaw.*]

So far as I can judge, German allegations of mass ill-treatment of German minority by Polish authorities are gross exaggeration, if not complete falsification.

2. There is no sign of any loss of control of situation by Polish civil authorities. Warsaw (and as far as I can ascertain the rest of Poland) is still completely calm.

3. Such allegations are reminiscent of Nazi propaganda methods regarding Czechoslovakia last year.

4. In any case it is purely and simply deliberate German provocation in accordance with fixed policy that has since March exacerbated feeling between the two nationalities. I suppose this has been done with object (a) creating war spirit in Germany, (b) impressing public opinion abroad, (c) provoking either defeatism or apparent aggression in Poland.


August 23, 1939, Berlin      64. Document 1780-PS

[*This entry is from the diary of Hitler's chief military adviser, Jodl.*]

Received order from Armed Forces High Command [*OKW*] to proceed to Berlin and take over position of Chief of Armed Forces Executive Office [*Operations*].

1100 hours-1330 hours [*11:00-1:30 p.m.*]: Discussions with Chief of Armed Forces High Command [*Keitel*]. X-day has been announced for 26 August. Y time has been announced for 0430 hours [*4:30 a.m.*].

[*This was not the only important event of this day. On August 23 the famous Russo-German non-aggression pact was signed.*]

August 25, 1939                    65. Document 1796-PS

[*This is another item from the "Notes to a War Diary" previously quoted.*]

In spite of the English guarantee to Poland, and therefore a war on 2 fronts becoming almost unavoidable, the Fuehrer decides to settle the account with Poland after having prevented encirclement by means of *an agreement with Russia.*

Same date                          66. Document TC-72 No. 68

[*In spite of Hitler's determination to settle the Polish question, the British guarantee to Poland, announced on this day, gave him pause. Because he was eager to avoid a conflict with England while working his will on Poland, Hitler, to the amazement and chagrin of certain German generals, called off the war for the time being and reopened negotiations with the British. His obvious aim was to get substantial gains in Poland and an agreement with England. In other words, another Munich. Equally obvious, he believed that thereafter events would run a course similar to the one they ran in Czechoslovakia. The following account is from the British Blue Book.*]

The following is a translation of the text of a verbal communication made to Sir Neville Henderson [*British Ambassador to Berlin*] by Herr Hitler at his interview on the 25th August:

By way of introduction the Fuehrer declared that the British Ambassador had given expression at the close of the last conversation to the hope that, after all, an understanding between Germany and England might yet be possible. He (the Fuehrer) had therefore turned things over in his mind once more and decided to make a move as regards England which should be as decisive as the move as regards Russia which had led to the recent agreement. Yesterday's sitting in the house of Commons and the speeches of Mr. Chamberlain and Lord Halifax had also moved the Fuehrer to talk once more to the British Ambassador. The assertion that Germany affected to conquer the world was ridiculous. The British Empire embraced 40 million square kilometers, Russia 19 million square kilometers, America 9½ million square kilometers, whereas Germany embraced less than 600,000 square kilometers. It is quite clear who it is who desires to conquer the world.

The Fuehrer makes the following communication to the British Ambassador:

1. Poland's actual provocations have become intolerable. It makes no difference who is responsible. If the Polish Government denies responsibility, that only shows that it no longer possesses any influence over its subordinate military authorities. In the preceding night there had been a further twenty-one new frontier incidents; on the German side the greatest discipline had been maintained. All incidents had been provoked from the Polish side. Furthermore commercial aircraft had been shot at. If the Polish Government stated that it was not responsible, it showed it was no longer capable of controlling its own people.

2. Germany was in all circumstances determined to

abolish these Macedonian conditions on their Eastern frontier and, what is more, to do so in the interests of quiet and order, but also in the interests of European peace.

3. The problem of Danzig and the Corridor must be solved. The British Prime Minister had made a speech which was not in the least calculated to induce any change in the German attitude. At the most, the result of this speech could be a bloody and incalculable war between Germany and England. Such a war would be bloodier than that of 1914 to 1918. In contrast to the last war, Germany would no longer have to fight on two fronts. Agreement with Russia was unconditional and signified a change in foreign policy of the Reich which would last a very long time.

Russia and Germany would never again take up arms against each other. Apart from this, the agreements reached with Russia would also render Germany secure economically for the longest possible period of war.

The Fuehrer had always wanted an Anglo-German understanding. War between England and Germany could at the best bring some profit to Germany but none at all to England.

The Fuehrer declared that the German-Polish problem must be solved and will be solved. He is, however, prepared and determined after the solution of this problem to approach England once more with a large comprehensive offer. He is a man of great decisions, and in this case also he will be capable of being great in his action. He accepts the British Empire and is ready to pledge himself personally for its continued existence and to place the power of the German Reich at its disposal if—

(1) His colonial demands which are limited and can be negotiated by peaceful methods are fulfilled and in this case he is prepared to fix the longest time limits.

(2) His obligation towards Italy is not touched; in

other words, he does not demand that England give up her obligations toward France and similarly for his own part he cannot withdraw from his obligations toward Italy.

(3) He also desires to stress the irrevocable determination of Germany never again to enter into conflict with Russia. The Fuehrer is ready to conclude agreements with England which, as has already been emphasized, would not only guarantee the existence of the British Empire in all circumstances as far as Germany is concerned, but also if necessary an assurance to the British Empire of German assistance regardless of where such assistance should be necessary. The Fuehrer would then also be ready to accept a reasonable limitation of armaments which corresponds to the new political situation, and which is economically tolerable. Finally, the Fuehrer renewed his assurance that he is not interested in Western problems and that a frontier modification in the West does not enter into consideration. Western fortifications which have been constructed at a cost of millions were final Reich frontier on the West.

If the British Government would consider these ideas a blessing for Germany and also for the British Empire peace might result. If it rejects these ideas there will be war. In no case would Great Britain emerge stronger; the last war proved this.

The Fuehrer repeats that he is a man of *ad infinitum* decisions by which he himself is bound and that this is his last offer. Immediately after solution of the German-Polish question he would approach the British Government with an offer.

August 29, 1939, Berlin        67. Document TC-72
                                              No. 78

[*On August 28 the British replied to the suggestions of Hitler thus: they would like an accord between Germany and themselves; but only after a peaceful*

158

*settlement of the difficulties now standing between Poland and Germany, a settlement which would be guaranteed by England, Germany and other powers. What England did not know at this time—among other things—was that the August 23rd agreement between Germany and Russia contained a secret protocol dealing with a shuffling of Polish provinces to the territorial advantage of both Germany and Russia. England also did not know, apparently, that Hitler was determined to "take" Poland willy-nilly, though he would have preferred, naturally, to do it without having to fight England and France if that could be arranged. With these facts in mind the following German reply is better understood.]*

Though sceptical as to the prospects of a successful outcome, the [*German Government*] are nevertheless prepared to accept the English proposal and to enter into direct discussions. They do so, as has already been emphasized, solely as a result of the impression made upon them by the written statement received from the British Government that they too desire a pact of friendship in accordance with the general lines indicated to the British Ambassador.

The German Government desire in this way to give the British Government and the British nation a proof of the sincerity of Germany's intentions to enter into a lasting friendship with Great Britain.

The Government of the Reich felt, however, bound to point out to the British Government that in the event of a territorial arrangement in Poland they would no longer be able to bind themselves to give guarantees or to participate in guarantees without the U.S.S.R. being associated therewith.

For the rest, in making these proposals the German Government have never had any intention of touching Poland's vital interests or questioning the existence of an independent Polish State. The German Government, accordingly, in these circumstances agree to accept the British Government's offer of their good offices in securing the dispatch to Berlin of a Polish Emissary with full powers. They count on the arrival of this Emissary on Wednesday, the 30th August, 1939.

The German Government will immediately draw up proposals for a solution acceptable to themselves and will, if possible, place these at the disposal of the British Government before the arrival of the Polish negotiator.

**August 30, 1939, Berlin**       **68. Document TC-72**
                                                   **No. 92**

*[The following is Ambassador Henderson's telegraphic report to Halifax of his, Henderson's, conversation with Ribbentrop as the British reply to the above note was given.]*

I told Herr von Ribbentrop this evening that his Majesty's Government found it difficult to advise Polish Government to accept procedure adumbrated in German reply, and suggested that he should adopt normal contact, i.e., that when German proposals were ready to invite Polish Ambassador to call and to hand him proposals for transmission to his Government with a view to immediate opening of negotiations. I added that if basis afforded prospect of settlement His Majesty's Government could be counted upon to do their best in Warsaw to temporize negotiations.

2. Herr von Ribbentrop's reply was to produce a lengthy document which he read out in German aloud at top speed. Imagining that he would eventually hand it to me I did not attempt to follow too closely the sixteen or more articles which it contained. Though I cannot therefore guarantee accuracy the main points were: restoration of Danzig to Germany; southern boundary of Corridor to be line Marienwerder, Grandenz, Bromberg, Schoenlanke; plebiscite to be held in the Corridor on basis of population of 1st January 1919, absolute majority to decide; international

160

commission of British, French, Italian and Russian members to police the Corridor and guarantee reciprocal communications with Danzig and Gdynia pending result of the plebiscite; Gdynia to be reserved to Poland; Danzig to be purely commercial city and demilitarized.

3. When I asked Herr von Ribbentrop for text of these proposals in accordance with undertaking in the German reply of yesterday, he asserted that it was now too late as Polish representatives had not arrived in Berlin by midnight.

4. I observed that to treat the matter in this way meant that request for Polish representative to arrive in Berlin on 30th August constituted in fact, an ultimatum in spite of what he and Herr Hitler had assured me yesterday. This he denied, saying that idea of an ultimatum was figment of my imagination. Why then I asked could he not adopt normal procedure and give me copy of proposals and ask Polish Ambassador to call on him, just as Herr Hitler had summoned me a few days ago, and hand them to him for communication to Polish Government? In the most violent terms Herr von Ribbentrop said that he would never ask the Ambassador to visit him. He hinted that if Polish Ambassador asked him for interview it might be different. I said I would naturally inform my Government so at once. Whereupon he said that while those were his personal views he would bring all that I had said to Herr Hitler's notice. It was for Chancellor to decide.

5. We parted on that note, but I must tell you that Herr von Ribbentrop's whole demeanor during an unpleasant interview was aping Herr Hitler at his worst. He inveighed incidentally against Polish mobilization, but I retorted that it was hardly surprising since Germany had also mobilized as Herr Hitler himself had admitted to me yesterday.

August 26, 1939, Rome          69. Document 1823-PS

[*Meantime Hitler's Ambassador in Rome, Macken-sen, had learned from Mussolini that Italy could not enter the coming war at an early date; indeed, the Duce thought it would be two or three years before Italy would be ready for a general conflict. However Hitler was assured that in every other way Italy stood one hundred percent behind him. This information, direct from Mussolini, was wired to Hitler on the 25th. The next day a message from Hitler, which follows, was read to Mussolini by Mackensen.*]

### Duce!

I have received the information concerning your final attitude. I respect the motives and influences determining your resolution. Perhaps it will neverthe-less be for the best. Of course, in my opinion, this will be true only if the world does not receive any inkling of the intended attitude of Italy, at least not till actual fighting starts. For this reason I beg you heartily to support my struggle psychologically in your press and any other means. I also beg of you, Duce, if it is possible for you to force at least England and France to immobilize certain parts of their strength, by demon-strative military actions, or to keep them in any case, in a state of uncertainty. But the most important thing is this, Duce: should, as mentioned, the big war start, the situation in the East will be solved, before the two Western powers can achieve any success. This winter, or at the latest by spring I intend to deploy in the West forces at least equal to those of France and England. The blockade will be of little effect, especially under the altered circumstances in the East and as a result of my autarchic preparations. Its danger during the progress of the war will not increase but decrease. Now I have a big favor to ask you, Duce. You and your people could help me most in this hard struggle by supporting me with Italian manpower, manpower for industrial as well as agricultural purposes. Should you later on in the course of developments be forced or be in a position to intervene, the intensified autarchic basis of the Reich would be of the utmost importance to you. In reiterating my entreaty for the granting of this special favor, I wish to thank you for all the efforts you have made in our common cause.                    Adolf Hitler


August 27, 1939, 10:00 p.m., Rome          70. Document
                                                                            1832-PS


[*About this time the word began to get about that negotiations were on again between Germany and Italy and the prospects of another "Czechoslovakia" were good. The following is a Mackensen memorandum of a telephone conversation between him and Ribbentrop apropos that matter.*]

According to authentic information, the rumors spreading in Rome, by way of the Italian embassy in Berlin, that a relaxation of the situation is to be noted and that conferences are being held. We want to state on the contrary, that just the opposite is true and that the situation is getting more serious from hour to hour. "The Armies are marching." It would be good if I would see to it that the rumor mentioned above should not be believed by the Duce and Ciano.


August 31, 1939, Berlin          71. Document TC-73
                                                    No. 112


[*The armies were indeed about to march. It will be recalled that the day before, August 30, Henderson and Ribbentrop had had their rather violent exchange. The British insisted upon negotiations being carried on through normal channels, the Germans demanded a special envoy. On this day Lipski, the Polish ambassador, was received by Ribbentrop. The following is from*] *the Polish White Book and reports what took place in that interview.*]

I was received by M. von Ribbentrop at 6:30 p.m.

I carried out my instructions. M. von Ribbentrop asked if I had special plenipotentiary powers to undertake negotiations. I said no. He then asked whether I had been informed that on London's suggestion the German Government had expressed their readiness to negotiate directly with a delegate of the Polish Government, furnished with the requisite full powers, who was to have arrived on the preceding day, August 30. I replied that I had no direct information on the subject. In conclusion M. von Ribbentrop repeated that he had thought I would be empowered to negotiate. He would communicate my demarche to the Chancellor.

Same day, a little later, Berlin     72. Document TC-73
No. 113

[*This is a monitored report of a German broadcast at 9:00 p.m., August 31.*]

It has once more been made clear as a result of a demarche which has meanwhile been made by the Polish Ambassador that the latter himself has no plenary powers either to enter into any discussion, or even to negotiate.

The Fuehrer and the German Government have thus waited two days in vain for the arrival of a Polish negotiator with plenary powers.

In these circumstances the German Government regard their proposals as having this time too been to all intents and purposes rejected, although they considered that these proposals, in the form in which they were made known to the British Government also, were more than loyal, fair and practicable.

September 1, 1939, Berlin        73. Document TC-73
                                              No. 147

[*In his final report to the Polish Foreign Office,
Ambassador Lipski had this to say.*]

In the early hours of September 1 I learned from the
wireless that German armed forces had invaded Poland,
and that the German air force had bombed a number of
Polish towns.

In the morning I received a note from the Ministry
of Foreign Affairs, stating that in the interests of my
personal safety I was not to leave the Embassy building.
At about 1 p.m. Prince Luborinerski called in my name
on the Director of the Protocol, Baron Dorenberg, and
asked for my passports.


September 3, 1939, Rome        74. Document 1831-PS
                                              (Coded Telegram).

[*The following document is a telegram sent by the
German Foreign Office in Berlin to Mackensen to
inform the latter of what Attolico, Italian Ambassador
in Berlin, has just communicated to Hitler. The Duce
got the nervous jitters, apparently, as the armies
clashed.*]

Italy sends the information, leaving, of course, every
decision to the Fuehrer, that it still has a chance to call
a conference with France, England and Poland on the
following basis: 1.  Armistice which would leave the
Army Corps where they are at present. 2. Calling the
conference within 2-3 days. 3. Solution of the Polish-
German controversy which would be certainly favorable for Germany as matters stand today.

This idea which originated from the Duce had its
foremost exponent in France.

Danzig is already German and Germany is holding

already securities which guarantee most of her demands. Besides, Germany has had already its "moral satisfaction." If it would accept the plan for a conference, it will achieve all her aims and at the same time prevent a war which already today has the aspect of being universal and of extremely long duration.

Duce does not insist on it, but he lays particular emphasis that above should be brought to the immediate attention of von Ribbentrop and of the Fuehrer.

The same day, Berlin                    *Ibid.* "Telegram Heading in Italian"

[*A personal reply from Hitler was immediately forthcoming.*]

Duce

I first want to thank you for your last attempt at a mediation. I would have been ready to accept, but only under condition, that there would be a possibility to give me certain guarantees that the conference would be successful. Because, for the last two days the German troops are engaged in an extraordinarily rapid advance in Poland. It would have been impossible to devaluate the bloody sacrifices made thereby by diplomatic intrigues. Nevertheless, I believe that a way could have been found if England would not have been determined to wage war under all circumstances. I have not given in to the English, because Duce, I do not believe that peace could have been maintained for more than ½ year or 1 year. Under these circumstances, I thought that, in spite of everything, the present moment was better for resistance. At present, the superiority of the German armed forces in Poland is too overwhelming in all fields that the Polish Army will collapse in a very short time [*sic*]. I doubt whether this fast success could be achieved in one or two years. England and France would have armed their allies to such an extent that the crushing technical superiority of the German forces could not have become so apparent any more. I am aware, Duce, that the fight that I enter, is one for life and death. My own fate does not play any role in it at all. But I am also aware that one cannot avoid such a struggle permanently and that one has to choose after cold deliberation the moment for resistance in such a way that the probability of the success is guaranteed and I believe in this success, Duce, with the firmness of a vouch. Recently you have given me the kind assurance that you think you will be able to help me in a few fields. I acknowledge this in advance with sincere thanks. But I believe also—even if we march now over different roads—that fate will finally unite us. If the National Socialist Germany were destroyed by the Western democracies, the Fascist Italy would also have to face a grave future. I was personally always aware of this community of the future of our two governments and I know that you, Duce, think the same. To the situation in Poland, I would like to make the brief remark that we lay aside, of course, all unimportant things, that we do not waste any man in unimportant tasks, but direct all on acts in the light of great operational considerations. The Northern Polish Army which is the Corridor [sic], has already been completely encircled by our action. It will be either wiped out or will surrender. Otherwise, all operations proceed according to plan. The daily achievements of the troops are far beyond all expectations. The superiority of our air force is complete, although scarcely one third of it is in Poland. In the West I will be on the defensive. France can here sacrifice its blood first. Then the moment will come when we can confront the enemy also there with the full power of the nation. Accept my thanks, Duce, for all your assistance which you have given to me in the past and I ask you not to deny it to me in the future.

Adolf Hitler

[*The Duce understood the undertones of the Hitler note and immediately got in his defensive rebuttal with the Fuehrer's Ambassador, Mackensen. The following is a telegram from the latter to the German foreign office.*]

Duce remarked, during the presentation of the Fuehrer's message, which took place in Ciano's presence at 0949 [*9:40 a.m.*], that he would forward his view point by letter. He explained somewhat as follows, during the ensuing conversation of half an hour: they never had considered in the least to let himself be used in an action of arbitration, which had as prerequisite the withdrawal of German troops. No man on earth can seriously consider the thought as worthy of discussion, to make such an offer to troops, which, furthermore, are advancing successfully. He refused such ideas with actual indignation, also he would not consider the "symbolic withdrawal" suggested by Paris. In view of the strong appeal by France to make one last attempt, he had forwarded the suggestion under the self-evidence [*sic*]. In this case, if we consider the agreement of the Fuehrer to the suggestion possible, he would perhaps even advise it. However, England, which is guilty for the entire development of the German-Polish conflict, did apparently not want to let it come to a compromise. He seemed to know, that the Polish Ambassador in London still exercised in the last minutes a decisive influence on the position at the British Cabinet. The declaration by England, which brought about the stage of war, and which France followed up the last, only hesitantly, is absolutely "diotic" [*sic*], brought about by people who apparently have never studied a map. For what form should a war take? It can only be waged on water, on land or in the air. Breaking out of the Maginot Line on land, over-running of the West Wall would be a hopeless undertaking, which will hardly be attempted by the French. Even if our fleet is modest, in any case the Navy cannot undertake anything decisive. The air force would attempt to drop a few bombs, maybe it would destroy this and that installation, but even that has nothing to do with the decision, especially if we limit ourselves in the air as well to the defensive. In brief, the delcaration of war is an absolutely absurd undertaking, because the only thing actually left would be the war of attrition and that would also be harmful to the one who declares it.

If the Fuehrer's message says that the Fuehrer and the Duce "would now go separate ways," he is of an entirely different opinion. On the contrary, the most complete agreement in respect to methods and goals prevails, and especially militarily, he has done everything to the last, what the Fuehrer desired of him, and he continues his preparation most intensively. The critical month for him is September [*sic*], after which even there, he will be armed for a successful defense. Already today, he ties down 400,000 men of the opponent by his measures on the Alpine frontier and in Africa. He will send to the Fuehrer, via the military attache (who is invited this evening to the home of General Pariani) all the details of his military measures with appropriate carbo-graphic material, which he also showed me and explained most thoroughly. I can leave the reporting on this to the military attache. I only wish to emphasize the Duce's remark, that the mobilization measures did not pass without any friction, but also that the spirit of those conscripted and of their families, thanks to the generous subsidy allotted to them, is excellent.

At the end, the Duce repeated his assurance of every assistance desired by us, particularly, in the question of workers and (on a suggestion of mine) by the Press.

Duce was in a confidential mood.

September 1, 1939, Berlin          76. Document TC-54

*[However involved the reasoning between the two dictators may have become, the simple declaration of the Fuehrer's to the armed forces the day he sent them into action was the very essence of outraged indignation, succinctly expressed.]*

To the Armed Forces—

The Polish Government unwilling to establish good neighbourly relations as aimed at by me wants to force the issue by ways of arms.

The Germans in Poland are being persecuted with bloody terror and driven from their homes. Several acts of frontier violation which cannot be tolerated by a great power show that Poland is no longer prepared to respect the Reich's frontiers. To put an end to these mad acts I can see no other way but from now onwards to meet force with force.

The German Armed Forces will with firm determination take up the struggle for the honor and the vital rights of the German people.

I expect every soldier to be conscious of the high tradition of the external German soldierly qualities and to do his duty to the last.

Remember always and in any circumstances that you are the representatives of National Socialist Greater Germany.

Long live our people and Reich!

Adolf Hitler.

*[And so "Case White" turned into World War II. With malice aforethought Hitler had managed to drive the world before him and engulf it in world catastrophe. The first act—Poland—was soon over, and Hitler, eager to cue himself into a greater development of the drama, looked to the West.]*

November 23, 1939          77. Document 789-PS

[*Part of the "Common Plan" of conspiracy and aggression is revealed in the minutes of a meeting Hitler held on this date with his military and naval commanders. The war with Poland has been brought to a victorious close but Hitler is finding his generals lethargic vis a vis war in the West. The object of this meeting is to pump enthusiasm into his leaders. Documentary evidence abundantly shows Hitler eager for attack in the West in the Fall of 1939, but the weather and the apathetic response of his commanders combined to postpone the action until Spring. In November, however, Hitler is hopeful.*

*The long, historical introduction is typical. He wants to prove to his generals he is omniscient. Much of the material in this document is repetitive, but is included here because of its intrinsic importance; it needs to be shown that the Hitlerian aims announced in this speech or that were not affairs of the moment, stray enthusiasms voiced capriciously, but rather genuine basic purposes taking on life and substance as the months and years passed. The defendants at Nurenberg squirmed as the prosecution labored the contents of this document*]

The purpose of this conference is to give you an idea of the world of my thoughts, which governs me in the face of future events, and to tell you my decisions. The building up of our armed forces was only possible in connection with the ideological education of the German people by the Party. When I started my political task in 1919, my strong belief in final success was based on a thorough observation of events of the day and the study of the reasons for their occurrence. Therefore I never lost my belief in the midst of set-backs which were not spared me during my period of struggle. Providence has had the last word and brought me success. On top of that I had a clear recognition of the probable course of historical events, and the firm will to make brutal decisions. The first decision was in 1919 when I after long internal conflict became a politician and took up the struggle against my enemies. That was the hardest of all decisions. I had, however, the firm belief that I would arrive at my goal. First of all, I desired a new system of selection. I wanted to educate a minority which would take over the leadership. After 15 years, I arrived at my goal, after strenuous struggles and many set backs. When I came to power in 1933, a period of the most difficult struggle lay behind me. Everything existing before that had collapsed. I had to reorganize everything from the beginning with the mass of the people and extending it to the armed forces. First reorganization of the interior, abolishment of appearances of decay and defeatist ideas, education to heroism. While reorganizing the interior, I undertook the second task: to release Germany from its international ties. Two particular characteristics are to be pointed out: secession from the League of Nations and denunciation of the disarmament conference. It was a hard decision. The number of prophets who predicted that it would lead to the occupation of the Rhineland was large, the number of believers was very small. I was supported by the nation, which stood firmly behind me, when I carried out my intention. After that the order for rearmament. Here again there were numerous prophets who predicted misfortunes, and only a few believers. In 1935 the introduction of compulsory armed service. After that militarization of the Rhineland, again a process believed to be impossible at the time. The number of people who put trust in me was very small. Then the beginning of the fortification of the whole country, especially in the west.

One year later Austria came, this step also was considered doubtful. It brought about a considerable reinforcement of the Reich. The next step was Bohemia, Moravia and Poland. This step also was not possible to accomplish in one campaign. First of all, the western fortification had to be finished. It was not possible to reach the goal all in one effort. It was clear to me from the first moment that I could not be satisfied with the Sudeten-German territory. That was only a partial solution. The decision to march into Bohemia was made. Then followed the election of the Protectorate and with that the basis of the action against Poland was laid, but I wasn't clear at that time whether I should start first against the East and then in the West, or vice versa. Moltke often made the same calculations in his time. Under pressure the decision came to fight with Poland first. One might accuse me of wanting to fight and fight again. In struggle I see the fate of all beings. Nobody can avoid a struggle if he does not want to lose out. The increasing number of people requires a larger living space. My goal was to create a logical relation between the number of people and the space for them to live in. The struggle must start here. No people can get away from the solution of this task or else it must yield and gradually die out. That is taught by history. First migration of people to the southwest, then adaptation of the number of people to the small space by emigration. In the last years, adaptation of the people to insufficient space, by reducing the number of births. That would lead to the death and weakening of the blood of the people. One acknowledgement is important. The state has a meaning only if it supports the maintenance of its population potential. In our case 82 million people were concerned. That means the greatest responsibility. He who does not want to assume that responsibility, is not worthy of belonging to the mass of the people. That gave me the strength to fight. No calculated cleverness is of any help, solution only with the sword. Since 1870 England has been against us. Bismarck and Moltke were certain there would have to be one more action. The danger at that time was of a two-front war. Moltke was at times in favor of a preventive war. The basic thought of Moltke was the offensive. He never thought of the defense. Many opportunities were missed after Moltke's death. In 1914 there came a war on several fronts. It did not bring the solution to these problems. Today the second act of this drama is being written.

For the first time in 67 years it must be made plain that we do not have a two front war to wage. That which has been desired since 1870 and considered as impossible of achievement has come to pass. For the first time in history we have to fight on only one front, the other front is at present free. But no one can know how long that will remain so. I have doubted for a long time whether I should strike in the east and then in the west. Basically I did not organize the armed forces not to strike. The decision to strike was always in me. Earlier or later I wanted to solve the problem. Under pressure it was decided that the East was to be attacked first. Now the situation is as follows: the opponent in the West lies behind his fortifications. There is no possibility of coming to grips with him. The decisive question is, how long can we endure this situation? Russia is at present not dangerous. It is weakened by many incidents today. Moreover, we have a pact with Russia. Pacts, however, are only held as long as they serve the purpose. Russia will hold herself to it only so long as Russia considers it to be to her benefit. Even Bismark thought so. Let no one think of the pact to assure our back.... Now Russia has far-reaching goals, above all the strengthening of her position in the Baltic. We can oppose Russia only when we are free in the West. Further Russia is striving to increase her influence on the Balkans and is striving toward the Persian Gulf. That is also the goal of our foreign policy. Russia will do that which she considers to benefit her. At the present moment it has retired from internationalism. In case she renounces this, she will proceed to Pan-Slavism. It is difficult to see into the future. It is a fact that at the present time the Russian army is of little worth. For the next one or two years the present situation will remain. Italy will not attack until Germany has taken the offensive against France. Just as the death of Stalin, so the death of the Duce can bring danger to us. Just how easily the death of a statesman [may] came I myself have experienced recently. [*The Nurenberg assassination attempt had just occurred.*] The time must be used to the full, otherwise one will find himself faced with a new situation. As long as Italy maintains this position then no danger from Yugoslavia is to be feared. Scandinavia is hostile to us because of Marxistic influences, but is neutral now. America is still not dangerous to us because of its neutrality laws. The strengthening of our opponents by America is still not important. The position of Japan is still uncertain, it is not yet certain whether she will join against England.

Everything is determined by the fact that the moment is favorable now, in six months it might not be so anymore.

As the last factor I must name my own person in all modesty: irreplaceable. Neither a military nor a civil person could replace me. Assasination attempts may be repeated. I am convinced of the powers of my intellect and of decision. Wars are always ended only by the destruction of the opponent. I shall strike and not capitulate. The fate of the Reich depends only on me. I shall deal accordingly. Today we have an advantage such as we have never had before. The British army has only a symbolic meaning. Every German infantryman is better than the French. Behind the Army stands the strongest armament industry in the world.

If the French army moves into Belgium in order to attack us, it will be too late for us. We must anticipate them. One more thing. U-Boats, mines and Luftwaffe can strike England effectively...However this can occur only if we have occupied Belgium and Holland. It is a difficult decision for me. None has ever achieved what I have achieved. I am setting this work on a gamble. I have to choose between victory and destruction. I choose victory. Breach of the neutrality of Belgium and Holland is meaningless. No one will question that when we have won.

[*Thus spoke Zurathustra.*]

# V

# From White to Yellow

## After an Exercise in the West

October 9, 1939, Berlin                78. Document C-62

[*The Polish war was over in less than six weeks. At its
conclusion Hitler made a "peace offer" to England and
France. He offered to guarantee the British empire and
French possessions in perpetuity in exchange for cessation of hostilities and allied recognition of Germany's
new position in Europe, including, of course, its Polish
gains. Since the allies were now convinced—finally—that
Hitler's ultimate aims were of Napoleonic dimensions, no
serious consideration was given to the offer, and the war
continued. Today American revisionist historians are
calling Roosevelt war-monger; they are charging that
America was tricked into entering World War II—that
Hitler could have been "stopped" at a peace conference in
1939. Says one of the leading exponents of this thesis—
Charles C. Tansill—in his back Door to War (p. 607):
"During the meetings of a peace conference in Washington (Goering had agreed to holding the conference
there—ed.) there would have been an opportunity to
focus the eyes of the world upon the ills of Europe and
attempt to remedy them. If the president had possessed
real courage and vision he would have welcomed these
German overtures and staged a peace conference that
would have saved both Poland and Czechoslovakia.
. . . In the long chapter of historical might-have-beens,
Roosevelt plays a prominent and dismal part." Elsewhere*

*Tansill refers to Hitler as entering the war with "many misgivings," and as offering to the world on October 6, 1939—the date of the peace bid referred to above—a "sane and moderate program." This interpretation of historical developments approaches the weird, and gives him who has a thorough knowledge of Hitler's aims and techniques a feeling that such an interpretation is a species of treason against humankind's efforts to understand his yesterdays so that his tomorrows may be better. Let the reader, for example, read the entire text of Hitler's October 6 Reichstag speech and then ask for himself of Mr. Tansill what purpose a historian has in so distorting data.*

*Hitler's plans to defeat the West were embodied in a plan which the government designated "Case Yellow." For reasons explained below its execution was postponed for several months. Meantime—again, as explained by the following documents—the decision to occupy Norway and Denmark was made. The code word for this was Weseruebung—Western Exercise. For some weeks, roughly from late January, 1940, to March, Hitler was unclear in his own mind as to the proper sequence of steps—should "Yellow" and "Weser" take place together or, if not, which should come first?*

*The Fuehrer, in formulating plans for "Yellow," decided to abandon the strategy of World War I's Schlieffen Plan and, instead of a grand movement designed to flank Paris, worked out Mannstein's suggestion of a bold attack to be launched in a northwesterly direction, the aim of which was capture of the French channel ports and destruction of the French and English armies. But as in the case of the Schlieffen Plan, this attack called for violation of neutral territory.*

*The first document in this section, signed by Hitler, is entitled, DIRECTIVE No. 6 FOR THE CONDUCT OF THE WAR.*

*The period between the conclusion of the Polish campaign and the opening of the attack against Norway is quite erroneously known as the period of the "phoney war."]*

1. If it should become apparent in the near future that England, and, under England's leadership, also France, are not willing to make an end of the war, I am determined to act actively and aggressively without much delay.

*[The reader who has come this far will clearly understand that Hitler was "determined to act actively and aggressively without much delay" whether England and France would have paused for more appeasement or not.]*

2. If we wait much longer, not only will Belgium and perhaps also Dutch neutrality be lost in favor of the Western powers, but the military strength of our enemies will grow on an increasing scale, the neutrals' confidence in a final German victory will dwindle, and Italy will not be encouraged to join us as a military ally.

3. Therefore I give the following orders for the further military operations:

*a.* Preparations are to be made for an attacking operation on the northern wing of the Western front, through the areas of Luxembourg, Belgium, and Holland. This attack must be carried out with as much strength and at as early a date as possible.

*b.* The purpose of this attacking operation will be—

To defeat as strong a contingent of the French operational army as possible as well as the allies fighting by its side, and at the same time to gain as large an area as possible in Holland, Belgium and Northern France as a base for conducting a promising air and sea war against England and as a glacis for the vital Ruhr area.

*c.* The timing of the attack depends on the readiness of tanks and motorized units for use,—this must be speeded up by every possible effort, also on the weather conditions then prevailing and the weather prospects ahead.

7. The camouflage used for these preparations must be that they are merely precautionary measures in view of the threatening concentration of French and English forces on the Franco-Luxembourg and Franco-Belgian borders.

8. I request the Supreme Commanders, to give me, as soon as possible, detailed reports of their intentions in the basis of this directive and from now on to keep me informed, via the OKW, of the state of the preparations.

October 13, 1939, Brussels          79. Document TC-34

[*Less than a week later the German Ambassador at Brussels handed to the Belgian Foreign Minister the following communication.*]

...the German Government regards it as appropriate to define now its own attitude towards Belgium.

To this end it makes the following declaration:

(2) The German Government considers that the inviolability and integrity of Belgium are common interests of the Western Powers. It confirms its determination that in no circumstances will it impair this inviolability and integrity, and that it will at all times respect Belgian territory, except, of course, in the event of Belgium's taking part in a military action directed against Germany in an armed conflict in which Germany is involved.

[*Similar declarations were made at the same time to the Netherlands and Luxemburg.*]

November 15, 1939, Berlin          80. Document C-62,
                                              "Fall Gelb"

[*Headed "Fall Gelb" ("Case Yellow") this memoran-*

*dum, signed by Keitel, explains why plans against Holland were made.*]

It is of not inconsiderable significance for the over-all strategy of the war to protect the Ruhr areas by moving the plane-spotting organization and the air defense as far forward as possible in the area of Holland.

The more Dutch territory we occupy, the more effective can the defense of the Ruhr area be made. This viewpoint must determine the choice of objectives made by the Army, even if Army and Navy are not directly interested in such a territorial gain. Therefore, the purpose of the Army's preparations must be to occupy—when a special order is received—the area of Holland, as far as the Grebbe-Maas line. It will depend upon the political and military attitude of the Dutch, as well as on the effectiveness of their flooding, whether it will be necessary and possible to push the objective still further.

Likewise, preparations must be made to take possession of the West Frisian islands, with the support of the Navy, at first with the exception of Texel, as soon as the Northern coast of Groningen is in our hands; these, too, are of great significance as bases for the A/C reporting service and England must be deprived of the possibility of seizing them for similar purposes.

November 20, 1939, Berlin     81. Document 440-PS

[*Hitler's Chief of Staff, Keitel, five days later issued "Directive No. 8."*]

1. The state of alert, to make the continuation of the initiated concentration of troops possible at any moment, must be maintained, for the time being. Only this will make it possible to exploit favorable weather conditions immediately.

The various components of the Armed Forces will make arrangements enabling them to stop the attack even if the order for such action is received by the High

Command as late as D-1 at 2300 hours [*11:00 p.m.*] The keyword

"Rhine" (—start attack)

or

"Elbe" (—withhold attack)

will be passed on to the High Command at the latest by this time.

The High Commands of the Army and Air Forces are requested after having determined the day for attack, to notify department L of the High Command of the Armed Forces immediately with regard to the mutually agreed hour of the commencement of the attack.

2. Contrary to previous orders, all measures intended against the Netherlands are to be carried out without special orders at the start of the general attack.

The reaction of the Dutch Armed Forces cannot be foreseen. The entering of our troops will take on the character of a friendly occupation wherever no opposition is encountered.

3. The *land operations* are to be carried out on the basis of the assemble directive of 29 October. The following is added to complete this directive:

*b.* The Dutch area, including the coastal West-Frisian Islands, without Texel for the time being, is to be seized as far as the Grebbe-Maas line, until further notice.

4. *The Navy* is authorized to take blockade measures for submarines against the Belgian and, contrary to the previous orders, also against Dutch harbors and waterways, in the night before the attack and from the time of the start of the blockade activities and the time of the land attack must also be kept as short as possible in the case of the use of submarines [*sic*].

5. The tasks of the *Air Force* remain unchanged.

November 7, 1939—January 20, 1940,
Berlin.                                    82. Document C-72

[*During this period Hitler and his advisers made changes in their plans as they awaited favorable weather*

*for the attack. This attack was postponed many times. At
the time, this was called the period of the "phoney war,"
and some analysts fancifully toyed with the idea that
Hitler was in negotiation with France and England and
that a heavily tilted Hitler compromise would be effected.
The captured German records show that the phoney war
was a figment of the analysts' imagination. Here are given
some of the memoranda captured by the Allies showing
the actual postponements.*]

On November 7 the Fuehrer and Supreme Commander of the Armed Forces, after hearing reports on the
meteorological and the railway transport situation, has
ordered:

A-day [*i.e., D-Day*] is postponed for the time being by
three days. The next decision will be made by 1800 hours
[*6:00 p.m.*] on 9 November 39.

On 9 November the Fuehrer and Supreme Commander of the Armed Forces, after hearing a report on the
meteorological situation, has decided:

The earliest date designated for A-day is 19 November.

On 13 November the Fuehrer and Supreme Commander, after receiving a report on the meteorological
situation, has decided:

The next decision on A-day will be made on Thursday,
16 November.

On 16 November the Fuehrer and Supreme Commander, after hearing a report on the meteorological
situation, has decided:

The next decision on A-day will be made on Monday,
20 November.

[*In December the memoranda were reading:*]

On 12 December the Fuehrer and Supreme Commander has ordered:

1. The next decision on A-day will be made by 1800
hours on 27 December.

2. Earliest date of next A-day therefore 1 January
1940.

3. Christmas leave to be arranged accordingly by the branches of the armed forces.

On 27 December the Fuehrer and Supreme Commander has made the following decision:

In view of the general meteorological situation, the date of the attack is further postponed, as far as can be foreseen by at least a fortnight.

On 10 January 1940 the Fuehrer and Supreme Commander of the Armed Forces, after receiving reports from the Commander in Chief of the Air Force, the Commander in Chief of the Navy, and the Chief of the General Staff of the Army, has ordered the following:

1. *A-day and X-hour:*

*A-day* is Wednesday, 17 January 40 [*The word and figure "Wednesday 17" were written in ink.*]

*X-hour* 15 minutes before sunrise at Aix-la-Chapelle on A-day=1816 hours [*sic*]. [*The time, 8:16 a.m. was also written in ink.*]

The code-name "Rhine" or "Elbe" . . . will be issued before 2300 hours [*11:00 p.m.*] on A-day minus 1, provided the weather forecast permits.

On account of the meteorological situation, the Fuehrer has decided to postpone A-day, probably to 20 January 40.


[*In the meantime the idea of a new operation to the North was born and developed. This idea was not originally Hitler's; as a matter of fact the Fuehrer was against the notion in the beginning, but it did not take him long to swing around to its support.*

*The idea was the invasion of Norway. Originally the idea of the project occurred, practically at the same time, to two of Hitler's lieutenants—Admiral Raeder and Alfred Rosenberg, the Nazi party's "philosopher." Raeder was thinking of naval bases; Rosenberg was a friend of Quisling who at this time was giving reports of an imminent invasion of Norway by the British and French (it will be remembered that the Russian-Finnish war was going on and that there was considerable agitation by Finnish sympathizers for Allied intervention which would, presumably, have to take place via Norway).*]


October 3, 1939, Berlin                83. Document C-122

[*This extract from the German Naval War Diary is a questionnaire sent out by Raeder, at the request of his Chief of Staff, concerning the desirability of obtaining bases in Norway. It will be noted that this is contemporaneous with the closing of the Polish campaign.*]

The Chief of the Naval War Staff considers it necessary that the Fuehrer be informed as soon as possible of the opinions of the Naval War Staff on the possibility of extending the operational base to the North. It must be ascertained whether it is possible to gain bases in Norway under the combined pressure of Russia and Germany, with the aim of improving fundamentally our strategic and operational position. The following questions must be given consideration:

a. What places in Norway can be considered as bases?

b. What bases can be gained by military force against Norway's will if it is impossible to carry out this without fighting?

c. What are the possibilities of defense after the occupation?

d. Will the harbors have to be developed completely as bases, or have they already decisive advantages as supply positions?

e. What decisive advantage would exist for the conduct of the war at sea in gaining a base in North Denmark e.g. Skagen?


October 9, 1939, Wilhelmshaven        84. Document C-5

[*From Doenitz, subsequently Hitler's successor as Fuehrer and Commander in Chief of the Armed Forces,*

184

*came this reply from his office of Operations Division.*]

I. Suppositions:
    a. A position outside the Shetlands—Norway Straits.
    b. Freedom from ice.
    c. Rail communications.
These suppositions apply only to Trondheim and Narvik.

II. *Advantages and disadvantages:*
    1. *Trondheim:*
    Advantages:
      a. Position within the fjord which is unaffected by artillery action from the sea.
      b. Deep water in the entry channels—difficult for the enemy to mine in their mining operations.
      c. Existence of several entry and exit routes.
      d. Protected areas directly in front of the harbor for exercises and entry.
      e. Southern position: i.e. short lines of communications to Germany, better climatic conditions, shorter route to the Atlantic.
      f. Basins which, according to the North Sea Handbook and instructions of the Navy office at Hamburg, are suitable for U-boats.
      g. Several industrial installations which facilitate the construction of repair- and supply installations.
    Disadvantages:
    Short distance from the bases of the British Air Force—danger from air attack.
    2. *Narvik:*
    Advantages:
      a., b., c., d., the same as Trondheim.
      e. Greater distance from the British bases—less danger of air attack.
    Disadvantages:
    a. Northern position: Long lines of communication to Germany, unfavorable climatic conditions, longer route to the Atlantic.

      b. Communications only from the Baltic—the Gulf of Bothnia is not free from ice.

      c. No basins—quay installations only in the bay.

      d. Very few industrial installations.

Trondheim is therefore the more favorable place.

III. The following is therefore proposed:

   1. Establishment of a base in Trondheim, including:

      a. Possibility of supplying fuel, compressed air, oxygen, provisions.

      b. Repair opportunities for overhaul work after an encounter.

      *c. Good* opportunities for accommodating U-boat crews.

      d. Flak protection, L.A. armament, petrol and M/S units.

   2. Establishment of the possibility of supplying fuel in Narvik as an alternative.

October, 1939, Berlin          85. Document C-66

[*Before the end of the war Admiral Raeder compiled notes for those who were writing a naval history of the war. The following is from a memorandum written by Raeder and given to Admiral Assman for naval history purposes.*]

During the weeks preceding the report on 10.10.39, I was in correspondence with Admiral Karls who, in a detailed letter to me, first pointed out the importance of the occupation of the Norwegian coast by Germany, I passed this letter on to C/SKI [*Chief of Naval War Operations*] for their information and prepared some notes based on this letter for my report to the Fuehrer which I made on 10.10.39, since my opinion was identical with that of Admiral Karls' while, at the same time I set out the disadvantage which an occupation of Norway by the British would have for us—control of the approaches to the Baltic, pressure on Sweden. I also mentioned the advantage for us of the occupation of the Norwegian coast outlet to the North Atlantic, no possibilities of British mine fields as in the year 1917-1918. Naturally at the time, only the coast and bases were considered; I included Narvik, though Admiral Karls, in the course of our correspondence hoped that Narvik might be excluded. (At that time we were able to use Murmansk and/or a special Russian Base.) The Fuehrer saw at once the significance of the Norwegian problem; he asked me to leave the notes and stated that he wished to consider the question himself.

Winter, 1939, Berlin     86. Document 007-PS Annex 1

[*This is from a report Rosenberg drew up to prove to what he then considered would be a Nazi dominated posterity that the Rosenberg Organization should receive primary credit for the Norwegian coup.*]

During the winter of 1938/1939, Quisling was privately visited by a member of the Bureau [*Rosenberg's party organization*]. When the political situation in Europe came to a head [*when, that is, Germany occupied Czechoslovakia in March, 1939*], Quisling made an appearance at the convention of the Nordic Society in Luebeck in June. He expounded his conception of the situation, and his apprehensions regarding Norway in the Scandinavian area, and to the advantages that would accrue to the power dominating the Norwegian coast in case of a conflict between the Greater German Reich and Great Britain. Assuming that his statements would be of special interest to the Marshal of the Reich, Goering, for aero-strategical reasons, Quisling was referred to Staff Secretary Koerner [*on Goering's staff*] by the Bureau. The State Director of the Bureau handed the Chief of the Reich Chancellery a memorandum for transmission to the Fuehrer. After the outbreak of German-Polish hostilities and of the Soviet-Finnish war, the tensions in

Scandinavia became more strained and facilitated the work of Anglo-Saxon propaganda. It began to appear possible that, under the pretext of altruistic aid to Finland, Great Britain might intend to occupy Norway, and perhaps Sweden, to complete the anti-German blockade in the North Sea for all practical purposes, and to gain comfortable airplane bases against Germany. The aim would have been to drag the Northern countries, too, into a military conflict with Germany. Apprehensive about this development, Quisling again appeared in Berlin in December, 1939. He visited Reichsleiter Rosenberg and Grand Admiral Raeder. In the course of a report to the Fuehrer, Reichsleiter Rosenberg turned the conversation once more to Norway. He especially pointed to Norway's importance should England, to tighten her blockade and under pretext of aid to Finland, take steps to occupy the country, with the Norwegians tacit consent. On the basis of his conversation with Quisling and at his own request, Grand Admiral Raeder, too, had been asked to see the Fuehrer. In consequence of these steps, Quisling was granted a personal interview with the Fuehrer on 16 December, and once more on 18 December. In the course of this audience the Fuehrer emphasized repeatedly that he personally would prefer a completely neutral attitude of Norway as well as the whole of Scandinavia. He did not intend to enlarge the theaters of war and to draw other nations into conflict. Should the enemy attempt to spread the war, however, with the aim of achieving further throttling and intimidation of the Greater German Reich, he would be compelled to gird himself against such an undertaking. In order to counter-balance increasing enemy propaganda activity, he promised Quisling financial support of his movement, which is based on Greater Germanic ideology.

December 12, 1939, Berlin          87. Document C-64

[*This is a Raeder memorandum covering a meeting of*

188

*Hitler, Raeder, Keitel, Jodl and Puttkamer (naval A.D.C. to Hitler) on this date. Raeder wrote up the memorandum immediately after the conference. Four days later, and as a consequence of this meeting, Hitler met Quisling for the first time. Up until this time Hitler had not known of Quisling.]*

1. C. in C. Navy has received Quisling and Hagelin [*Quisling's deputy, working in Germany*]. Quisling [*says Raeder*] creates the impression of being reliable and states that:

As a result of the Russo-Finnish conflict, anti-Germany feeling in Norway is even stronger than hitherto. England's influence is very great—especially through Storthing [*Norwegian parliament*]; President Hambro (Jew, a friend of Hore-Belisha [*former British war minister*]), all powerful in Norway just now. Quisling is convinced that there is an agreement between England and Norway for the possible occupation of Norway. Danger of Norway's occupation by England is very great—possibly very shortly. [*This prod was used by Quisling continually*]. From 11/1/40 onwards the Norwegian Parliament and therefore the Norwegian Government is unconstitutional as Parliament, in defiance of the constitution, prolonged its term by a year [*the British parliament prolonged its term five years*]. This would give an opportunity for a political re-shuffle. Quisling has good connections with officers of the Norwegian Army and has supporters in important positions (for example, Railways). In such an event Quisling is ready to take over the Government and to call upon Germany for help. He is also ready to discuss preparations of a military character with the German Armed Forces.

C. C. Navy points out that with such offers one never knows how far the people concerned were wishing to further the ends of their own party or how much they have German interests at heart. Therefore caution is indicated—Norway must be prevented at all costs from falling into England's hands. That might have a decisive effect upon the war; for Sweden would be completely under England's influence and it would bring the war into the Baltic, thus preventing completely the activities of the German Navy in the ocean and the North Sea. The Fuehrer, too, said that a British occupation of Norway would be unbearable. C. in C. Navy pointed out that occupation by Germany of positions on the coast would naturally produce strong British counter-measures to stop the export of ore from Narvik, and that this would bring about surface warfare off the Norwegian coast, to which the German Navy was not equal for any length of time. This was one weak spot of the occupation.

The Fuehrer thought of speaking to Quisling personally so that he might form an impression of him. He wanted to see Rosenberg once more beforehand, as the latter has known Quisling for a long while. C. in C. suggests that if the Fuehrer forms a favorable impression, the OKW should obtain permission to make plans with Quisling for the preparation and carrying out of the occupation—a. By peaceful means, that is, German forces summoned by Norway. b. To agree to do so by force (Fuehrer agrees).

[*It should be pointed out that the "peaceful" means referred to are those used in the case of Austria, when Seyss-Inquart "summoned German troops to prevent civil war."*]


January 27, 1940, Berlin          88. Document C-63


[*It will be recalled that simultaneously with consideration of the Norway development Hitler was daily hoping to launch the attack in the West—Case Yellow. As Norway came more and more to seem important he became uncertain as to which operation should precede which or whether they should be put into effect at the same time. By this date Hitler was sufficiently concerned over Norway to order Keitel to make out the following directive:*]

Re: Study "N"

The Fuehrer and Supreme Commander of the Armed Forces desires that work on the Study "N" be continued under his personal and immediate influence and in closest collaboration with the conduct of the war as a whole. For these reasons the Fuehrer has ordered me to take charge of the further preparations.

For this purpose a working staff will be found within the High Command of the Armed Forces, this staff will at the same time represent the neucleus of the future operations staff.

I request the High Command of the Services to appoint each one officer suitable as Ia [*operations*] and, if possible, trained in questions of organization and supply. The Officer for Intelligence Abroad will furnish the information, and the Armed Forces General Staff will furnish the transport expert, one officer for signal communications and one officer for general questions of territorial administration.

The date when the staff will convene will be communicated later.

All further preparations will be conducted under the code word "Weseruebung" [*Western Exercise*].


March 1, 1940, Berlin          89. Document C-174

[*Some five weeks after Keitel's order was issued Hitler supplemented it with this directive:*]

1. The development of the situation in Scandinavia requires the making of all preparations for the occupation of Denmark and Norway by a part of the German Armed Forces.

[*The addition of Denmark, a nation the violation of*

*whose neutrality not even the ultra-suspicious of the Nazis charged against England, was purely Hitler's idea; Raeder felt it to be a useless provocation.*]

This operation should prevent British encroachment on Scandinavia and the Baltic; further, it should guarantee our air base in Sweden and give our Navy and the Air Force a wider start line against Britain. The part which the Navy and the Air Force will have to play, within the limits of their capabilities, is to protect the operation against the interference of British Naval and Air striking forces.

In view of our military and political power in comparison with that of the Scandinavian states, the force to be employed in the "Fall Weseruebung" will be kept as small as possible. The numerical weakness will be balanced by daring actions and surprise execution. On principle, we will do our utmost to make the operation appear as a *peaceful* occupation, the object of which is the military protection of the Scandinavian States. Corresponding demands will be transmitted to the Governments at the beginning of the occupation. If necessary, demonstrations by the Navy and Air Force will provide the necessary emphasis. If, in spite of this, resistance should be met with, all military means will be used to crush it.

2. I put in charge of the preparations and the conduct of the operation against Denmark and Norway the Commanding General of the XXI Army Corps . . . General v. Falkenhorst.

In questions of the conduct of operations the above named is directly under my orders. The staff is to be completed from all three branches of the Armed Forces.

The force which will be selected for the purpose of "Fall Weseruebung" will be under separate command. They will not be allocated for other operational theaters.

The part of the Air Force detailed for the purpose of the "Weseruebung" will be tactically under the orders of Group XXI. After the completion of their task, they will revert to the command of Ob.d.L. [*Goering.*]

3. The crossing of the Danish border and the landings in Norway must take place *simultaneously*. I emphasize that the operations must be prepared as quickly as possible. In case the enemy seizes the initiative against Norway, we must be able to apply immediately our own counter-measures.

It is most important that the Scandinavian States as well as the Western opponents should be *taken by surprise* by our measures. All preparations, particularly those of transport and of readiness, drafting and embarkation of troops, must be made with this factor in mind.

In case the measures for embarkation can no longer be kept secret, the leaders and the troops will be deceived with fictious objectives. The troops may be acquainted with the actual objective only after putting to sea.

March 30, 1940, Berlin        90. Document C-151

[*This Doenitz-Godt order gives further particulars.*]

## Operation order "HARTMUT" [*Toughness*]
## Occupation of Denmark and Norway

This order comes into force on the code word "Hartmut" With its coming into force the orders hitherto valid for the boats taking part lose their validity. The day and hour are designated as "Weser-Day" and "Weser-Hour" and the whole operation is known as "Weseruebung." Situation: the operation ordered by the code word has as its objective the rapid surprise landing of troops in Norway. Simultaneously Denmark will be occupied from the Baltic and from the land side. The primary requisite for .success once the landing has been accomplished is the hindering of enemy counter-measures, above all of troop landings, until an adequate number of troops has been put ashore. With this object, orders have been given for the full committment of all naval forces. The Naval force will as they enter the harbor fly the British flag until the troops have landed, except presumably at Narvik.

April 4, 1940, Berlin ·        91. Document C-115

[*These items are taken from an unsigned file of naval operations' orders. The "Sperrbreechers" referred to are barrage-breaking vessels.*]

General Orders. (a) The Sperrbreechers will penetrate inconspicuously and with lights on into Oslo Fjord, distinguished as merchant steamers. (b) Challenges from coastal signal stations and lookouts are to be answered by the deceptive use of names of English steamers. I lay particular stress on the importance of not giving away the operations before zero-hour.

Behavior during entrance into the harbor. All ships darkened lights to be put on only by order of the Flag Officer Reconaissance Forces.

No personnel on deck except gun crews and other upper deck action stations. All challenges in morse [*code*] by Norwegian ships will be answered in English. In answer to questions a text with something like the following content will be chosen:

"Calling at Bergen for a short visit; no hostile intent."

Challenges to be answered with names of British Warships:

| | |
|---|---|
| "Koeln" | —H.M.S. "Cairo" |
| "Bremse" | —H.M.S. "Calcutta" |
| "Koenigsberg" | —H.M.S. "Faulknor" |
| "Karl Peters" | —H.M.S. "Halcyon" |
| "Leopard" | —British Destroyer |
| "Wolf" | —British Destroyer |
| E-Boats | —British motor torpedo boats. |

Arrangements are to be enabling British war flags to be

illuminated. Continual readiness for making smoke.

Prepared Signals, Group III, for possible traffic with passing ships and with land during entry into Bergen harbor.

Following is laid down as guide principle should one of our own units find itself compelled to answer the challenge of passing craft.

To challenge (in case of "Koeln") H.M.S. "Cairo."

In order to stop: (1) Please repeat last signal. (2) Impossible to understand your signal.

In case of a warning shot: "Stop firing. British ship. Good-friend."

In case of an inquiry as to destination and purpose: "Going to Bergen. Chasing German steamers."


February 5-April 30, 1940,
Berlin                                  92. Document 1809-PS

[*Colonel-General Jodl, chief of operations of OKW and Hitler's most intimate military adviser, recorded "Weser" items, among others, in the diary which he kept during this period. The following are from that diary.*]

5 February:
Special Staff "Weser Exercise" meets and is welcomed by Chief of Armed Forces High Command; gets instructions.
Representative of air force is still missing.

6 February:
3:30 p.m.; conference with General Jeschonneck [*Luftwaffe's Chief of Staff*], Col. v. Waldan and Col. Warlimont [*Jodl's deputy*].
Air Force submits following question:
Does X-time remain unchanged? Yes. Deceptive action intolerable for Army Group C on A-1 day. Navy is not interested in Walcheren [*Netherlands island in province of Zeeland, in North Sea*]. Does not see any

danger from the English side. New idea: carry out action H[*olland*] and Weser Exercise only and guarantee Belgium's neutrality for the duration of the war.

[*Jodl here refers to "Case Yellow"—the invasion of Belgium, Holland and France. No serious consideration was given, apparently, to this "new idea" by Hitler. He had not at that time quite made up his mind whether "Yellow" or "Weser" should take place together, or, if not, which should come first.*]

21 February:
Fuehrer talks to General von Falkenhorst and charges him with preparations of the Weser Exercise. Falkenhorst accepts gladly. Instructions to each of the three branches of the armed forces.

26 February:
Fuehrer raises question, whether it is better to undertake the Weser Exercise before or after "Yellow."
Chief of the Air Force charged with examining this problem. Fuehrer decides that Navy will have to wait with starting of mine laying by means of planes until situation will permit large-scale employment of air force.

28 February:
I make the following proposition to the Chief of the Armed Forces High Command and after that to the Fuehrer: "Case Yellow" and "Weser Exercise" have to be prepared in such a manner that they will become quite independent from one another regarding time and strength. Fuehrer completely agrees with that proposition if there is any possibility for it.

29 February:
Fuehrer wishes also to have a strong group at Copenhagen and detailed elaboration in which way the individual coastal batteries are to be overpowered. Commander-in-Chief of the Air Force is instructed to

make out immediately the order for Army, Navy and Air Force, and Chief "WZ" order concerning increasing the staff.

According to my proposals [*get*] transport ships immediately and with them bring horses over here from East Prussia.

3 March:
Fuehrer expresses his opinion about the necessity of prompt and strong action in Norway, very sharply. No delay by branches of Armed Forces. Rapid acceleration is necessary.

Commander-in-Chief of the Air Forces is against any proposition to subordinate Air Forces to XXI Corps.

Fuehrer decides to undertake Weser Exercise before case "Yellow," with several days interval.

[*As it turned out there was a month's interval. The reference below to Weser Exercise South is to Denmark.*]

4 March:
Fuehrer orders that the Air Force shall provide the anti-aircraft battalion for the Weser Exercise South.

3rd mountain division to be ready in Berlin already on March 6th.

10:00 a.m.: Chief of Air Force is informed.

5:00 p.m.: General Bodenschatz [*an Air Force general*] complains about exclusion of the Field Marshal [*Goering*] from Weser Exercise. He said that 110 officers of the Air Force had been consulted in advance. Such subordination is intolerable.

Mad at K[*eitel*]
I certify this error.

5 March: 3:00 p.m.:
Big conference with the 3 Supreme Commanders about Weser Exercise, Field Marshal vents his spleen, because he was not consulted before-hand. He dominates

the discussion and tries to prove that all previous preparations are good for nothing.

7 March:
Falkenhorst with Commander-in-Chief of the Air Force. The preparations have now materialized. The Fuehrer signs a directive containing all changes subsequent to the conference of March 5th. Nothing is to be changed any more, now.

8 March:
Fuehrer wishes to have issued special orders for the Weser Exercise in another form. They are to be divided into military orders which have to be made known to the tactical troops and into general instructions concerning actions of the Plenipotentiary of the Reich.

10 March:
The news about the Finnish-Russian negotiations are very favorable, from a political point of view.
The French press rages about it because they consider it necessary to cut Germany off from the Swedish ore. In a military way, the situation is disturbing for us, because, if peace should be concluded soon, the motivation for the prepared action of the group Falkenhorst will be difficult.

12 March:
Conclusion of peace between Finland and Russia deprives England, but us too, of any political basis to occupy Norway.
The preparations are ready to the extent that March 20th could be W-day. However, unfavorable ice conditions compel post-ponement by 1-2 days.

13 March:
Fuehrer does not yet give order for "W." He is still looking for some justification.

14 March:

English keep vigil in the North Sea with 15-16 submarines; the reason is doubtful; either to prevent a German action [*sic*]. Fuehrer has not yet decided how to justify the Weser Exercise. Wrong news report in the American newspapers.

Commander-in-Chief of the Navy is in doubt, whether it is still important to play at preventive war [*?*] in Norway. The question is, if it wouldn't be better to carry out case "Yellow" before the Weser Exercise.

The danger in that case is that the English will immediately get a foothold in Narvik, because we would have started with neutrality violation.

26 March:
The Fuehrer is back.
Discussions about deadlines for operations.
Fuehrer sticks to it: first Weser Exercise, dark nights necessary for it. Commander-in-Chief of the Navy reports, urges to start laying mines with planes as 1270 mines will already be on hand at end of April. Fuehrer wants to think it over some more.

28 March:
Individual naval officers seem to be luke-warm concerning Weser Exercise and need stimulus.
In the evening the Fuehrer steps into the map room and explains sharply that he will not be content with the navy again quitting the Norwegian ports right away. Narvik, Trondheim, and Oslo will have to remain occupied by naval forces. Bad impression on ground forces.

29 March:
Talk with Commander-in-Chief of the Navy, 12:00 a.m. Wants decision about committment of air mines.
Fuehrer talks to him alone about retaining of ships. Admiral of the Fleet rejects Narvik, but wants to examine, if Trondheim cannot be set up as a base immediately.

1 April:

1:00 p.m.: Falkenhorst again gives general report about Weser Exercise. Breakfast, then discussion with all commanding officers primarily concerned.

Fuehrer has very good impression about thoroughness of preparations.

2 April:

3:30 p.m.: Commander-in-Chief of the Air Force, Commander-in-Chief of the Navy, and General von Falkenhorst are with the Fuehrer. All confirm end of the preparations. Fuehrer orders carrying out of Weser Exercise for April 9th.

3 April:

Movements of the first 3 ships of the leading echelon started at 2:00 a.m. Lt. Commd. Junge reports at 1600 hours that the three ships have instructions how to act against the Norwegians.

4 April:

Slight alarm, as some news from Norway indicates increased preparations. Sweden has asked what preparations for troop shipments in Stettin are supposed to mean.

Fuehrer drafts the proclamations. Piepenbrock, Chief of Counter-Intelligence service 1, returns with good results from the talk with Quisling in Copenhagen.

News that two armored coastal vessels are in Narvik and that 2 submarines are expected.

5 April:

Weser exercise runs according to plan. Some alarm report from the source of a Belgian agent appear unworthy of belief.

6 April:

Weser Exercise runs according to plan. The high pressure area over the North Sea, which was predicted yesterday, is not taking place and that favors the action of the Navy. Fuehrer puts great emphasis on the fact that the

200

families of deserters will be checked carefully. Navy records long English radio message, but is unable to decipher it.

3:00 p.m.: General Gerke reports that his movements according to plan [*sic*].

5:00 p.m.: Report that Luetzow is dropping out and can go to Oslo only, because auxiliary engines did not take part. Fuehrer agrees to this decision.


7 April:

No disquieting news. *Hipper* with destroyer seems to have been reported by an English submarine on Sunday morning, April 7th.

Prince Axel of Denmark has the intention to visit Field Marshal Goering on Monday.


8 April:

Day of highest tension. The English put three mine fields in the Norwegian territorial waters and make that public.

Leading echelon is far off [*course?*] with several ships because of lack of pilots.

Only one ship near Narvik; everything else seems hardly beyond Bergen.

Boat Rio de Janeiro is torpedoed; since horses and men in uniform are landed, the impending project becomes known to the Norwegians.

Group Hipper gets into battle with an English destroyer and annihilates it.


9 April:

The surprise effect succeeds in Bergen, Trondheim, Narvik, and from the air in Stavanger. Not at Christiansand and at Oslo.


April 27, 1940, Berlin          93. Document 1809-PS, from April 27, 1939, on.

*[By this date the Western "exercise" had developed into a German military triumph and the Fuehrer accordingly turned his thoughts back to "Case Yellow."]*

27 April:
Fuehrer voices intention to start with case "Yellow" between 1st and 7th of May. I point out that the Air Force and the Transportation Chief have to be officially notified 3 days ahead of time.

29 April:
Fuehrer decides: Air Force can commit another 2 groups (new) in Norway on Tuesday and Wednesday, but must be ready for Yellow on Sunday.

1 May:
Fuehrer orders that starting Saturday, May 4th, everything must be in readiness to start operations for case Yellow the following day, when ordered.

3 May:
After evaluation of the Weather, Fuehrer decides that X-day will not be before Monday, 6 May.

Prepared White Book concerning unneutral actions of Holland and Belgium does not seem to satisfy the Foreign Office completely. To my mind the material is more than sufficient.

4 May:
Fuehrer himself wants to make comprehensive report about the campaign in Norway. He is furious about it that people other than himself meddle with this reporting. He stated that the Armed Forces High Command is his staff. Fuehrer designates Tuesday, May 7th as X-day.

5 May:
Fuehrer has finished justification for case "Yellow." Wednesday, May 8th, is designated as A-day.

6 May:

Detailed orders for May 8th for A-day are issued, and for transmission of the codewords Augsburg and Danzig.

7 May:
Fuehrer railroad train was scheduled to leave Finkenkrug at 4:38 p.m.

But weather remains uncertain and therefore, the order valid up to this time is rescinded.

11:00 a.m.: The Field Marshal with Bodenschatz and Jeschonnek at the Fuehrer's.

3:00 p.m.: Admiral of the Fleet Raeder.

Fuehrer very much agitated about new postponement, as there is danger of treachery particularly in brown leaflets [?]. Talk of the Belgian Envoy to the Vatican to Brussels [*sic.*] permits the deduction that treason has been committed by a German personality who left Berlin for Rome on April 29th.

8 May:
Alarming news from Holland, cancelling of furloughs, evacuation, roadblocks, other mobilization measures; according to reports of the counter-intelligence service the British have asked for permission to march in but the Dutch have refused.

According to reports the measures of the Dutch are partly directed against the coast [*that is, against England*] and partly against us. It is not possible to obtain a clear picture, whether the Dutch don't work hand in hand with the English or whether they actually want to defend their neutrality against the first attacker. Evaluation of the weather shows slow improvement of the whole situation, but development fog in the next few days still have to be taken into consideration.

Fuehrer does not want to wait much longer.

Field Marshal wants postponement until the 10th at least.

Chief of the Armed Forces High Command [*Keitel*] presses for early action. Fuehrer is much agitated; then he consents to postponement until May 10th, which is against his intuition, as he says. But not one day longer.

Departure of Envoy Kieritz, who was scheduled to leave at 12:57 p.m. is stopped at the last minute. Is not supposed to leave until the last minute.

[*Kieritz was probably one of the diplomats who presented Germany's note of "explanation" to either Belgium, Holland, or Luxemburg.*]

9 May:
Fuehrer decides to fall in on May 10th for sure. Departure with Fuehrer train at 5:00 p.m. for Finkenkrug.

After report Jeschonnek that weather situation will be favorable on the 10th, the code word Danzig is given at 8:00 p.m.

The same to the Commander-in-Chief of the Air Force.

10 May:
Morning arrival at Emskirchen still during darkness. At 5:30 a.m. in the Eagle's nest.

May 10, 1940, Brussels          94. Document TC-58

[*The official Belgian account gives "the other view" on this day.*]

From two o'clock in the morning, the Dutch wireless stations announced, time after time, that aeroplanes going from East to West were flying over various localities in the Netherlands. It was impossible to ascertain the importance and significance of this information, but all the signs pointed in the same direction. The Government decided there and then to introduce a state of seige and to arrest suspected persons in the Eastern provinces so as to prevent internal action against our lines of defense.

As the night wore on, there was a fairly long lull. When dawn was about to break, the peace of the capital had not been disturbed.

From 4:30 information was received which left no shadow of doubt; the hour had struck. Aircraft were first reported in the east. At five o'clock came news of the bombing of two Netherlands aerodromes, the violation of the Belgian frontier, the landing of German soldiers at the Eben-Emael Fort, the bombing of the Jemelle station.

While the Minister for National Defense was checking this information, Brussels was suddenly awakened to a radiant dawn at 5:17 a.m. by the mournful sound of the sirens, and soon the windows of the Ministry of Foreign Affairs, where the chief members of the Government were still assembled, were shaken by the firing antiaircraft artillery and German bombs dropped on the Evere aerodrome and on several parts of the town.

It was at once decided to appeal to Belgium's guarantors, and this was done.

At 8:30 the German Ambassador came to the Ministry of Foreign Affairs. When he entered the Minister's room, he began to take a paper from his pocket. M. Spaak stopped him: "I beg your pardon, Mr. Ambassador, I will speak first." And in an indignant voice, he read the Belgian Government's protest: "Mr. Ambassador, the German Army has just attacked our country. This is the second time in twenty-five years that Germany has committed a criminal aggression against a neutral and loyal Belgium. What has happened is perhaps even more odious than the aggression of 1914. No ultimatum, no note, no protest of any kind has ever been placed before the Belgian Government. It is through the attack itself that Belgium has learned that Germany has violated the undertakings given by her on October 13th, 1937, and renewed spontaneously at the beginning of the war. The act of aggression committed by Germany, for which there is no justification whatever, will deeply shock the conscience of the world. The German Reich will be held responsible by history. Belgium is resolved to defend herself. Her cause, which is the cause of Right, cannot be vanquished."

The Ambassador was then able to read the note he had brought: "I am instructed by the Government of the Reich," he said, "to make the following declaration: In order to forestall the invasion of Belgium, Holland, and Luxemburg, for which Great Britain and France have been making preparations clearly aimed at Germany, the Government of the Reich is compelled to ensure the neutrality of the three countries mentioned by means of arms. For this purpose, the Government of the Reich will bring up an armed force of the greatest size, so that resistance of any kind will be useless. The Government of the Reich guarantees Belgium's European and colonial territory, as well as her dynasty, on the condition that no resistance is offered. Should there be any resistance, Belgium will risk the destruction of her country and the loss of her independence. It is therefore in the interest of Belgium that the population be called upon to cease all resistance and that the authorities be given the necessary instructions to make contact with the German Military Command."

In the middle of this communication, M. Spaak, who had by his side the Secretary-General of the Department, interrupted the Ambassador: "Hand me the document," he said, "I should like to spare you so painful a task." After studying the note, M. Spaak confined himself to pointing out that he had already replied by the protest he had just made.

[*Thus "White" turned to "Yellow." And Hitler had only begun to manipulate his palette.*]

# VI

# Sea Lion and Felix

*There'll Always Be an England*

July 16, 1940, Fuehrer's Headquarters,
Ziegenberg                    95. Document 442-PS

[*Four days after the launching of "Yellow," Holland
surrendered. Two weeks later Belgium surrendered.
Twenty-four days after that—France surrendered. It
was at this point in world history that Hitler danced his
little jig. To him France's fall meant the soon collapse
of England; things were going much better even than he
had planned. But no quick word of surrender came
from the British. And as the days passed without such
word Hitler sadly concluded he would have to choke it
out of them. He therefore reluctantly issued the order
embodied in the following document. Only eighteen
miles of water separated the two armies. But that
watery stretch was a living, roiling nightmare to the
German Fuehrer.*

*"Sea Lion" was the code name given the plans for
invasion.*]

Since England, despite her militarily hopeless
situation still shows no sign of willingness to come to
terms, I have decided to prepare a landing operation
against England, and if necessary to carry it out.

The aim of this operation is to eliminate the English
homeland as a basis for the carrying on of the war
against Germany, and if it should become necessary to
occupy it completely;

To this end I order the following:

1. The *Landing* must be carried out in the form of a surprise crossing on a broad front approximately from Ramsgate to the area west of the Isle of Wight, in which air force units will take the roll [sic] of artillery, and units of the navy the roll [sic] of the engineers. Whether it is practical to undertake subordinate actions, such as the occupation of the Isle of Wight or of County Cornwall, before the general landing is to be determined from the standpoint of every branch of the armed forces and the result is to be reported to me. I reserve the decision to myself. The preparations for the entire operation must be completed by *mid-August*.

2. To those preparations also belong the creation of those conditions which make a landing in England possible.

a. The English air-force must morally and actually be so far overcome, that it does not any longer show any considerable aggressive force against the German attack.

b. Mine channels must be created.

c. By means of a closely concentrated mine-barrier the strait of Dover on both *Flanks* as well as the western entrance to the channel in the approximate line Aldemey-Portland must be sealed off.

d. The area in front of the coast must be dominated and given artillery protection by strong coastal artillery.

e. Tying down of the English naval forces in the North Sea as well as in the Mediterranean (by the Italians) is desired, whereby it must now be attempted that the English naval forces which are in the homeland be damaged by air and torpedo attack in strength.

3. Organization of the leadership and of the preparations;

Under my command and according to my general directions the supreme commanders will lead the forces to be used from their branches of service. The command-staffs of the supreme commander of the army, the supreme commander of the Navy, and the supreme commander of the air-force must from 1 August on be located within a radius of at least [*most?*] 50 km. from my headquarters. Lodging the command staffs of the supreme commanders of the army and navy together at Giessen appears practical to me.

The project bears the code name "Seeloewe."

*a. Army:* will draw up the operational plan and the transport plan for all units of the 1st wave to embark. The Army furthermore distributes the means of transport to the individual crossing groups and establishes the embarkation and landing points in agreement with the Navy.

*b. Navy:* will secure the means of transport and will bring them corresponding to the desires of the Army and according to the requirements of seamanship into the individual embarkation areas. Insofar as possible ships of the defeated enemy states are to be procured. It will protect, along with the airforces employed to guard the movement, the entire crossing of the channel on both flanks. As great an amount of *very heavy artillery* as possible is to be employed as quickly as possible to secure the crossing and to protect the flanks from enemy operations from the sea.

Independent of this, the heaviest available platform batteries are to be opposite the Straits of Dover, so emplaced under concrete that they can withstand even the heaviest aerial attacks and thereby dominate the Straits of Dover under any circumstances in the long run, within their effective range.

The technical work is the responsibility of the Todt Organization.

[*This organization was the labor group which built the West Wall and provided the engineering miracles which attended so frequently the action of Germany's armed forces.*]

*c. Mission of the Air Force is:* To hinder interference from the enemy air force. To overcome coastal defenses which could do damage to the landing

209

position, to break the first resistance of enemy troops and to smash reserves which may be coming up.

I request proposals on the use of parachute and glider troops. In this regard it is to be determined whether it is worth-while here to hold parachute and glider troops in readiness as a reserve to be quickly committed in case of emergency.

5. I request the Supreme Commanders to submit to me as soon as possible:

*a.* The intentions of the Navy and Air Force for achieving the necessary conditions for the crossing of the channel.

*b.* The construction of the coastal batteries in detail (Navy).

*c.* A survey of the tonnage to be employed and the methods of getting it ready and fitting it out. Participations of civilian agencies? (Navy).

*d.* The organization of aerial protection in the assembly areas for troops about to cross and the means of crossing (Air Force).

*e.* The crossing and operations plan of the army, composition and equipment of the first crossing wave.

*f.* Organization and measures of the Navy and the Air Force for carrying out the crossing itself, security of the crossing and support of the landing.

*g.* Proposals for the committment of parachute and glider troops, as well as for the attachment and command of anti-aircraft, after an extensive gain of territory on English soil has been made (Air Force).

*h.* Proposals for the location of the command staffs of the supreme commanders of the Army and of the Navy.

*i.* The position of the army, navy and air force on the question whether and what subsidiary actions before the general landing are considered practical.

*k.* Proposals of the army and navy on the overall command *during* the crossing.

[*But the condition considered primary by Hitler*

*before this vast scheme could be put into motion, i.e.,
"Morally and actually overcoming the English air
force," was never achieved and so the plan died
in birth. After the initial time set, the Fall of 1940,
talk was made from time to time in Hitler quarters to
the effect that possibly "soon" the plan would be
executed, but it appears that a tacit understanding was
fairly generally held that the invasion would never come
off; defeat of Britain was still envisioned but not by this
means.*]

November 12, 1940,
Fuehrer's Headquarters                96. Document 444-PS

[*Some four months later, a host of other matters was
occupying Hitler's mind. The following is his general
Directive No. 18.*]

The preparatory measures of Supreme Hq. for the
prosecution of the war in the near future are to be made
along the following lines:

1. *Relations with France.* The aim of my policy
towards France is to cooperate with this country in the
most effective way for the prosecution of the war
against England. For the time being France will have
the role of a "non-belligerent power"—she will have to
tolerate German military measures on her territory,
especially in the African colonies, and to give support,
as far as possible, even by using her own means of
defense. The most pressing task of the French is the
defensive and offensive protection of their French
possessions (West and Equatorial Africa) against
England and the deGaulle movement. From this initial
task France's participation in the war against England
can develop fully.

For the time being, the conversations with France
resulting from my meeting with Marshal Petain are
being carried on—apart from the current work of the

armistic commission—entirely by the foreign office in cooperation with the Supreme Command of the Armed Forces.

2. *Spain and Portugal.* Political steps to bring about an early Spanish entry into the war have been taken. The aim of *German* intervention in the Iberian peninsula (code name Felix) will be to drive the English out of the Western Mediterranean. For this purpose:

*a.* Gibraltar will be taken and the Straits closed.

*b.* The British will be prevented from gaining a foothold at another point of the Iberian peninsula, or the Atlantic Islands.

The preparation and execution of this operation is intended as follows:

*Section I.*

*a.* Reconnaissance troops (officers in civilian clothes) make the necessary preparations for the action against Gibraltar and for taking over aerodromes. As regards disguise and cooperation with the Spaniards they will comply with the security measures of the Chief of Foreign Intelligence.

*b.* Special units of the Foreign Intelligence Bureau are to take over the protection of the Gibraltar area, in secret cooperation with the Spaniards.

*c.* The units intended for this operation will be kept in readiness away from the French-Spanish border and information will be withheld from the troops, at this early stage.

*Section II.*

*a.* Units of the Air Force, directed by observation at Algeciras, will, at a favorable moment, carry out an air attack from French soil on the units of the British fleet lying in the port of Gibraltar, and will force a landing on British aerodromes after the attack.

*b.* Shortly after this the units intended for use in Spain will cross the Franco-Spanish frontier on land or in the Air.

*Section III.*

*a.* Attack for the seizure of Gibraltar by German troops.

*b.* Mobilization of troops to march into Portugal should the British gain a foothold there. The units intended for this will march into Spain immediately after the units intended for Gibraltar.

*Section IV.*

*a.* Support by the Spanish in closing the Straits after the seizure of the Rock from the Spanish-Morroccan side as well, if required. As for the *strength* of the units to be used for operation "Felix" the following will apply:

*Army:* The units intended for Gibraltar must be in sufficient strength to seize the Rock even without Spanish assistance.

Apart from this, a smaller group must be apart to aid the Spaniards in the unlikely event of the British attempting to land at a different point on the coast.

*Air Force:* Sufficient forces will be detailed for the air attack on Gibraltar to guarantee substantial success.

For the subsequent operations against naval objectives and for the support of the attack on the Rock mainly dive-bomber units are to be transferred to Spain.

*Navy:* Provision is to be made for U-boats to attack the British-Gibraltar-Squadron, particularly when they leave harbor, which they are expected to do after the air raid.

The commanders in chief of the Navy and Air Force are examining how the Spanish defense of the Canaries can be supported and how the Cape Verde Islands can be occupied.

I also request that the question of an occupation of Maderia and the Azores be examined and also the advantages and disadvantages that would arise from this for the conduct of the war at sea and in the air.

[*But the "political steps to bring about an early Spanish entry into the war" faltered and failed. Franco,*

Spain's dictator, was not unwilling to join a victorious Hitler in mutual adventures. But before such a partnership could be formed the Nazi juggernaut bogged down in the Russian winter of 1941 and Franco decided to wait a while. In the following months Hitler's legions drove afresh into Russia, but by that time Allied landings in Africa and the great German defeat at Stalingrad gave the Caudillo his definitive answer. Unlike Mussolini, Franco took a second look. As a consequence, Case Felix, as Sea Lion, never materialized.]

# VII

## Case Barbarossa
### Hitler Sees Red

[*From June, 1940 to June, 1941, England was the only great power standing against the Nazi force. From the Atlantic to the Pripet Marshes, from Norway to the Balkans Hitler either directly or indirectly controlled the European continent.*

*From the fall of France to the autumn of 1941 Hitler mulled over plans to invade and subdue England. In the end he abandoned the idea for reasons given above. During late autumn and the following winter English and German planes reciprocally bombed targets of all kinds. The Fuehrer was convinced the British were beaten only they were stubbornly refusing to admit it. To make these foolish people admit it might take a little time. Meanwhile every reason existed for getting on with "the last opponent"—Russia. Time was on the Soviets' side; with every passing month their consolidation of power in the buffer states grew stronger; with every passing month their military potential increased. The German leader reasoned thus with Poland crushed, France occupied, England to all intents and purposes beaten, there was no good reason why the ultimate aim of Nazi planning should not now be driven toward.*

*In the summer of 1940 Hitler began to implement that "Ultimate aim."*]

[*The following is an affidavit sworn to by General
Walter Warlimont, General Jodl's deputy. Here we
learn that Hitler originally intended to attack Russia
within a month or two after the fall of France, but was
dissuaded by tactical considerations.*]

On 29 July, 1940, I, as head of the defense
department of the OKW Operations Staff, together
with a number of other officers of the defense
department, attended a conference at Bad Reichenhall
called by General Jodl. At this conference Jodl
announced that Hitler intended to attack the U.S.S.R. in
the Spring of 1941. Sometime previous to this meeting
Hitler told Keitel that he wanted to launch the attack
against the U.S.S.R. during the fall of 1940. Keitel
argued that it would be impossible to launch such a
campaign that Fall because of the purely military
difficulties presented by the transportation of troops
from West to East and by the deployment of such
forces in the East, especially considering that the
necessary physical preparations for the deployment of
the masses of troops to be gathered for the attack had
not as yet been ordered. In addition Keitel argued that
only a few weeks of operational weather could be
expected due to the Fall weather conditions in Russia;
that the army could establish a number of additional
divisions by the Spring of 1941; that the problem of
motorized equipment, very necessary in an area such as
Russia where communication facilities, such as rail-
roads and roads, were limited, would be under control
by Spring of 1941; that the technical development of
armored vehicles and tanks, as well as an increase in
their numbers, could be expected by the Spring of 1941.
Keitel's arguments prevailed and by the time of the 29
July conference, mentioned above, the date for the
intended attack had been moved up to the Spring of
1941.

[*In another affidavit Warlimont says:*]

The first directive for the planned campaign against the U.S.S.R. in the Spring of 1941 was issued in August 1940. This directive was issued under the code word "Aufbau Ost" and was entirely camouflaged, not mentioning the U.S.S.R. nor the eventual attack. Its purpose was to make the necessary physical preparations in the deployment areas in the East so that the masses of troops to be gathered for the attack could be properly deployed. The first directive in which the intention to attack the U.S.S.R. was stated was that of 18 December 1940, issued under the code word "Barbarossa."

By early February 1941 the movement of troops to the border for assembly for the attack had already begun.

The campaign was originally scheduled to begin earlier than 22 June 1941, on 15 May 1941, but the Balkan operations against Yugoslavia and against Greece forced a postponement.

Same time, Fontainebleu, France      99. Document 3014-PS

[*Corroborative evidence is given in the form of an affidavit by General Ernst Koestring of the German Cavalry and military attache in Russia.*]

During August of 1940 the German military attaches were assembled at Fontainebleu, the Headquarters of the OKH [*Army*], for their yearly consultation with the OKH. I was there in my capacity as military attache in Moscow. On about the 6th or 8th of that month I was summoned by General Halder, Chief of the General Staff of the Army, who told me that he had received an order from the Fuehrer to prepare for operations against the U.S.S.R. As a consequence, General Halder said, he would very soon have to ask me many questions. He warned me that I was one of the very few who knew about this and that the fact that I did, had been recorded. If I told anyone of this plan, even my superiors, I should be aware of what would happen to me.

At this meeting the only other person present was a General Staff Officer, a Major whose name I cannot remember, but who was very close to General Halder. He took notes of the interview.

In November of 1940 I was instructed by O Qu IV [*Chief Quartermaster IV, Lieutenant-General von Tippelskirch*] to tell the Russian General Staff that inasmuch as the operations in the West had been concluded the Germans intended to replace the older men in the East with younger men so that the former could be employed in German production.

[*By "operations in the West had been concluded" is meant major land operations.*]

A further reason for this substitution to be offered to the Russian General Staff was that training and supply conditions were better in the East and there was no danger of attacks from the air there. I was to give the Russian General Staff this story and tell them that the German General Staff assures that there is no reason for them to be alarmed by these measures.

Fall, 1940                               100. Document 2353-PS

[*Preliminary economic preparation was made for the coming attack against Russia. The following extract is from a compilation of "Basic Facts for a History of German War and Armaments Economy" composed under the direction of General Georg Thomas, head of the Military Economy Organization. Rather typically, economic preparation was, though ostensibly*] *coordinated—as all things were supposed to be in the coordinated Reich—a jungle of overlapping jurisdictions. Thus Thomas' organization figured in it and competed with Goering's Four-Year-Plan staff; and both of these struggled with Rosenberg's organization when the latter became Reich Commissioner for Eastern Territories. It was a totalitarian state in a very limited sense.]*

1. There is no longer any mention of an Invasion of England but only a siege of England.

2. Aerial defence of the homeland was placed at the top of the list for the first time.

3. The prospective big action (Russian) mentioned for the first time and its postponement to some later date admitted as possible.

Shortly before—on Nov. 6, 1940—Reichmarshal Goering, for the first time made a statement to the effect, that we should prepare ourselves for a long war.

At the beginning of December, instructions were received, that for the time being there was no question of an Invasion of England, and that the "Seeloewe" preparations should merely be concluded.

In November, 1940, the Chief of Wi Rue [*War Economy*] together with Secretaries of state Koerner, Neumann, Backe and General von Hannekan were informed by the Reichmarshal of the action planned in the East.

By reason of these directives the preliminary preparations for the action in the East were commenced by the office of Wi Rue at the end of 1940.

The preliminary preparations for the action in the East concluded first of all the following tasks:

1. Obtaining of a detailed survey of the Russian Armament industry, its location, its capacity and its associate industries.

2. Investigation of the capacity of the different big armament centers and their dependency one on the other.

3. Determine the power and transport system for the

industry of the Soviet Union.

4. Investigation of sources of raw materials and Petroleum.

5. Preparation of a survey of industries other than armament industries in the Soviet Union.

These points were concentrated in one big compilation, "War Economy of the Soviet Union" and illustrated with detailed maps, etc.

Furthermore a card index was made, containing all the important factories in Soviet-Russia, and a lexicon of economy in the German-Russian language for the use of the German War Economy Organization.

The Fuehrer issued the directive that, in order to camouflage German troop movements, the orders Russia has placed in Germany must be filled as promptly as possible. Since the Russians only made grain deliveries, when the Germans delivered orders placed by the Russians, and since in the case of individual firms these deliveries to Russia made it impossible for them to fill orders for the German armed forces, it was necessary for the Wi Rue office to enter into numerous individual negotiations with German firms in order to coordinate Russian orders with those of the German from the standpoint of priority. In accordance with the wishes of the Foreign Office, German industry was instructed to accept all Russian orders, even if it were impossible to fill them within the limits of the time set for manufacture and delivery.

1940-1941                                  101. Document C-66

[*Admiral Raeder had not approved the Hitler decision to attack Russia. Towards the end of the war, when engaged in the task of compiling a history of the war as it concerned naval activities Raeder had submitted to him certain items for confirmation and exposition. The following account is from a memoran-*

*dum written by Raeder dealing with some of those items.*]

The Fuehrer very early had the idea of one day settling accounts with Russia, doubtless his general ideological attitude played an essential part in this. In 1937-38 he once stated that he intended to eliminate the Russians as a Baltic power; they would then have to be diverted in the direction of the Persian Gulf. The advance of the Russians against Finland and the Baltic States in 1939-1940 probably further strengthened him in this idea.

The fear that control of the air over the Channel in the autumn of 1940 could no longer be attained—a realization which the Fuehrer, no doubt, gained earlier than the Naval War Staff, who were not so fully informed of the true results of air raids on England (our own losses)—surely caused the Fuehrer, as far back as August and September, to consider whether—even prior to victory, in the West—an Eastern campaign would be feasible with the object of first eliminating our last opponent on the Continent. The Fuehrer did not openly express this fear, however, until well into September.

The Fuehrer's remark of 21 July 1940 is an indication of reflections of this kind ("It is of course our duty to give careful consideration to the question of America and Russia!").

Doubtless during September 1940 the possibility of an Eastern campaign was mentioned rather often by the Fuehrer, for *I* was *worried* that the war should take a wrong turn (being diverted from the main danger "England"), and this caused me to have an interview with the Fuehrer, tete a tete, "even outside my own department" on 26 June [*sic*] 1940, concerning the significance of the Mediterranean and North Africa, after I had *first* made a thorough report on these questions, on *6 September 1940.* In this interview of 26 September 1940 my statement—"It is questionable whether an attack on Russia from the North is necessary," removed all doubt that there had been talk during the previous weeks of the Eastern operation. It is in keeping with the Fuehrer's usual mode of procedure for him to exercise personal reserve in the first instance in this matter viz-a-viz the *Chief of Naval War Staff*, whose concept would *necessarily* be a different one. In this connection the Supreme Command of the Army will be able to give fuller details, since it was primarily concerned in the preparations, and will have been addressed by the Fuehrer on the matter. I would particularly point out here—quite apart from the Eastern operation—how I have attempted to impress on the Fuehrer the decisive importance for the war of the question of the Mediterranean and North Africa (when I reported to the Fuehrer on 6.9 and 26.9.40). After this discussion on 26.9 the Fuehrer told Kapitan Zur von Puttkamer that this report had been especially valuable to him, and that he could, in the light of it, review his own opinions, and see whether he was "in the right perspective."

3. At that time (*a* 1 above [?], the Fuehrer was firmly resolved on a surprise attack on Russia, regardless of what was the Russian attitude to Germany—this, according to reports coming in, was frequently changing. The communication to Matsuoka was designed entirely as a camouflage and to insure surprise.

4. [*Apparently Raeder had been criticized by some of his colleagues for not showing enthusiasm for "Barbarossa." In the notes upon which Raeder is here expounding reference is made to his "abbreviated remarks" regarding the attack on Russia with the implication that Raeder was allowing his opposition to the plan to manifest itself publicly. Here the Admiral contradicts that notion.*] The expression "greatly abbreviated" describes the representations I have always made while at 1 SKL [*Naval Operations*],— memorandums, which were not so much German essays, or very exhaustive, as notes, and thus easier to

put into report form. By means of the notes I could more briefly and forcefully present this report, which without doubt gave a particularly clear and significant picture of the situation. The Fuehrer, whose primary interest was in setting in motion Barbarossa (thus, for instance, he wanted to employ the German Air Forces principally on the Eastern Front)—naturally took a special interest in those points in connection with which fuller aid could be secured from the Italians. It would be a mistake to conclude, from the expression "greatly abbreviated," that there was "reserve" on my part on this subject, to which I have always given the greatest publicity.

5. In view of previous statements by the Fuehrer, and the contrast in ideology, I personally have always doubted that the Fuehrer believed from the very beginning that the Russo-German pact would last. I think that the pact arose solely out of the need of the moment and that the Fuehrer (in spite of his speech in the Reichstag on 1.9.39) *in no way* intended it to be a *Permanent solution* of the Russian problem. After the campaign against Poland he had contented himself in the first instance with a frontier line which would, with the help of an Eastern wall, afford an effective defense against Russia. In my opinion it was only later—when, on the one hand, the first successes in Russia had been gained, and on the other, when the prospects of turning North Africa to good account were fading—that it became his aim to make the feeding of Europe dependent on the Ukraine, this plan bringing with it *permanent* opposition to Russia. [*Raeder had never been known for close understanding of political matters. Here he demonstrates a typical naivete.*] Though nothing was actually said, this would involve giving up all thoughts of targets for which a certain measure of sea power was required, that is, it would mean striving for a pure continental policy.

6. The Fuehrer kept his plans [*re Russia*] most carefully secret from the Italians. I believe that Stalin is our *greatest* enemy—a statesman at home and abroad,

a soldier and an organizer on a prodigious scale, a Titanic genius seeing far into the future. I consider it extremely probable that in 1937 and 38 Stalin came to recognize, through the efforts of the United States ambassador, as described by Davies in "Mission to Moscow," that Russia could play an important part in a subsequent conflict between the Anglo-Saxon races and Germany, and that he thereupon began to speed up his armaments. The pact with Germany was of a kind which would help him toward the realization of the first part of his scheme—Eastern Poland, the Baltic countries, Bessarabia and perhaps the Balkans and the Dardannelles. The gains of 1939-40 were indeed great. In 1940-41 Stalin had no reason to march against Germany. Germany's surprisingly great successes against France and the Balkans impressively demonstrated her strength to him and perhaps even awakened fear of her. Stalin therefore cannot have intended to take the initiative in attacking this strong Germany in 1941, but while continuing to arm, he must have wanted to wait and see whether the subsequent course of the war between Germany and the Anglo-Saxon powers would offer him a favorable opportunity—he knew from Davies that the USA would join in sooner or later. Whether in this connection he favored a push towards the Rhine, passing through the Scandinavian countries, or to the North Atlantic, or in the direction of the Mediterranean to the Dardennelles, or through Persia to the Indian Ocean, or finally towards India, must have depended entirely on the course of the struggle between Germany and the Anglo-Saxon powers. As I see it, it does do justice to the importance of Stalin to assume that he intended "to start the war against Germany in the Autumn of 1941." It is true that an essential part of his armament was made ready for this deadline. I have sometimes been in doubt whether, for Stalin, the ideological point of view had not taken second place long ago in favor of a tremendous effort to use to the full the opportunity he was offered of realizing the schemes of Peter the Great. Was the announcement of the dissolution of the Commintern [*1943*] perhaps a hint to Germany that an understanding between Germany and Russia would have been possible even then, and that, after the Russian territories had been regained a peaceful relationship would have been possible between the two States, who, taking the long view, are both threatened by the USA?

Many remarks and plans indicate that the Fuehrer calculated on the final ending of the Eastern campaign in the autumn of 1941, whereas the Supreme Command of the Army (General Staff) was very skeptical.

September 6, 1940, Fuehrer's headquarters
102. Document 1229-PS

[*This is a Jodl memorandum sent to the counter-intelligence service abroad.*]

For the work of our own intelligence service as well as for the answer to questions of the Russian intelligence service, the following directives apply:

1. The respective total strength of the German troops in the East is to be veiled as far as possible by giving news about a frequent change of the army units there. This change is to be explained by movements into training camps, regroupings.

2. The impression is to be created that the center of massing of troops is in the Southern part of the Gouvernement, in the Protektoram'and in Austria, and that the massing in the North is relatively unimportant.

3. When it comes to the equipment situation of the units, espec. of the armoured divisions, things are to be exaggerated, if necessary.

4. By suitable news the impression is to be created that the anti-aircraft protection in the East has been increased considerably after the end of the campaign in the West and that it continues to be increased with

captured French material on all important targets.

December 10, 1940,
Fuehrer's headquarters          103. Document 446-PS

[*"Directive Nr. 21" is the official Hitler directive for Barbarossa.*]

## Directive Nr. 21
### Case Barbarossa

The German Armed Forces must be prepared to *crush Soviet Russia in a quick campaign* before the end of the war against England.

For this purpose the *Army* will have to employ all available units with the reservation that the occupied territories will have to be safeguarded against surprise attacks.

For the Eastern campaign the *Airforce* will have to free such strong forces for the support of the Army that a quick completion of the ground operations may be expected and that damage of the Eastern German territories will be avoided as much as possible. This concentration of the main effort in the East is limited by the following reservation: That the entire battle and armament area dominated by us must remain sufficiently protected against enemy air attacks and that the attacks on England and especially the supply for them [*sic*] must not be permitted to break down.

Concentration of the main effort of the Navy remains unequivocally against England also during an Eastern campaign.

If occasion arises I will order the concentration of troops for action against Soviet Russia eight weeks before the intended beginning of operations.

Preparations requiring more time to start are—if this has not yet been done—to begin presently and are to be completely by 15 May 1941.

Great caution has to be exercised that the intention

of an attack will not be recognized.

The preparations of the High Command are to be made on the following basis:

*I. General Purpose:*

The mass of the Russian *Army* in Western Russia is to be destroyed in daring operations by driving forward deep wedges with tanks and the retreat of intact battle-ready troops into the wide spaces of Russia is to be prevented.

In quick pursuit a (given) line is to be reached from where the Russian Airforce will no longer be able to attack German Reich territory. The first goal of operations is the protection from Asiatic Russia from the general line Volga-Archangelsk. In case of necessity, the last industrial area in the Urals left to Russia could be eliminated by the Luftwaffe.

In the course of these operations the Russian Baltic Sea Fleet will quickly erase its bases and will no longer be ready to fight.

Effective intervention by the Russian *Airforce* is to be prevented through forceful blows at the beginning of the operations.

IV. It must be clearly understood that all orders to be given by the commander-in-chief on the basis of this letter of instructions are precautionary measures, in case Russia should change her present attitude toward us. The number of officers to be drafted for the preparations at an early time is to be kept as small as possible. Further co-workers are to be detailed as late as possible and only as far as each individual is needed for a specific task. Otherwise, the danger exists that our preparations (the time of their execution has not been fixed) will become known and thereby grave political and military disadvantages would result.

V. I am expecting the reports of the commanders-in-chief on their further plans based on this letter of instructions.

The preparation planned by all branches of the Armed Forces are to be reported to me through the

November 14, 1940-January 24, 1941
104. Document C-170

[*This is a series of entries in a file-diary found by the Allies among the papers of the Navy High Command. The whole file is devoted to Russo-German relations.*]

14 Nov. *Naval Supreme Commander with the Fuehrer: Fuehrer is* "still inclined" *to instigate the conflict with Russia. Naval Supreme Commander [Raeder] recommends putting it off until the time after the victory over England since there is heavy strain on German Forces and the end of warfare not in sight.* According to the opinion of the Naval Supreme Commander Russia will not press for a conflict within the next year, since she is in the process of building up her Navy with Germany's help—38 cm turrets for battle ships, etc.;—thus during these years she continues to be dependent upon German assistance.

27 Dec. *Naval Supreme Commander with the Fuehrer:* Naval Supreme Commander emphasizes again that strict concentration of our entire effort against England as our main enemy is the most urgent need of the hour. On the one side England has gained strength by the unfortunate Italian conduct of the war in the Eastern Mediterranean and by the increasing American support.

[*Italian forces at this time were giving ground steadily and rapidly in Africa. General Wavell, British commander in this area, had, in the late days of 1940, reversed the Italian offensive, driving Mussolini's ill-trained forces out of Tobruk and Bardia, capturing over 25,000 prisoners, and ending the dream the Duce had of a quick conquest of Egypt.*]

On the other hand, however, she can be hit mortally by a strangulation of her ocean traffic, which is already taking effect. What is being done for submarine and naval-air force construction, is much too little. Our entire war potential must work for the conduct of the war against England; thus for the Navy and air force every fissure of strength prolongs the war and endangers the final success. *Naval Supreme Commander voices serious objections against Russia campaign before the defeat of England.* Fuehrer desires all possible advancement of submarine construction; present construction figures (12 to 18 per month) are too low. "*Generally, however, the last continental enemy must be removed under all circumstances because of the present political development (Russia's leaning to mix in Balkan affairs), before he could come to grips with England.* Thus the army must obtain the necessary strength. After that, full concentration on air force and navy can follow."

28 Dec. The political situation is changed by Russia's unreliability, as evident in the Balkan states; consequent rearmament of the army is necessary. Emphasis on navy and air force against England is not to be impaired.

[*Russia had edged into Bessarabia and a part of Bucovina; she was also interested in trying to affect to her advantage the political situation in Yugoslavia and Bulgaria. By this time she had already absorbed Esthonia, Latvia and Lithuania.*]

8 Jan. [*1941*] *Naval Supreme Commander with the Fuehrer:* Fuehrer declares; [*sic*] Russia's position in case of the imminent German action in Bulgaria not yet cleared. Russia needs Bulgaria for the assembly of troops against the Bosporus. Hope on USA, Russia keeps England together.

[*Germany was determined that she and not Russia would dominate Bulgarian politics.*]

Diplomatic preparation by England in Russia recognizable; England's aim is to set in motion Russian power against us. Stalin is to be regarded as an ice cold blackmailer. With USA and Russian entry into the war, very great burden for our conduct of the war. *Therefore, every possibility of such a threat must be excluded from the very beginning.* If the Russian threat can be removed, we can continue the fight against England under very tolerable conditions. Russia's collapse means considerable relief of burden for Japan, and increased danger for USA.

11 Jan. Signing of new, far-reaching agreements between Russia and Germany (Economical, resettlement and border questions).

12 Jan. Russian government denies foreign reports that she agrees with entry and stay of German troops in Bulgaria. Question was never mentioned by Germany to Russia. Denials give cause for concern in Bulgaria.

13 Jan. Russian press stresses strongly the German-Russian economic agreement, and emphasizes *that the Anglo-Saxon powers would never succeed in disturbing the good relationship between the two powers.*

18 Jan. *Fuehrer anticipates disturbance of the relations to [sic] Russia* as the result of the Balkan operations. [*This item refers to Italy's ill-fated invasion of Greece, an effort which Germany later had to take up in order to prevent serious Axis losses in men, material and face.*] Fears for the Roumanian oil area.

20 Jan. *Speech of Stalin: He works untiringly for the strengthening of the Russian fleet and army....* "The international situation is complicated and confused and even Russia is threatened by the danger of war."

22 Jan. Declaration in the House of Commons by Under Secretary of State Butler: England has repeatedly tried during the past year, to come to *closer political cooperation* with Russia. Russian government has not reacted on that.

24 Jan. *Conference Fuehrer-Duce:* Statements of the Fuehrer: great importance of Finland because of nickel

resources; *it shall not be touched any more* [*by Russia*].—Russian complaints because of German concentration in Roumania have been received but were rejected. USA even in case of entry into the war not a serious danger. *Greater danger, despite favorable political and economic treaties, Russia. Therefore tying down of considerable forces on the Russian border. There is no danger as long as Stalin lives....*

February 3, 1941, Fuehrer's headquarters
105. Document 872-PS

[*At this time Hitler was busy planning in a number of directions. "Sea Lion," the cross-channel attack against England, was so modified as to be in effect annulled; "Sonnenblume"—Sunflower—was being polished up: intervention on a broad front and on a large scale in North Africa; "Marita," aid to Italy in Greece was considered. But most important was Barbarossa. In the meeting of February 3, Hitler went over certain details of the project with Keitel, Jeschonnek (Goering's Chief of Staff), Brauchitsch, Halder and others. The following are notes made by a captain whose name on the "minutes" is illegible.*]

*Chief of the Army General Staff* [*Halder*]—
1. Enemy strength approximately 100 Infantry divisions, 25 Cavalry divisions, approximately 30 mechanized divisions. *Our own strength about the same, far superior in quality.*

[*The Germans' estimate of their own quality vis a vis Russian material was proved, when the armies clashed, quite mistaken.*]

In estimating the leading personalities, Timoshenko is the only outstanding figure. The only one, that is, according to General Koestring [*German military attaché in Moscow*].

231

Details of the strength and organization of the Russian divisions are *important only* in that even the Infantry Divisions include a comparatively large number of tanks, though the material is bad and merely thrown together.

In the case of mechanized divisions, we have superiority with regard to tanks, weapons and artillery. The Russians are superior in numbers, we in quality.

The Russians are normally equipped in artillery. Materials likewise inferior. The command of the artillery is insufficient. The Russian operational intentions are unknown. Strong forces are at the frontier. Any retreat could only be on a small scale since the Baltic States and Ukraine are vital to the Russians for supply reasons. Fortification work is in progress on the Northern and Southern flanks.

There is no fresh information on the communications system.

6 armored divisions are required from the "Marita" operation; of these the 2 training divisions are for the 1st line, a further 2 from Roumania itself for the Southern Group, the last 2 divisions are reserves from the Northern Group. It all depends on the Balkan situation (Turkey's attitude).

*Fuehrer*—When the die has been cast, the Turks will not make any further moves. No special protection of the Balkans is therefore necessary. One dangerous moment will be if North Africa is cleared by the British, thus enabling the British to operate in Syria with unhampered forces.

[*Halder then went into some detail concerning tactics in the Russian campaign.*]

*Fuehrer*—mentioned that the operational areas were enormous, that the enemy troops could be successfully encircled, only if the encirclement were *complete* (Cavalry divisions). The immediate surrender of the Baltic States, including Leningrad and the Ukraine [*sic*] cannot be expected at once. It is, however, possible that after the initial defeat, the Russians, knowing our operational aims, will retreat on a large scale and prepare for defense further East behind some barrier.

In this case the North, regardless of the Russians in the East, will be cleared. From there (a favorable supply-base) a thrust in the rear of the Russians without a frontal attack. It is essential to wipe out large sections of the enemy and not put them to flight. This will be accomplished if we occupy the flanking areas with the strongest possible forces. Then, with the enemy held in the center, he can be maneuvered out of it from the flanks.

Chief of Army General Staff—The Finns will probably make a strategic concentration in the South.

Fuehrer—assumed that Sweden would join with us at a price. The price: the Aaland Islands (not our possessions)

[*The Aaland Islands belonged to Finland.*]

There is no question of a union between Finland and Sweden as this would not suit the European New Order.

Norway must be under protection; no repercussions are desired from that quarter.

*Chief of Army General Staff*—Position of Hungary. If Hungary is not to participate, we must withdraw from Hungary. The destination of the march will be given as Roumania. At the last minute the direction will change toward the Russian frontier. Hungary will permit anything so long as she is given the corresponding political assurances. Agreements with all states taking part (with the exception of Roumania) can be made only at the eleventh hour. With Roumania it is a matter of life and death.

Army groups and High Commands are being withdrawn from the West. There are already considerable reinforcements though still in the rear area. From the middle of April, Hungary will be approached about the march through. Felix is now no longer possible [*the capture of Gibraltar, with Spain's help*] as the main part of the artillery is being entrained.

*C-in-C Army* [*Brauchitsch*]—requested that he no longer have to employ 5 control divisions for [*Marita*], but might hold them ready as reserves for commanders in the West.

*Fuehrer*—when Barbarossa commences, the world will hold its breath and make no comment.

*Conclusions:*

1. *Barbarossa.*

*a.* The Fuehrer on the whole was in agreement with the operational plan. When it is being carried out, it must be remembered that the *main aim* is to gain possession of the Baltic States and Leningrad.

*b.* The Fuehrer desires that the operation map and the plan of the disposition of forces be sent to him as soon as possible.

*c.* Agreements with neighboring states, who are taking part, may not be concluded until there is no longer any necessity for camouflage. The exception is Roumania with regard to the reinforcing of the Moldan.

*d.* It must, at all costs, be possible to carry out Attila [*occupation of Unoccupied France.*]

*e.* The strategic concentration for Barbarossa will be camouflaged as a faint for Seeloewe [*Sea Lion*] and the subsidiary measure Marita.

February 4-28, 1941                    106. Document C-170

[*From the Navy High Command File-Diary:*]

4 Feb. *Naval Supreme Commander with the Fuehrer: Naval Supreme Commander* explains operational plans in a Russian incident, emphasizes especially the necessity for the seizure of Murmansk/Polarnoje, so that England cannot take a foothold there.

5 Feb. Requests of Chief, Naval Operations for air support in case "Barbarossa" cannot be fulfilled completely because of lack of forces. Fuehrer points out as an especially important naval mission, *rapid organization of the supply line to Leningrad.*

18 Feb. Chief, Naval Operations insists on the occupation of Malta *even before "Barbarossa."* Measures for the covering up of the preparations for "Barbarossa." Concentration movements against Russia are to be put forth as the *"greatest undertaking of deception* [*in*] *the history of war,* [*"*] which serves to distract from the last preparations of the invasion against England. Even in the armed forces the impression is to be kept up that the invasion is being prepared further. Liaison contact with Sweden, Finland, Hungary, Slovakia, Roumania is to be made as late as possible.

[*But sooner in the case of Rumania than in the case of the others.*]

23 Feb. Instruction from Supreme Command, Armed Forces that seizure of Malta is contemplated for the fall of 1941 after the execution of "Barbarossa."

24 Feb. Proclamation by Marshal Timoschenko: the entire Soviet nation, despite the successes of the neutrality policy must keep itself in constant readiness for the danger of an enemy surprise attack!

28 Feb. Russian needs for the execution of her reform plans, a period of peace of several years. Russia's foreign policy is thus marked by her *will for neutrality and avoidance of conflicts with strong opponent.*

March 9, 1941, Fuehrer's headquarters 107. Document 874-PS

[*Reichminister Fritz Todt at this time was, among other things, head of the "Organization Todt," a vast*

235

*organization of labor battalions the work of which chiefly was construction of roads and fortifications and repair of bridges. It will be remembered that Todt was the constructor of the famous "Siegfried Line." Here is a brief letter to Todt from OKW dealing with Barbarossa.*]

Honorable Reich Minister:

For the missions which the Fuehrer has assigned to the Armed Forces in the East, extensive measures for the diversion and deception of friend and foe are necessary prerequisites for the success of operations.

The Supreme Command of the Armed Forces has issued guiding rules for the deception in accordance with more detailed directives of the Fuehrer. These rules aim essentially at continuing preparations for the attack against England in an increasing degree. Simultaneously the actual preparations for deployment in the East should be represented as a diversionary maneuver to divert from plans which are being pursued for an attack against England. In order to insure success for these measures, it is indispensable that these same principles are being also followed on the part of the organization Todt.

March 4-April 29, 1941          108. Document C-170

[*From the Navy High Command File-Diary:*]

4 Mar. Bulgaria's consent to the German entry is disapproved in Moscow; [*On March 1st German troops entered Bulgaria with the consent of the Bulgarian government.*] other reports also point to a *stiffening of Russian* attitude because of events in Balkans; however, a basic change of the Russian attitude is not anticipated. Bulgaria joins the Axis. Chief, Naval Operations informs the General Staff of the Army that possibilities of support for the army by naval warfare in

the Black Sea in case of "Barbarossa" are only limited.

15 Mar. According to report from diplomatic circles, improvement of relations between Russia and England.

16 Mar. Reports from agents: *Russians prepare for mobilization* on the Baltic coast.

17 Mar. Signs of Russian partial mobilization noticeable on the Western border.

20 Mar. After long negotiation, Yugoslavia joins the three-power pact, after restricting German concessions, German declaration of guarantee and promise of territorial gains (Exit to the Aegain [sic]).

22 Mar. US press emphasizes cooling off of German-Russian relations, conviction that Russia will not let herself be drawn into war.

22 Mar. *Russian-Turkish non-aggression pact* in case of attack by third power.

3 April *Balkan Operations delayed "Barbarossa" at first for about 5 weeks.* All measures, which can be constructed as *offensive actions,* are to be stopped according to Fuehrer order.

[*It will be recalled that at the time of the coup in Yugoslavia, when the pro-Nazi government was overthrown, Germany decided to occupy that country. On April 6th she invaded Yugoslavia and Greece. Within three weeks German troops were victorious.*]

8 Apr. Fear of Germany still a decisive factor of Russian policy, change in neutrality only anticipated in case of serious weakening of Germany; but increasing coolness unmistakable.

10 Apr. Russian war council, under Timoshenko: State of emergency and *increased military preparations for all units on Western front.*

13 Apr. *Conclusion neutrality pact Russia/Japan.*

10 [*sic: 19*] Apr. German Balkan successes lead to the "*return of Russia to the previous correct attitude.*"

Conclusion of Russian-Japanese pact "shows failure of the Anglo-American attempts to activate Russia against the three powers of the pact." English attempts, however, are being continued. Russian attitude toward Germany further impressed, however, military preparations on the Russian border proceed.

20 Apr. Naval Supreme Commander with Fuehrer: Naval Supreme Commander asks about result of Matsuoka's visit [*Matsuoka at this time was the Japanese Foreign Minister*], and evaluation of Japanese-Russian pact. Fuehrer has informed Matsuoka, "that Russia will not be touched if she behaves friendly according to the treaty. Otherwise, he reserves action for himself."

[*Thus did Hitler "confide" in his allies.*]

Japan-Russia pact has been concluded in agreement with Germany, and is to prevent Japan from advancing against Vladivostok, and to cause her to attack Singapore. *Above standpoint of the Fuehrer has affected Russia's position favorably who is now behaving very correctly and does not expect an attack.*

*Naval Supreme Commander* asks "what opinion the Fuehrer has about the *presently recognizable new Russian change of mind in a decisive pro-German sense. Fuehrer* replies as above.

21 Apr. Relief of tension. Russian-Finland. Russia at present eager to avoid every incident.

24 Apr. Naval attaché in Moscow reports *considerable extent of rumors: danger of war Germany-Russia*, fed by transient travellers from Germany. English Ambassador *predicts* as day of outbreak of war *June 22!* [*The Ambassador hit it right on the head.*]

25 Apr. According to the declarations in the English House of Commons, no great progress in the improvement of Anglo-Russian relations; English efforts will be continued.

29 Apr. Moscow radio reports landing of four German transports with 12,000 men in Finland.

[*After a conversation with Goering on this day Hitler drew up his time-table, and decided other Barbarossa details.*]

1. *Timetable Barbarossa:*
The Fuehrer has decided: Action Barbarossa begin 22 June. From 23 May maximal troop movements, performance schedule. At the beginning of operations the OKH [*Army High Command*] reserves have not yet reached the appointed areas.

2. *Proportion of actual strength in the plan Barbarossa:*
Sector North: German and Russian forces approximately of the same strength.
Sector Middle: Great German superiority.
Sector South: Russian superiority.

3. *Russian strategic concentration:*
Continued movements of strong forces to the German-Russian boundary.

4. *Estimate of the Supreme Commander of the Army of course Barbarossa will take.*
Presumably violent battles of the frontiers, duration up to 4 weeks. In course of the following development weaker resistance may be expected.
*Opinion of Russian soldiers:* A Russian will fight, on appointed spot, up to the last breath.

5. *Conversations with Finland* are approved by the Fuehrer.

6. *Conversations with Hungary* are only possible in the last third of May. The Fuehrer believes the Hungarians will be prepared to carry out defensive operations on the Russian border, but they will not allow any German attack from Hungary.

7. *Conversations with Roumania* will be possible only at a very advanced date.

8. *Concealment of conversations* with friendly countries: projected German assault in the West, hence

Eastern Front must be covered. Participation of friendly countries only as a purely defensive measure.

*[From the Navy High Command File-Diary:]*

1 May. Proclamations by Stalin and Timoshenko on account of first of May [*sic*], show that Russia is striving with all means at her disposal *to keep out of the war*, and on account of the fluid international [*situation*] *to prepare for any eventualities*. Further urgent war preparations and measures for the protection of the Russian western border.

5 May. English radio speaks of stronger indication of German attack on Russia.

6 May. Appointment of Stalin as chairman of the council of peoples' commissioners [*premier*] according to the Chief Naval Operations this means: concentration of the entire power, strengthening of the government authority and "desire to continue the present foreign policy, *avoidance of conflict with Germany*."

*[And, he might have added, affording a pivotal point in the government around which the people of the U.S.S.R. might rally if Russia were attacked. Stalin took Molotov's place.]*

7 May. The appointment of Stalin is evaluated in neutral countries—even in the USA—*as an indication of closer cooperation with Germany and of an all-inclusive agreement between Germany and Russia.*

10 May. Moscow withdraws diplomatic recognition from the Norwegian, Belgian, Yugoslavian representations (apparently a friendly gesture toward Germany). In the opinion of the Naval Attaché Stalin "*the bearer of German-Soviet cooperation!*"

17 May. Evaluation of Russian circles in Turkish diplomatic circles: Russia wants to satisfy Germany by

the last Russian declaration, by the expulsion of the diplomats of territories, occupied by the Germans, and above all, by extensive deliveries, and also to relieve all doubts on the political scene. One can count on a new German-Russian understanding, for the purpose of which Stalin took over the office of prime-minister!— (Report from the Embassy).

22 May. *Supreme Naval Commander with the Fuehrer: Supreme Naval Commander* declares all preparations for the holding back of the war materials consigned to Russia have been made. In the near future it will be explained to the Russian navy that, because of our own need, there may be small delays in the deliveries, without endangering the whole. *Fuehrer* agrees.

29 May. Begin[*ning*] of the preparatory warship movements for "Barbarossa."

4 June. Outwardly, no change in the relationship Germany-Russia. Russian deliveries continue to full satisfaction. Russian government is endeavoring to do everything to prevent a conflict with Germany.

6 June. *Ambassador in Moscow reports* . . . Russia will only fight if attacked by Germany. Situation is considered in Moscow much more serious than up to now. All military preparations have been made quietly—as far as can be recognized only defence. *Russian policy still strives as before to produce the best possible relationship to Germany as good* [*sic*].

7 June. From the report of the Ambassador in Moscow. . . . All observations show, that Stalin and Molotov, who alone are responsible for Russian foreign policy, [*so says this German naval commentator*] *are doing everything to avoid a conflict with Germany*. The entire behavior of the government as well as the attitude of the press, which reports all events concerning Germany in a factual, indisputable manner, support this view. The loyal fulfillment of the economic treaty with Germany, prove the same thing.

14 June. Speech by the *Fuehrer* before the highest armed forces of the commands about the background

and intended execution of "Barbarossa."

17 June. *Supreme Command, Armed Forces (OKW) confirms "D" day 22 June.*

21 June. Reconnaissance of the Baltic theater of operations shows Russian readiness, laying of mine barriers, but no striking movements, no symptoms that Russians are set for imminent German operations. Apparently, battle ships still continue target practice!

The contemplated German offensive mine barriers were laid according to plan, apparently unnoticed, the German submarines are in alert positions and assembling, also the S-flotillas. All shipping will be stopped from 8:00 p.m. on.

June 20, 1941.                         111. Document 1058-PS

[*Rosenberg, Commissioner-designate for Eastern lands, had many ideas as to just what circumstances and situations should flow from a successful military attack upon Russia. Before a group of his assistants, two days before the attack opened, Rosenberg made these statements.*]

The job of feeding the German people stands, this year, without a doubt, at the top of the list of Germany's claims on the East; and here the southern territories and the northern Caucasus will have to serve as a balance for the feeding of the German people. We see absolutely no reason for any obligation on our part to feed also the Russian people with the products of that surplus territory. We know that this is a harsh necessity, bare of any feelings. A very extensive evacuation will be necessary, without any doubt, and it is sure that the future will hold very hard years in store for the Russians. A later decision will have to determine to which extent industries can still be maintained there (wagon factories, etc.). The consideration and execution of this policy in the Russian area proper is for the German Reich and its future a tremendous and by no means negative task, as might appear, if one takes only the harsh necessity of the evacuation in consideration.

[*Note particularly the Nazi positive orientation:*]

The conversion of Russian dynamics towards the East is a task which requires the strongest characters. Perhaps, this decision will also be approved by a *coming* Russia later, not in 30 but maybe in a 100 years. For the Russian soul has been torn in the struggle of the last 200 years. The original Russians are excellent artistic craftsmen, dancers, and musicians. They have certain hereditary talents, but these talents are different from those of the Western people. The fight between Turgnjew and Dostoevski was symbolic for the nation. The Russian soul saw no outlet either way. If we now close the West to the Russians, they might become conscious of their own inborn, proper forces and of the area to which they belong. A historian will maybe see this decision in a different light, in hundreds of years than it might apply to a Russian today.

Undated. 112. Document 1039-PS

[*This extract is from a memorandum found in Rosenberg's files titled "Report on the Preparatory Work in Eastern European Questions." There wasn't much that this confidant of Hitler's and party mystic overlooked.*]

I may say that all the work, inasmuch as it is at all possible under present condition, is in full swing. Aside from the General and Chief Commissariats more than 900 Regional Commissariats are planned, which must all be manned by political leaders, representatives of the department and officials of the Reich Ministry of the Interior. The work in the East differs basically from the conditions in the West. Whereas we can count on every technical installation and a cultured population here in the big cities, that is not the case in the East. There literally everything will have to be prepared and taken along, additionally for the gigantic spaces—not only an auto park but a great number of typewriters, office material, above all medical supplies and much more down to the bed sheets. It does not appear possible to accomplish such a project suddenly in 14 days, therefore all these arrangements had to be set in full motion already now on my responsibility on the basis of the Fuehrer's decree.

The structure of my office itself is temporarily organized as follows in carrying out the Fuehrer's order. I have requested Gauleiter and Reichsstatthalter Dr. Meyer as permanent representative. He had negotiated personally and thoroughly, through the whole time with all pertinent offices, in order to develop all aspects down to the details. A political department has been founded for the execution of the substantial work, under my co-worker of many years Dr. Leibbrandt, who prepares the various books and pamphlets for information. A great number of propaganda leaflets have been composed by him which will then have been scattered over the Russian front in huge numbers by the armed forces. Also for a specific time other leaflets are ready which are addressed directly to the individual races. I do not care to decide on this date for myself, and will lay these originals before the Fuehrer at the first opportunity with the request to check the contents and determine the time of the eventually approved appeals. The political department is also undertaking a thorough investigation of all these, with the exception of the Russians, who eventually can be used as advisers for the administration of the various nationalities. Continuous discussions about this subject are under way with representatives of the OKW, the propaganda ministry, etc. Secondly, a department economic-political cooperation has been founded under direction of Oberbereischsleiter Malletke. Department of "Law, Finance, and Administration" has been taken over by Regierungspraesident Runte. A department for Culture and Science is as yet unoccupied since the development of this question does not appear urgent. Also the department "Enlightenment and Press." It is occupied by Major of the Air Force Carl Cranz, deputy Job Zimmerman. Integrated here are co-workers who command the Russian, Ukrainian, and other languages. The wishes of the Reich Press Chief for setting up one press chief for each Reichskommissar are under discussion in order to decide them in that sense if possible.

Thus I hope that when, after preliminary conclusion of the military action the Fuehrer has the possibility for a report from me, I shall be able to report to the Fuehrer for reaching preparations [*sic*], up to those points of special and personal nature which the Fuehrer alone can decide.


June 21, 1941, "Rosenberg Chancellery"
113. Document 1034-PS

[*On this day before the attack on Russia Rosenberg held a conference with some of his more important assistants. Rather typically the discussion ended on details of the kind of a uniform the Rosenberg staff would wear.*]


With regard to the question of putting the commissioners to be employed into uniform, Dr. Rosenberg stated that the organizations did not wish to give up their own (field-grey) uniforms and badges. The general opinion was that it was impossible for German-government officials to enter the Eastern territories in different uniforms; also, the (field-grey) color, in which the Armed Forces in the East would have provoked awe and respect for the German people, was held to be indispensible for the successful carrying out of their government functions. Party Member Gohdes said that Reichs-organizationsleiter Dr. Ley recommended the creation of a new unitary uniform for the Commissioners serving in the East. The Armed Forces were willing to set aside dark-brown cloth for 5,000 uniforms. Reichsleiter Rosenberg took it upon himself personally to submit the question of supplying uniform to the decision of the Fuehrer.

Arising from the question of supplying uniform, it was then discussed whether a special "Ostfuehrers Corps" [*Eastern Leaders' Corps*] as an organization of the National-Socialist Party should be created. An organization of this kind would then not only have the right to wear a unitary uniform, but it would imbue its members with the esprit de corps which was necessary for the fulfillment of the tasks which were to be carried out in the East. If the German was to enter the Eastern territory as master, he must be moulded as a unit both inwardly and outwardly. This inner regimental training could exert a certain counter-effect above all against the moral danger of "Space-Experience" and the depressing effect of foreign nationality. When this subject had been further discussed, it seemed more urgent than ever to achieve the purpose of creating an Ostfuehrer Corps of this kind which would be a unit in itself.

September 3, 1940-June 22, 1941    114. *Proceedings,*
                                       Volume VII,
                                       pp. 2545-256

[*The following is given for two reasons: 1) it summarizes Barbarossa; 2) it is direct testimony at Nurenberg by one of the generals most intimately concerned with the planning of Barbarossa—Field Marshal Paulus, who surrendered to the Russians at Stalingrad after one of the most sanguinary battles of modern times. Later Paulus headed a pro-Soviet committee of German affairs.*]

From personal experience, I can state the following: On 3 September 1940 I took office with the High

Command of the Army as Chief Quartermaster I of the General Staff. As such I was deputy to the Chief of the General Staff, and had in addition to carry out the instructions of a general operational nature which he delegated to me.

When I took office I found in my sphere of work, among other things, a still incomplete operational plan, dealing with an attack on the Soviet Union. This operational plan had been worked out by the then Major General Marx, Chief of the General Staff of the 18th Army, who for this purpose had been temporarily transferred to the High Command of the Army.

The Chief of the General Staff of the Army, General Oberst Halder, turned over to me the continuation of the work which was ordered by the Supreme Command of the Armed Forces, on the following basis:

An investigation was to be made as to the possibilities of an attack against the Soviet Union, with regard to the terrain, the points of the attack, the manpower needed, and so forth. In addition it was stated that altogether about 130 to 140 German divisions would be available for this operation. It was furthermore to be taken into consideration that from the beginning Roumanian territory was to be utilized for the deployment of the German southern army. On the northern flank the participation of Finland in the war was taken into account, but was ignored in this operational plan of the army.

Then, in addition, as a basis for the plan which was to be worked out, the aims—the instructions of the OKW—were given: First, the destruction of those parts of the Russian Army stationed in the west of Russia, to prevent the units which were fit for fighting from escaping deep into Russia; second, the reaching of a line from which the Russian air force would be unable to attack Germany territory effectively, and the final aim was reaching of the Volga-Archangel line.

The operational plan which I just outlined was completed at the beginning of November and was followed by two military exercises with the command of which the General Staff of the Army entrusted me. Senior officers of the General Staff of the Army were also assigned. The basic strength requirements assumed in these military exercises were: The launching of one army group south of the Pripet territory, specifically from southern Poland and from Roumanian territory, with the aim of reaching the Dnieper-Kiev line and south of it; north of the Pripet territory another army group, the strongest, from the area around Warsaw and northward, with the general direction of attack being the Minsk-Smolensk line, the intention being to direct it against Moscow later; then a further army group, namely Army Group North, from the area of East Prussia, with the initial direction of attack being through the Baltic States toward Leningrad.

The conclusion which was drawn from these military exercises was at that time that in case of actual hostilities provision should be made firstly for reaching the general line Dnieper-Smolensk-Leningrad, and then the operation was to be carried forward if the situation developed favorably, supply lines, *et cetera* being adjusted accordingly. In connection with these military exercises and for the evaluation of the theoretical experience gained therefrom, there was a further conference of the Chief of the General Staff of the Army and the chiefs of the general staffs of the army groups which had been planned for the East. And further, in connection with this conference, there was a speech about Russia by the then chief of the section Foreign Armies East, Colonel Kinsel, describing Russia's geographic and economic conditions, the Red Army et cetera. The most significant point here was that no preparations whatever for an attack by the Soviet had come to our attention.

With these military exercises and conferences which I have just described the theoretical considerations and plans for this offensive were concluded. Immediately thereafter, that is on 18 December 1940, the Supreme Command of the Armed Forces issued Directive Number 21. This was the basis for all military and economic preparations which were to be carried out. In the Supreme command of the Army this directive resulted in going ahead with the drafting and working out of directions for troop deployments for this operation. These first directives for troop deployment were authorized on 3 February 1941 by Hitler after a report by the Commander-in-Chief of the Army at Obersalzburg; thereupon they were forwarded to the troops. Later on several supplements were issued. For the beginning of the attack the Supreme Command of the Armed Forces had calculated the time which would make it possible for large troop movements to be made on Russian territory. That was expected from about the middle of May on. Preparations were made in accordance with this. Then at the end of March this date underwent a change, when Hitler decided, due to the development of the situation in Yugoslavia, to attack this country.

Because of his decision to attack Yugoslavia, the date foreseen for the beginning of the attack had to be postponed by about five weeks, that is, to the last half of June. And, indeed, this attack then did place on 22 June 1941.

In conclusion, I confirm the fact that the preparation for this attack on the Soviet Union, which actually took place on 22 June 1941, dated back to the autumn of 1940.

June 22, 1941                              115. Document C-170

*[From the Navy High Command File-Diary:]*

22 June. Begin[*ning*] of hostilities against Russia. Our own operations were not disturbed by the enemy, although they are taking place in his immediate vicinity. The outbreak of hostilities has stimulated movements and activity of Russian Naval forces only moderately. Symptom of energetic offensive reaction against the German attack cannot be recognized on the evening of the first day on the enemy's side.

[*Some three weeks after the German attack on
Russia a conference was called by Hitler for the
purpose of deciding, as Goering later sadly put it, "what
to do with the bear's skin." The fact that the bear had
so far only been shot at and not shot seemed to disturb,
however, Goering only.*

*Here we get a glimpse of what the New Order in the
East would have looked like had the Nazi armies
triumphed over Russia.*

*The document is a memorandum written up by
Martin Bormann (who took Hess's place after the
latter's flight to England in May, 1941). Bormann
attended the conference as did Rosenberg, Keitel,
Goering and Lammers (Chief of the Reich Chancellery).
This was a long meeting during which many items came
up for discussion. It might be pointed out that
Bormann and Goering did not get along well; and both
disliked Rosenberg.*]

*Memorandum for the record.*

By order of the Fuehrer: he held today at 3:00 p.m.
in his quarters a conference attended by Reichsleiter
Rosenberg, Reich Minister Lammers, Field Marshal
Keitel, the Reich Marshal and myself. The conference
began at 3:00 p.m. and, including a break for coffee,
lasted until about 8:00 p.m.

By way of introduction the Fuehrer pointed out, he
desired first of all to make some funadmental
statements. Several measures had to be taken without
delay; this was confirmed, among other events, by an
assertion made by an impudent Vichy newspaper that
the war against the Soviet Union was a war waged by
Europe, and that, therefore, it had to be conducted for
the benefit of Europe as a whole. Obviously the Vichy
paper meant to say by these hints that it ought not be
the Germans alone who benefited from this war, but
that all European states ought to profit by it.

Now it was essential that we did not publicize our aims before the world; also there was no need for that, but the main thing was that we oursleves knew what we wanted. By no means should we render our task more difficult by making superfluous declarations. Such declarations were superfluous because we could do everything where ever we had the power, and what was beyond our power we could not do anyway.

What we told the world about the motives for our measures ought to be conditioned, therefore, by tactical reasons. We ought to act here in exactly the same way as we did in the case of Norway, Denmark, Holland, and Belgium. In these cases too we did not publish our aims, and it was only sensible to continue in the same way.

Therefore we shall emphasize again that we were forced to occupy, administer, and secure a certain area; it was in the interest of the inhabitants that we provide order, food, traffic, etc., hence our measures. This need not prevent our taking all necessary measures— shooting, resettling, etc.—and we shall take them.

But we do not want to make any people into enemies prematurely and unnecessarily. Therefore we shall act as though we wanted to exercise a mandate only. At the same time we must know clearly that we shall never leave those countries.

Our conduct therefore ought to be:

1. To do nothing which might obstruct the final settlement, but to prepare for it only in secret;

2. To emphasize that we are liberators.

In particular:

The Crimea has to be evacuated by all foreigners and to be settled by Germans only.

In the same way the former Austrian part of Galicia will become Reich territory.

Our present relations with Roumania are good, but nobody knows what they will be at any future time. This we have to consider and we have to draw our frontiers accordingly. One ought not be dependent on the good will of other people [*here, it may be pointed out, speaks the very spirit of Nazism*]; we have to plan our relations with Roumania in accordance with this principle.

On principle we have now to face the task of cutting up the giant cake according to our needs, in order to be able:

first, to dominate it,
second, to administer it, and
third, to exploit it.

The Russians have now ordered partisan warfare behind our front. This partisan war again has some advantage for us; it enables us to eradicate everyone who opposes us.

Principles:

Never again must it be possible to create a military power west of the Urals, even if we have to wage war for a hundred years in order to attain this goal. Every successor to the Fuehrer should know: Security for the Reich exists only if there are no foreign military forces west of the Urals; it is Germany who undertakes the protection of this area aginst all possible dangers. Our iron principle is and has to remain:

*We must never permit anybody but the Germans to carry arms!*

This is especially important; even when it seems easier at first to enlist the armed support of foreign subjugated nations, it is wrong to do so. In the end this will prove to be to our disadvantage unconditionally and unavoidably. Only the German may carry arms, not the Slav, not the Czech, not the Cossack nor the Ukrainian!

On no account should we apply a wavering policy such as was done in Alsace before 1918.

[*There might be some argument about how "wavering" that policy was. The Alsatians were pretty effectively ruled from Berlin, but not entirely. Moreover*

252

*there was some opposition to this stern policy. Perhaps this is the wavering that Hitler alludes to.*]

What distinguishes the Englishman is that he pursues constantly *one* line and *one* aim. In this respect surely we have to learn from the Englishman. Therefore we ought never to base our actions on single contemporary personalities: here again the conduct of the British in India towards the Indian princes etc. ought to be an example: it is always the soldier who has to consolidate the regime.

We have to create a Garden of Eden in the newly occupied eastern territories; they are vitally important to us; as compared with them colonies play only an entirely subordinate part.

Even if we divide up certain areas at once, we shall always proceed in the role of protectors of the Right and of the people. The terms which are necessary at this time should be selected in accordance with this principle: we shall not speak of a new Reich territory only, but of the task which became necessary because of the war.

In particular[.]

In the Baltic territory the country up to the Duna will now have to be administered in agreement with Field Marshal Keitel. Reichsleiter Rosenberg emphasizes that in his opinion a different treatment of the population is desirable in every district (Kommissariat). In the Ukraine we should start with a cultural administration, there we ought to awake the historical consciousness of the Ukranians, establish a university at Kiev, and the like.

The Reich Marshal makes the counter statement that we had to think first of securing our food situation, everything else could come later.

*(Incidental question: is there still anything like an educated class in the Ukraine, or are upper class Ukrainians rather to be found only as emigrants outside present day Russia?)*

Rosenberg continues, there were certain independent movements in the Ukraine which deserved furtherance.

The Reich Marshal asks the Fuehrer to indicate what areas had been promised to other states.

The Fuehrer replies, Antonescu desired Bessarabia and Odessa with a strip (of land) leading north-westward from Odessa.

Upon objections made by the Reich Marshal and Rosenberg, the Fuehrer replies that the new frontiers desired by Antonescu contained little outside the old Roumanian frontiers.

The Fuehrer states furthermore that nothing definite has been promised the Hungarians, Turks and Slovaks.

Then the Fuehrer submits for consideration whether the former Austrian part of Galicia ought to be added at once to the government; upon objections having been voiced the Fuehrer decides that this part shall not be added to the government but should only be subordinated likewise to Reichminister Frank (Lwow).

The Reich Marshal thinks it was right to incorporate into East Prussia several parts of the Baltic country, *e.g.* the Forest of Bialystock.

The Fuehrer emphasizes that the entire Baltic country will have to be incorporated into Germany.

At the same time the Crimea, including a considerable hinterland (situated north of the Crimea) should become Reich territory; the hinterland should be as large as possible.

Rosenberg objects to this because of the Ukrainians living there.

(Incidental question: It occured to me several times that Rosenberg has a soft spot for the Ukrainians; thus he desires to aggrandize the former Ukrain to a considerable extent.)

The Fuehrer emphasizes furthermore that the Volga Colony too will have to become Reich territory, also the district around Baku; the latter will have to become a German concession (Military Colony).

The Finns wanted East Carelia, but the Kola

Penninsula will be taken by Germany because of the large nickel mines there.

The annexation of Finland as a federated state should be prepared with caution. The area around Leningrad is wanted by the Finns; the Fuehrer will raze Leningrad to the ground and then hand it over to the Finns.

[*A discussion of which officials should rule which parts, Ukraine, Moscow area, Crimea, etc. ensued after which the following matters were taken up.*]

Reichsleiter Rosenberg than broached the question of securing the administration of the Eastern Areas.

The Fuehrer tells the Reich Marshal and the Field Marshal he had always urged that Police Regiments should be provided with armored cars; this has proved to be quite necessary for police operations within the newly occupied eastern territories, because a Police Regiment equipped with the appropriate number of armoured cars of course could perform many services. Otherwise, though, the Fuehrer pointed out the protection was very slight. However, the Reich Marshal was going to transfer all his training fields to the new territories, and if necessary even Junkers 52 could throw bombs in case of riots. Naturally this giant area would have to be pacified as quickly as possible; the best solution was to shoot anybody who looked sideways.

Field Marshal Keitel emphasizes the inhabitants themselves ought to be made responsible for their things because it was of course impossible to put a sentry in front of every shed or railway station. The inhabitants had to understand that anybody who did not perform their duties properly would be shot, and that they would be held responsible for each offense.

Upon a question of Reichsleiter Rosenberg the Fuehrer replied newspapers also—e.g. for the Ukraine—would have to be re-established, in order to obtain means of influencing the inhabitants.

*After the interval* the Fuehrer emphasized we had to understand that the Europe of today was nothing but a geographical term; in reality Asia extended up to our previous frontiers.

Reichsleiter Rosenberg then described the organizational arrangement he intended to establish; he did not intend to appoint a Permanent Deputy of the Reich Commissioner ahead of time, but always the most efficient of the General Commissioners would be called upon to deputize for the Reich Commissioner.

Rosenberg will set up four departments in the office of the Reich Commissioner: first for the general administration,
second for politics,
third for economics,
fourth for engineering and architecture.
*(Incidental remark: The Fuehrer emphasizes that activities on the part of the churches are out of the question. Papen had sent him through the Foreign Office a long memorandum in which it was asserted now was the right moment to reintroduce the churches; but this was completely out of the question.)*

Reichsleiter Rosenberg applies for appropriate premises to house his administration; he applies for the premises of the Commercial Mission of the Soviet Union in Lietzenberger Street; the Foreign Office though, were of the opinion that these premises were extraterritorial. The Fuehrer replies that this was nonsense; Reich Minister Lammers was charged to inform the Foreign Office they were to hand over these premises to Rosenberg at once and without any negotiations.

Rosenberg then proposes to detail a liaison officer to the Fuehrer; his adjutant Koeppen was to be appointed; the Fuehrer agrees and adds that Koeppen would become the opposite number to Hewell.

[*Hewell was a legation counsellor, Ribbentrop's liaison agent with Hitler.*]

A longer discussion takes place concerning the jurisdiction of Reich SS Fuehrer [*Himmler*]; obviously at the same time the participants have in mind the jurisdiction of the Reich Marshal.

The Fuehrer, the Reich Marshal and others reiterate that Himmler was to have no greater jurisdiction than he had in Germany proper; but this (much) was absolutely necessary.

The Fuehrer repeats emphatically this quarrel would soon subside in practice; he recalls the excellent collaboration between Army and Air Force at the front.

In conclusion it is decided to call the Baltic country Ostland.

[*Five months after this conference of grandiose planning Hitler's armies faltered in the vast cold spaces of Soviet Russia; the next year they encountered* Stalingrad—*and the Hitler era began to fade. But back of Britain and Russia, sustaining them with resources of all kinds in the beginning and finally collaborating in a crescendo of fearful armed might, stood the United States. Both Britain and Russia officially admitted that the absence of U.S. help would have meant victory for Hitler.*

*Time tends to soften and blur memories. But some memories we cannot afford to coddle in this way if we are to learn from bitter experience. Some fresh understanding of the way our memories of the Hitler years have served us can be gained by turning to the record of certain events that have occurred in the decades since the war's end. Those events make up the chief portion of the Afterword.*]

# VIII

# Aftermath

## Nazis In The U.S.

It has been nearly forty years since the Thousand Year Reich went up in flames. Throughout these decades some Americans have indulged certain feelings, have developed certain behavioral patterns strikingly similar to those prominent in the Germany destroyed at such fearful cost. Examples are easy to cite: the Third Reich's permanent war economy, once condemned by us as the cancerous growth of authoritarian evil, is now our cherished guarantor of prosperity; Germany's Gestapo, SS, SA, and related units are now mirrored in our CIA, FBI, NSC, DIA, NIC, etc.; before Hitler we had never, from our beginnings, sanctioned a peacetime conscript army—for 30 years after Hitler we maintained one of the largest in the world, and we feel a little anxious now without it; during the 1930s and 1940s we expressed indignant scorn at Nazi Germany's journalistic forays into blatant chauvinism and crude prejudice as practiced, for example, by Julius Streicher's notorious *Der Sturmer*. So luxuriant has been the growth of our own hate journals and at the same time so little known by many Americans that quotations *in extenso* are not out of order. The following are typical samples.

*Action,* a bi-monthly founded in 1961. It began as the voice of "Sons of Liberty, A National Political Committee," went on to become the mouthpiece for "The American Nationalist Movement" and, beginning in 1967, often spoke for the American Nazi Party. In the late

1960s it regularly reported on "patriotic" efforts to counter the activity and influence of civil rights groups such as Blacks, Jews, and pacifists. It also stressed, of course, the danger of communist infiltration and propaganda. The excerpt below is from the January/February 1968 issue.

On hand to greet the Communist forces of revolution was a detachment of American Nazi Stormtroopers under the command of Major Allen Vincent. In contrast to the unhealthy bodies of the peace marchers, each Stormtrooper was the very image of vigorous American manhood; clean shaven, physically fit, and sharply uniformed, with jackboots and blazing Red-White and black Swastika armbands. As they marched into the park, an audible shudder was heard from the Communist ranks, and many of the Comrades began to panic and disperse.

The *National Christian News,* a Florida based monthly, is against integration. The Civil Rights Bill is a "vicious, Godless Law". This periodical is also against the "anti-Christ World Council of Churches, against the United Nations, and against the idea of universal brotherhood. It is sympathetic to the regime of Adolf Hitler, claiming that the Nazis helped protect the world from the "Jew-Communists". An article in the 1968 issue calls television "The Electric Jew". It has replaced the family altar and the Holy Bible in millions of homes. "From this satanic devil box comes [*sic*] forth all the slogans and perverted lies parroted by the Anti-Christ from throughout the world."

The *National Renaissance Bulletin* is a 10-page Newsletter out of New York City. The following excerpt is from its April, 1968 issue.

Germany was... the first modern nation to throw into the dustbin the outmoded ideas of "equality", "democracy", for these byproducts of 19th Century liberalism and rationalism are myths and have no place in the new 20th Century Age of Authority, which is the next stage of our historical development. She replaced them by the new BIOPOLITICS based on NATURAL LAW. Her new Socialism was ETHICAL SOCIALISM which superceded [*sic*] both the selfish individualism of 19th Century capitalism and the hate-based negative madness of Bolshevism. (Both Capitalism and Bolshevism are of Jewish origin and can continue in the face of the New Age only as symbols of cultural malady.)

Most of America's Nazi-inspired journals print material that is quite indistinguishable in content; to read one is to read all. A final excerpt, from *White Power,* a bimonthly tabloid (Arlington, Virginia) with a circulation of about 30,000, illustrates this sameness.

[Members of the Party recently celebrated the 80th anniversary of the birth of Adolf Hitler.]....84 persons gathered at the country estate of an Arlington-area supporter to celebrate the most joyous day in the National Socialist calendar. An afternoon of feasting and rifle and pistol-shooting was followed in the evening by an address by the National Leader.... He called April 20, 1889, the most significant date in Aryan history....

The National Leader concluded by reminding his listeners that Adolf Hitler still lived as long as there were Aryan men and women dedicated to his teachings....

..........................................................................

To the strains of the Badenweiler March, the Leader's personal march, the traditional bonfire was lit. As the flames leaped upward into the dark night sky, the Horst Wessel Song [Germany's national anthem during the Hitler regime] was played, followed by the militant anthem, White Men to Arms.

The Preface of the *Official Stormtroopers Manual,*

issued by the American Nazi Party [after 1969 called the White Power Party], ends with the words "Heil Hitler!" In it Hitler is referred to as "one of the greatest men to walk the earth in twenty centuries." The Manual makes clear that the Aryan *race* alone among all races is "creative." Holding that democracy "is rule by mobs... by the mediocre," the Manual goes on to argue for the establishment of an "Authoritarian Republic." As for Blacks, their "destiny lies in Africa.... Those blacks who wish to remain here will be strictly segregated on reservations with the classification of subjects rather than citizens." [In Nazi Germany, Jews were forced to wear the six-pointed Star of David in all public places.] Jews, the Manual flatly states, "are insane. The Jews as a race are paranoic.... This sick people must be stopped before they drag the world down with them." The method of stopping them is clearly spelled out: "The extent of [their] traitorous conspiracy requires a large scale of execution.... the tradition of gas chambers drives traitors frantic and helps to expose them." The Manual concludes with the reminder that "Hitler and his followers rooted out Communism in Germany and brought happiness and prosperity to this once sad land."

Across the past three decades certain ominous events have occurred which, against the backdrop of the sentiments professed above, should cause Americans of every race, religion, and cultural level to feel deep concern. They need to be tracked and kept in our national consciousness if the heritage and promise of American democratic life do not come, one dark day, to be fed into a new Fuhrer's shredder of holy hate. Though not chosen at random, the following "diary items" are only samples of happenings the scope of which is large and varied.


December 12, 1946                    Atlanta, Georgia


Dr. James H. Sheldon, chairman of the Non-Sectarian Anti-Nazi League, was charged today with engaging in illegal activities by Mr. Emory Burke, president of the anti-Jewish, anti-Black "Columbians, Inc." Burke's action followed publication of a report on "alleged activities and aims of the Columbians through the office of the Attorney-General of Georgia. Two members of the Anti-Nazi League had infiltrated the Columbians and had gathered information that made up most of the Attorney-General's report. Code sections on which the warrants were based were "similar to those under which Mr. Burke [was] indicted recently" and charged by the grand jury with usurping powers of police officers. Dr. Sheldon told reporters that what had happened in Atlanta, fantastic as it may seem, "is being laid as groundwork for similar activities in many of our principal cities."

"I intend," Dr. Sheldon said, "immediately as head of the league to call on and appoint a committee of outstanding leaders of the bar to join me in formulating and obtaining the enactment of adequate state legislation that will be airtight and not leave any loopholes for those threatening once again to destroy what we won in a tragic war."

April 27, 1953                    County of New York

The membership committee of the Medical Society of the County of New York voted 8-3 to admit Dr. G. Arnold. Admission of Dr. Arnold was opposed by a group of physicians on the grounds that the Medical Society should not accept into its membership a former Nazi Storm Trooper, which the records showed Dr. Arnold to be. The majority of the committee said it did not believe political discrimination should be allowed to affect membership application. Opposing members made such an issue of it, however, that the general body rejected Dr. Arnold's application.

January 15, 1960                    Washington, D.C.

Navy officials said today that "steps had been taken to discharge George Lincoln Rockwell... as a commander in the Naval Reserve." Rockwell was in World War II and the Korean War as a naval officer. He recently applied for a permit to open headquarters in Arlington, Virginia for his American Nazi Party.

January 16, 1960                          Flushing, Queens

Three youths were arrested yesterday for threatening to "invade the Fresh Meadows section of Queens and beat up some Jews." Police found in the home of one of the youths "swastikas, armbands, a recording of Hitler speeches, blank membership cards, and notes filled with anti-Semitic and obscene scribblings."

On the same day elsewhere:
A 12-year-old boy was arrested in Long Island for drawing swastikas on the walls of a laboratory.
In Mt. Vernon, New York, "a swastika was found pencilled on the front door of a Jewish convalescent home."
Detroit police detained a 14-year-old boy who told them he was the Fuehrer of a Nazi club.
In Chicago police sought vandals who had smeared swastikas on about 50 tombstones they had kicked over in a Jewish cemetery.

January 26, 1960                          New York City

After a rally held by the Committee to Stop the Revival of Nazism and Anti-Semitism, Rabbi Harold Maratech paused to talk with several men who had been inmates of Nazi concentration camps. Three young men approached them, flung out their arms in the Nazi salute, and shouted "Heil Hitler!" When Rabbi Maratech told them this was a democracy one of the youths, later identified as a member of the Renaissance Party [see above] said, "This is a

Republic, and as for the constitution, I'll shove it down your throat." The three youths were arrested.

January 30, 1960                    Kansas City, Missouri

Investigation of the January 29th bombing of a synagogue revealed the existence of a neo-Nazi party cell in each of two Kansas City high schools. In East and Southeast High Schools police discovered scores of youth enlisted in Nordic Reich groups. Nazi uniforms and swastikas were worn, and in a school locker a paper was found that proclaimed "Our leader is Adolf Hitler. The war ended in 1945. The ideas of National Socialism have not died." Thirteen students were suspended.

February 1, 1960                    Norwalk, Connecticut,
                                     and Fair Lawn, New Jersey

Two former University of Virginia students were charged with painting swastikas on a synagogue in Norwalk.

A Fair Lawn elementary school was damaged by fire today. Firemen found swastikas and Stars of David and obscenities chalked on a number of walls.

June 23, 1960                        New York City

George Lincoln Rockwell, here to void a ban against his speaking in Central Park, said he had designed an emblem for the American Nazi Party that included the seal of the United Nations. "By putting the United Nations within the swastika," he said, "we symbolize that the world is with us and the Jews are on the outside."

July 8, 1960                               Bronx, New York

Although not on the Attorney-General's list of subversive organizations, the American Nazi Party was involved in the discharge of a Bronx man from the Marine Corps. Officials of the Corps believed membership in that party warranted such action.


November 12, 1960                    Los Angeles, California

Roy H. Heard, 38, night editor of the City News Service, was killed today. He had been working on an article exposing Nazi youth activities in southern California. Two young men were held for questioning.


January 16, 1961                      Boston, Massachusetts

George Lincoln Rockwell and three of his followers were stoned by a group of anti-Nazis in attempts to prevent Nazis picketing "Exodus", a film depicting the terrors and trials of Jews making their way from four Nazi concentration camps to Israel. Members of the group carried signs reading "Fight Nazism Now" and "Remember Auschwitz."


May 25, 1961                          New Orleans, Louisiana

The leader of the American Nazi Party and nine of his Stormtroopers were arrested today for picketing the showing of the film "Exodus." They carried signs reading "America for Whites, Africa for Blacks, Gas Chambers for Traitors." The American Nazis wore swastika armbands and brown uniforms. Rockwell said he could "put 150 men on the streets of America at any time." He insisted that he had been invited to come to New Orleans by "very high, respectable people."

July 8, 1961                    Washington, D.C.

A thirteen-year-old boy and four of his companions passed the local headquarters of the American Nazi Party last night on their way home from a high school dance. They will probably remember the incident for some time. According to police, who were alerted by a resident in the area, the boys were dragged into the Party headquarters, handcuffed, and quizzed about their religion. Two Party members were charged with felonious assault. In defense they alleged that neighborhood boys had been in the habit of throwing rocks at their headquarters offices.


August 4, 1961                    Queens, New York

U.S. Representative Seymour Halpern requested the Department of Defense to dismiss Schyler D. Ferris from the Army Map Service after Ferris acknowledged that he belonged to Fighting American Nationalists, an organization associated with the American Nazi Party. Officials at the Department of Defense said they had been investigating Ferris after receiving reports that he had picketed a movie house in Philadelphia when it was showing the film "Exodus." Ferris is a former Marine captain.


January 18, 1965                    Selma, Alabama

Martin Luther King, Jr. was assaulted today in Selma as he was helping Blacks to register for voting. His assailant, James Robinson, is a member of the National States Rights Party. Later in the day George Lincoln Rockwell and several other members of the American Nazi Party showed up in the vicinity of the projected Black demonstration to ridicule the Negroes by staging "a blackface show on the street while the Negroes were lined up to register....At one point Robinson turned on Rockwell and accused him of being [an FBI] spy. 'Where are your Nazis, Mr. Ratwell?' the Alabaman asked."


December 16, 1966            Arlington, Virginia

The leader of the American Nazi Party announced organizational and other Party changes today. The name of the organization has been changed to National Socialist White People's Party. The rallying cry "Sieg Heil!" has been changed to "White Power!"


August 25, 1967            Arlington, Virginia

George Lincoln Rockwell, head of the National Socialist White People's Party, was shot and killed today. His assassin, John Patler, is a former captain in the Party's Stormtroopers. He had been ejected from the Party a month ago for "fermenting dissension between fair-skinned and dark-skinned Nazis." Until recently Patler had been in charge of a Nazi printing plant in Spotsylvania, Virginia.

Party officials announced that Rockwell's successor will be Matthias Koehl, a former Marine and a former student at the University of Virginia. He is a native of Milwaukee, Wisconsin. Speaking of the founder of the Party Koehl said, "I think he will go down in history as one of the greatest living [sic] Americans and one of the greatest white men of all time."

Shortly after the slaying two boys approached the Party's headquarters. They were stopped by an armed Stormtrooper who shouted at them "Get off this property! Move! And wipe those silly grins off your face." When he cocked his rifle, the boys turned away.

267

March, 1968                                          Carbondale, Illinois

Matthais Koehl, new head of the National Socialist White People's Party, addressed students at Southern Illinois University today. He said that Germany's Third Reich had been a desirable development. Objection to its concentration camps was hypocritical nonsense, he implied, since the objectors didn't seem to find too much wrong with Bolshevik Russia's camps for detainees. He lamented infiltration of the media by Jews, and declared that the war in Vietnam should be "handled as Nazi Germany dealt with its problems, by exterminating the enemy."


January 21, 1973                                        Cleveland, Ohio

Members of the National Socialist White People's Party attended a city council meeting wearing swastika armbands. They were ordered out of the chambers. [Subsequently they appealed the order and won their case.]


June 6, 1974                                      San Francisco, California

Miss Sandra Silva, a member of the National Socialist White People's Party and a $514 a month clerk in the city's Police Department, said in an interview today that her long journey into loneliness had happily ended when she joined the Party in 1971. Until then, she said, she had felt "all by myself. I was glad to know there were other people like me." She said she liked discipline, the military, and Adolf Hitler. Dislikes included Jews, Communists, and trouble makers who threatened white supremacy. She said she believed accounts of German concentration camps and their atrocities were pure fabrications. When asked what she did for recreation she replied, "Anything to do with the Nazi party is fun."

June 15, 1974                    Mount Holly, New Jersey

Police arrested two members of the National Socialist
White People's Party here today and found in their car
four loaded automatic weapons, including carbines and
rifles. Police are searching for a third person, allegedly a
self-proclaimed Nazi.


December 18, 1976                        New York City

Prominent leaders of Judaism staged a protest today
outside the headquarters of the National Council of
Churches. Their action was in support of demands that
the Council oust Archbishop Valerian Trifa from its
membership. Trifa, according to the Jewish leaders, had
murdered many Jews and Christians in Rumania in 1941.
The Rabbis accused the Archbishop of being a one-time
member of the Rumanian Iron Guard, a Fascist
organization that collaborated with the Nazis in World
War II.


February 14, 1977                    New Rochelle, New York

Frederick Cowan was a card-carrying member of the
National States Rights Party, noted for its anti-Black,
anti-Jewish activities. Three weeks ago he was repri-
manded by his supervisor at his place of employment for
refusing to move an article of furniture for a customer.
The supervisor, Norman Bing, was a Jew. Today Cowan
"awoke early, donned a T-shirt (emblazoned 'White
Power') . . . , a khaki shirt, and brown pants. He loaded his
weaponry—a rifle, four pistols, and a hunting knife—into
the trunk of his [car] and drove to the Neptune [moving
company's] parking lot. . . ." Standing near the entrance
way were Joseph Hicks, 59, Frederick Holms, 54, and
James Green, 44, all black men. Cowan shot and killed all
three and then "began to prowl the corridors of the two-

story office building, bellowing: 'Where's Norman? I'm gonna blow him away.'"

Bing saved himself by hiding under an office desk. When police were notified of the shootings they sent a squad car to the scene. Cowan promptly killed the officer who stepped out and called on him to drop his rifle. "Then, in a fury, he sprayed the employee cafeteria with rifle fire, killing Pariyarathu I. Varghese, 32, an Indian immigrant electrician.

Police searched his rooming quarters later and found a small arsenal of weapons, pictures of Himmler and Hitler, and a Nazi propaganda book in which Cowan had written: "Nothing is lower than black and Jewish people except the police who protect them."

The head of the National States Rights Party, J.B. Stoner, said, "The FBI caused niggers to start harassing Cowan on the job. Apparently the FBI's to blame for the whole incident."


March 28, 1977                 San Francisco, California

The Rudolph Hess Bookstore opened today. It specializes in Nazi literature and racist periodicals. Situated in a Jewish neighborhood, the store quickly attracted bristling attention and bitter comment. "It's not a bookstore," one resident of the area said, "It's a hate store."

The room was leased to the occupants by Nathan Green, who said he had had no prior knowledge of what kind of literature his new tenants would handle. Green, a Polish immigrant who had been an inmate of Auschwitz concentration camp, said he would evict the new lessees if he could. The Nazi group declared it would fight any such action.

Jewish residents of the neighborhood sacked and burned the Nazi bookstore established there six days ago. In apparent retaliation, vandals shattered the stained-glass windows of B'Nai Emunch, a nearby synagogue. Nine district police stations have mobilized special patrols to prevent the outbreak of further violence in the embattled neighborhood.

No national poll results show what proportion of the American public approves of the events described above. The preponderant attitude is surely negative. Still, it is true that millions of Americans daily tune in on a "comedy" take-off on the Nazi treatment of World War II prisoners. Its particular feature is the ingenious capers Hogan and his fellow inmates think up to outwit their bungling overlords. No TV producer has yet offered to the public a series of programs dealing with the comic aspects of a cancer ward. The fact that "Hogan's Heroes" essentially does this with a deep running cultural cancer is, to put it mildly, distressing. At best it reveals offensive ignorance; at worst it reflects a latent tolerance of the intolerable. In either case, the informed conscience is made uneasy by the prospect of a new Nazi beast slouching, to borrow from Yeats, toward some Bethlehem to be born.

# THE UNTOLD STORY OF

# DOUGLAS MacARTHUR

## BY FRAZIER HUNT

**The definitive story of one of the most controversial military men of all times, told by a reporter with a background of information and experience that better fitted him than any other to tell the intimate MacArthur story.**

### $2.50 ★ #25101

---